THE LAS Corinth

THE LAST Corinthian

Mike Thompson

The Cricketing Life of

MJK SMITH

pitch

First published by Pitch Publishing, 2023

Pitch Publishing
9 Donnington Park,
85 Birdham Road,
Chichester,
West Sussex,
PO20 7AJ
www.pitchpublishing.co.uk
info@pitchpublishing.co.uk

A CIP catalogue record is available for this book from the British Library.

ISBN 978 1 80150 638 0

Typesetting and origination by Pitch Publishing

Printed and bound in Great Britain by TJ Books, Padstow

Contents

Foreword

MY FIRST encounter with Mike Smith was in my debut match for Warwickshire in May 1955 against Oxford University. I didn't cover myself in glory, failing to trouble the scorers. The following year I played against Mike again in his final year as captain of Oxford, and twice with him when he captained Warwickshire against Scotland and when he was included in Warwickshire's team against the touring Australians. In that latter match Mike top-scored for us with 55 against the bowling of Ray Lindwall, Keith Miller, Ron Archer and Richie Benaud, and it was apparent then what a fine player he was. I, sadly, got another duck, bamboozled by Benaud.

Because he had previously represented Leicestershire, Mike was not able to play in Championship matches for Warwickshire on leaving university under an MCC ruling which made players changing counties take a year out. Aware of his record, though, both the older and younger members of our squad were excited at the prospect of him joining us as captain in 1957. He did not make an immediate impact with the bat but finished the season topping the Warwickshire batting averages and scoring over 2,000 runs. He would do the same for the next five years, even making over 3,000 in 1959.

Mike strongly favoured the leg side and was particularly severe on off-spinners. One innings in particular stands out in my memory. It was against Gloucestershire at Stroud in 1959 and we needed 318 to win, having been 142 behind in the first innings. Mike's 182 not out included five sixes and 28 fours, as he dispatched Gloucestershire's top-class spinners, Sam Cook, John Mortimore and David Allen, to all parts of the ground. Victory was secured by four wickets. My late great friend and fellow Coventrian, Tommy Cartwright, who started at Warwickshire on the same day as me in 1952, thought it was the greatest innings he had ever seen, as did I. Mike was also an outstanding fielder at forward short leg, never flinching, even after having had his wrist broken fielding there. He took some fantastic catches in that position for both Warwickshire and England and set a fine example to the team.

But it was as a captain that Mike really excelled. He was an inspiring leader who allowed the bowlers to set their own fields, never criticised fielders for dropped catches or berated batsmen for getting out cheaply. And he never made excuses for his own failures. The only things he insisted on were fitness, effort and good behaviour. He always played to win, but never unfairly. His calmness under pressure, modesty and good humour earned him the affection and respect of team-mates and opponents alike. Mike treated everybody as equals and under his leadership we were a very happy band. I will forever remember a dressing room that was full of laughter, fun and optimism.

Mike will go down in the annals of Warwickshire cricket as one of its greatest players and captains, and it was an honour and pleasure to play for and with him. Mike Thompson's book is carefully researched and I enjoyed the many eyewitness accounts and anecdotes. It is a fitting tribute to a man of great warmth and integrity, and to one of cricket's finest sportsmen.

Jim Stewart
Warwickshire player, 1952–69

Preface

AT THE beginning of 2022 I wrote to Mike Smith to ask him if he would be interested in my writing a book on his cricketing career. I was aware that an excellent biography of him had been written a few years earlier by Douglas Miller, but I had in mind something more detailed, focusing only on his achievements on the cricket field as a player and a captain. Somewhat to my surprise he readily agreed, with the caveat that his memory was not as good as it once was. I was in no way deterred by this, believing that this could be compensated for by the enormous fund of published records of the game, supplemented by the recollections of his contemporaries.

Ever since I developed an interest in first-class cricket in the mid-1950s, MJK Smith has been one of my favourite players. I later got to know Mike in 1973 when I joined his burgeoning squash club, Wootton Court, near Kenilworth. Mike doesn't remember me from Wootton Court, as the club had around 600 members and was the 'in place' to be in that area in the mid-1970s. I do remember, though, having extensive conversations with him about cricket, his elegant wife Diana serving behind the bar and me bowling to his then 12-year-old son Neil in the cricket net he had set up in the grounds. My wife and I had our wedding reception at Wootton Court in 1975, and Mike tells me that on one occasion Diana tripped on a badly fitted carpet and dropped the wedding cake, but happily that wasn't at our reception.

I stayed with Mike at his home in Warwickshire for a weekend in early 2022, where he was the perfect host. He has been widowed for some years, and his elder daughter Barbara and son Neil both live not far away and visit him regularly. Whilst there, he kindly gave me the contact details of several of his former Warwickshire team-mates – Alan Smith, who took over the captaincy from him in 1968; Bob Barber, who joined Warwickshire from Lancashire in 1963; David Brown, who now runs a horse-breeding stud in Worcestershire; and Dennis Amiss, John Jameson and Jim Stewart, who all live in Warwickshire. Over the next three months I was to visit them all and was always warmly received. I have also had telephone conversations with many of his Test colleagues and county opponents, and not one has had a bad word to say about him, although some considered him a bit too defensive as a captain in the field, with an over-reliance on seam. 'To end a career without enemies in a divisive game like cricket is quite an achievement,' says the cricket historian and author David Frith.[1]

Mike had an outstanding career as a player at university and for Warwickshire, breaking records at Oxford including the unequalled feat of centuries in three successive Varsity matches and playing rugby for England in his final year. He was also elected president of Vincent's, a club for outstanding sportsmen. He broke batting records as captain of Warwickshire in 1959, scoring 3,245 runs, the first time 3,000 had been exceeded since Len Hutton managed it in 1949. He was not quite so successful as a batsman at Test level, often being dismissed by pace early on, but, when set, he was capable of making a big score and always played for the team rather than for himself. His major contribution, though, was as a captain who had the complete loyalty and trust of his players, and he was also an outstanding and courageous short leg fielder.

---

1 Conversation with David Frith.

He was liked and respected by opponents probably better than any other English captain, and relations between opposing countries always ran smoothly when he was in charge.

He was democratic in his approach without being too easily influenced, competitive without being aggressive, utterly straightforward in all his dealings, and unfailingly cheerful and good-humoured, except perhaps when he knew he had received a bad decision or his authority was challenged. He treated everybody as equals, irrespective of rank or class, was modest to a fault, and never complained or made excuses for failure. Mike is a man who, in the words of Kipling's poem, could talk with crowds and keep his virtue and walk with kings without losing the common touch. He is truly one of the last Corinthians.

It has been a great pleasure and a privilege to undertake the task of writing about England's only living double international, and it is my sincere hope that this book will provide a lasting memento to a unique cricketer, whose like we shall not see again. I went with Mike to Edgbaston in early September 2022 to watch a county match and it was like being with royalty. He was greeted with warmth and respect by doorkeepers and committee members alike. An ageing doorman whispered to me as Mike was picking up the tickets, 'What a player and what a lovely man.'

Acknowledgements

I HAVE received a great deal of help in researching, writing and producing this book. First and foremost, I am indebted to the following players I have met for discussions: Bob Barber, Dennis Amiss, David Brown, Alan Smith, Jim Stewart, John Jameson and Harold Rhodes. They have all been most helpful in the information and anecdotes they have provided. In the words of the Bard, 'Old men forget', but not these former cricketers, most of whom are now in their eighties; their memories of past events are quite remarkable.

I am also grateful to those who replied to my letters requesting information: Ossie Wheatley, John Barclay, Sir Geoffrey Boycott, Peter Parfitt, Eric Russell, Farokh Engineer, Robin Hobbs, Raman Subba Row, Micky Stewart, Roy Virgin, Pat Pocock, Bob Taylor, Fred Rumsey, John Price, Doug Padgett and Bobby Parks. There is no substitute for an eyewitness account and I have had most interesting conversations with all these former players, who without exception have the highest regard for Mike as a player, captain and man. 'Brilliant people-manager,' says Boycott.[2] 'It was an honour to play against him,' says Engineer.[3] I would like to thank Bob Barber and David Frith for casting their eye over my chapter on the Australian tour of 1965/66 and to Jim Stewart,

2 Conversation with Sir Geoffrey Boycott.

3 Conversation with Farokh Engineer.

Mike's friend and former Warwickshire team-mate, so nearly a double international for cricket and rugby himself, for writing the foreword.

I would also like to mention two lesser-known players who featured in the 1956 Varsity match on opposite sides but did not go on to play county cricket, Victor Clube and Michael James. They were classmates and friends at St John's School, Leatherhead who left in the same year, 1955, to attend Oxford and Cambridge respectively. Victor was an off-spinner who took the scalps of seven Test players, including Clyde Walcott and Everton Weekes, and later went on to become a world-renowned astrophysicist. It was his letter, in response to mine, that brought Michael James to my notice. Michael, in his freshman year in 1956, made a century against the touring Australians. He also played rugby for Cambridge as a prop forward, and Bob Barber, a contemporary, remembers that he used to strengthen his back muscles by lifting beds with his neck! On leaving university he embarked on a teaching career before joining the Foreign and Colonial Office and, while serving in Guyana, was instrumental in helping Alvin Kallicharran obtain a visa enabling him to play cricket in England. After university Michael played for Berkshire for several years, topping the Minor Counties averages in 1962 with 1,068 runs at 76.28, ahead of players like Boycott, John Edrich, Dennis Amiss and Brian Bolus.

I have consulted many cricket books in the course of my research, a full list of which is given in the bibliography. My principal source has been *Wisden*, on which I have relied for their scorecards and match reports. I have also consulted numerous biographies, accounts of tours and newspaper articles, most of them supplied from Mike's scrapbooks, kept first by his mother, then by his mother-in-law, and afterwards by his late wife Diana. Most of the photographs in the book are from Mike's personal collection. I would also like to thank Bobby Parks for sending me a photograph of a bat owned by his father Jim and autographed by the whole England tour squad in Australia in 1965/66. I had written to Jim a few weeks before he died, not realising he was ill, and understandably did not get a reply. Bobby found my letter when going through his dad's effects and thoughtfully got in contact with me by email.

My greatest thanks, though, are due to Mike himself, whose love for and interest in the game still shines through brightly. For someone whose cricket was played in a different era his views are surprisingly modern, and he is enthusiastic about the limited-overs game. He sees cricket as entertainment and, in his view, if that's what the public want, that's what you have to give them.

This undertaking has been tinged with a certain degree of sadness with the realisation that the majority of the names mentioned in the book are now fallen oaks in cricket's memory lane. I am therefore indebted to authors such as Stephen Chalke and Douglas Miller, who had the opportunity to write biographies about and interview some of the players who have passed on. I have made several borrowings from these books, with their permission and, I hope always, with the appropriate acknowledgements. I have also made considerable use of Colin Schindler's perceptive biography of Bob Barber, Jack Bannister's *The History of Warwickshire County Cricket Club* and Leslie Duckworth's *The Story of Warwickshire Cricket.*

The contact I have had with former players has been both stimulating and nostalgic and the opportunity to get first-hand accounts invaluable. I have, I am pleased to say, brought about a couple of reunions: Jim Stewart with his friend Eric Russell, with whom he had lost contact, and likewise school friends, Michael James with Victor Clube, who has lived abroad for the last 30 years or so. I must also mention the assistance given to me by my friend

Chris Finch, the Speaker Secretary of the Dorset Cricket Society, who must have one of the largest collections of cricket books in the UK and even had an extension built on his property to house them. He has kindly lent me a dozen books from his library. I would also like to thank the following people for proofreading my book and their comments: my brothers, Peter and Bryn, both cricket nuts, Peter still playing for Kent over-70s and Bryn for Cheshire over-60s; my wife, Jenny, who is quick to spot my errors (not only in my written work!); and my son Chris, who has missed his vocation as an editor.

My thanks are also due to my publishers, Pitch Publishing, in particular Bruce Talbot for his meticulous editing, Graham Hales for his immaculate typesetting and preparation of the index and to Duncan Olner of Olner Design for his strikingly attractive cover.

CHAPTER 1

A Leicestershire Village Childhood

MICHAEL JOHN Knight Smith was born in Leicester on 30 June 1933 and grew up in Broughton Astley, a village in Leicestershire not far from Hinckley. His father Maurice was born in 1909 and grew up in the neighbouring village of Narborough. Mike's mother Muriel, née Bird, was born in 1906 in Broughton Astley, where the family lived thereafter. Muriel's father Tom was the village blacksmith, a trade that had been handed down through several generations of Birds from the beginning of the 18th century. Mike's maternal great-grandfather, also Tom, appears in the 1881 census as a blacksmith and publican, as does his great-great-grandfather John Bird in the 1851 census. Mike knew they had a smithy, but was unaware of the pub.

Although Mike's father was keen on sport and played for the village cricket team, his mother's side of the family boasts a more impressive sporting pedigree. His uncle Bill played football for Coventry City; Bill's daughter and Mike's cousin Di Batterham played hockey for England; and her twin brother David was a flying winger who scored 86 tries for Leicester Tigers in 13 seasons with them. Another cousin, Ken, who died young, was also a very talented local cricketer.

Mike's middle name of Knight derives from his paternal great-great-grandfather, Charles Knight, whose daughter Anne

Elizabeth Knight married Albert Smith in 1877. Their son Charles was given the Knight surname as a second Christian name, a not uncommon practice in the past. It has continued to be passed down.

Mike attended the then only primary school in Broughton Astley and showed a keen interest in sport from an early age. Apparently, he was given a train set at the age of nine but, according to his father, showed little interest in it, preferring to play football and cricket on the local recreation ground and practise his ball skills by endlessly bouncing a ball off the garden wall.[4] It was during his school holidays that Mike coincidentally came into contact with Colin Cowdrey who, dispatched from India by his parents to boarding school in England, spent part of his holidays at his uncle's farm in Croft, a village close to Broughton Astley. These two schoolboys playing cricket together could hardly have imagined that one day they would become England cricket captains.

4 *MJK Smith: No Ordinary Man*, Douglas Miller.

CHAPTER 2

Cricket at Stamford School

WHEN MIKE had reached the age of ten, his father decided to send him to Stamford School in Lincolnshire as a boarder, believing he would derive more benefit from this type of experience than at a state school.

Mike maintains his mother was more nervous about the arrangement than he was, although he admits to having been very shy at that age. He soon fitted in, his precocious sporting talent a valuable passport to social acceptance. He was selected for the under-14 cricket team in his first year there.

His captain was Colin Dexter, a good all-round sportsman who, after a 12-year career as a classics teacher, following the onset of deafness, went on to become a celebrated crime writer and the creator of the acclaimed *Inspector Morse* TV series. Two years later, shortly before his 13th birthday, Mike was in the school First XI. He made his debut against local rivals Oakham, scoring 48 before he was run out, having been slowed down, according to his sports master, Bill Packer, by his oversized pads. The team photo from that year shows a diminutive figure sitting in front of much bigger boys seated and standing behind him.

Mike played in the school's First XI for six years, captaining sides containing older boys in two of his last three, in spite of the natural distinction which is usually governed by age.

His batting statistics there are as follows:

	Runs	*Average*	*Highest score*
1946	118	19.66	48
1947	437	48.55	91 not out
1948	310	20.66	60
1949	540	54.00	94
1950	480	48.00	105 not out (against Oakham)
1951	654	65.40	116 not out

In 1951 Mike sometimes also gave himself a bowl, taking 15 wickets at 16.93, although the team's principal spin bowler was left-armer Ray Smith, who played for Leicestershire from 1956–1960.

In 1950 Mike was selected to play for the Rest XI against Southern Schools at Lord's. He scored 3 and 15 not out in a drawn game, falling in the first innings to the bowling of John May, Peter May's younger brother, who later went on to play Minor Counties cricket for Berkshire. The Southern Schools side included some notable future players: Colin Cowdrey, Micky Stewart, Dennis Silk and Charles Williams. Asked what his first experience of playing at Lord's was like, Mike said: 'It was exciting – you get there and you're gobsmacked.'

The following year Mike was again selected for the Rest against Southern Schools at Lord's. This time he did much better, making 88 in a rain-affected drawn game. Colin Ingleby-Mackenzie, John Pretlove and Charles Robins, Walter Robins' son, were in opposition, and Michael Melluish and Bob Gale were in his side. No doubt on the strength of this innings, Mike was selected for the Public Schools against a strong Combined Services team which included future Test players Fred Titmus, Micky Stewart and Keith Andrew. Mike was run out in both innings but finished on the winning side with only a few minutes to spare, thanks to spirited knocks from Ingleby-Mackenzie and Nigel Paul, who later played a few games for Warwickshire before Mike joined them.

While at Stamford, Mike benefitted from the dedicated attention of HE (Bill) Packer, who taught French and coached the cricket and rugby teams. A pupil there himself in the 1920s, Bill had captained the First XI for three years and the First XV for two years before going on to St Edmund Hall, Oxford where he won a blue for rugby as a fly-half. His rugby career was prematurely curtailed when he suffered a serious back injury after a collision with a goal post. He was a lifelong devotee of the school and even got married in the school chapel in 1936. Bill Packer must have seen a reincarnation of himself in Mike and he would have enjoyed following Mike's subsequent cricket and rugby achievements. He wrote of Mike, 'As a captain at school he was superb … and boys of his era have always said that they never enjoyed their cricket as much as they did under Mike's leadership.'

Prior to the matches at Lord's, Mike had played one game for the Leicestershire Second XI at the age of 16, and he made his debut for the First XI as an 18-year-old. In a drawn game against Northamptonshire, batting at number seven, he was out for 0, caught Fiddling, bowled Nutter, a source of subsequent amusement to Mike. This was really no disgrace as Bert Nutter was a seasoned professional who had commenced his career with Lancashire in 1935, joining the county on the same day as Cyril Washbrook. After the war, he moved to Northants, playing for them for six seasons. In 1948 against the touring Australians, the 'Invincibles', he took 5-57 with his accurate fast-medium bowling on a good wicket, including the scalps of Lindsay Hassett, Sid Barnes, Sam Loxton and Ron Hamence. Ken Fiddling played for Northants from 1947–53, having previously been with Yorkshire. During his career he took 226 catches and 76 stumpings. To complete a miserable debut, Mike dropped an easy catch in Northamptonshire's only innings.

Leicestershire persisted with Mike and he played two more games for them that season, one against Derbyshire on a sporting pitch at Burton-on-Trent and the second at Grace Road. He fared no better in these, being bowled by Cliff Gladwin for a duck in the first innings of the Derbyshire game and getting out lbw to 'Dusty' Rhodes for 4 in the second innings. Leicestershire were dismissed for 45 in their first innings and, if it was any consolation to Mike, four other players made ducks. In the second match against Kent, Mike made 1, caught by Cowdrey at slip off Doug Wright. He did, however, catch Godfrey Evans, who made 101 out of Kent's first-innings total of 158. After this inauspicious start to Mike's county career things could only get better.

CHAPTER 3

National Service and Oxford

AS WAS quite common practice at the time, Mike decided to do his National Service, then obligatory, before going to university. Whether he could have got into Oxford immediately is debatable, as a credit in School Certificate Latin was an essential entry requirement for Oxbridge and Latin was not one of Mike's strong suits. In the event, he passed it at the third attempt during his National Service. Mike was surprisingly not offered a commission but was quite happy as a sergeant based in and around Aldershot, where he was allowed plenty of time for good quality sport. One of his Army contemporaries was Micky Stewart, and it was a matter of some surprise to him that Mike, with his school record, was never asked to represent the Combined Services XI.[5]

In the autumn of 1953 Mike went up to St Edmund Hall, Oxford, the college of his former sports master. 'Maybe someone pulled a few strings,' says Mike modestly, but it is more likely that his sporting prowess played a major part, as the college had recently gained a new principal who put a high value on sporting achievement. This was to be the start of a sensational three years on the sporting front at Oxford. Mike impressed immediately by scoring a century in the trial match. On the strength of this he

5 Conversation with Micky Stewart.

was one of only two freshmen selected for the first match against Gloucestershire. Colin Cowdrey, that year's captain, won the toss and batted in what was the only innings in a match ruined by rain. Cowdrey made a sparkling 78 and Mike, batting at number five, a patient 104 not out in three and a half hours. Oxford declared at 309/9, after which no further play was possible, thus depriving Mike of the chance to see Arthur Milton and Tom Graveney bat.

In the next game against Yorkshire, Oxford were dismissed for 58, Fred Trueman accounting for Cowdrey for 0 and Mike for 11 among his 5-8 from ten overs. A lot of professionals avoided the matches against Oxford and Cambridge, but Fred saw it as an opportunity to pick up a number of cheap wickets, which for him it usually was. 'Fred was a great bowler', says Mike, 'and he was always a challenge with his late outswing.' Mike did better in the second innings with 46, before being bowled by Ray Illingworth. Charles Williams,[6] batting at number three, made 53 out of an Oxford total of 239. Oxford had been made to follow on but they staved off defeat, the last pair holding on for a rather undeserved draw.

In the following match against Kent, Cowdrey asked Mike to open the batting on the promise that if it didn't work out he could revert to his number four position. Mike performed well in the second innings with 50 not out to help his side to a draw. He retained this position for the game against Lancashire, which

6 Charles Williams (1933–2019) was educated at Westminster School and at Christ Church, Oxford, gaining an MA in classics. He made his first-class debut for Oxford in 1952 and captained the university in his final year. He played 42 matches for Oxford during his three years there and later 40 matches for Essex. He went on to enjoy a successful career in banking and was a director of Mirror Group Newspapers from 1985–92. He was awarded the CBE in 1980 and was created a life peer in 1985 as Baron Williams of Elvel, sitting in the House of Lords as a Labour peer. He wrote highly regarded biographies of Don Bradman, Charles de Gaulle, Konrad Adenauer, Maréchal Pétain and Harold Macmillan as well as *Gentlemen and Players*, a detailed account of the ending of amateurism in cricket.

also ended in a draw after an exciting finish, Lancashire closing two runs short with three wickets standing. This would have been Mike's first encounter with Bob Barber, then still a schoolboy, who was later to play for Mike many times for both Warwickshire and England. Mike continued to open the batting for the remainder of the season and the start of the following one.

Towards the end of May Oxford entertained the Pakistan touring team in the Parks. Cambridge had enjoyed a high-scoring draw with them the previous week and Oxford were hoping to go one better. Batting first, Oxford made 253, of which Mike scored 53. Oxford's number ten, David Fasken, made a hard-hit 61. Fazal Mahmood, Pakistan's opening fast bowler, took 5-54. Pakistan replied with 392, Abdul Kardar, the captain and a former Oxford blue, making 79, as did Maqsood Ahmed. Oxford's second innings, after a stand of 51 between Mike (43) and Charles Williams (48), fizzled to a tame 169 all out. Pakistan knocked off the 34 runs required for the loss of one wicket.

In the next fixture against Middlesex, which ended in a rain-affected draw, Mike made 86 and 15 not out, again opening the batting. He was up against Fred Titmus, later to become a highly valued England team-mate, but Mike held him off for many of the 47 overs Titmus bowled in the match.

Oxford suffered their first defeat of the season at the hands of Worcestershire, who beat them by the narrow margin of 11 runs in a match with three declarations. Don Kenyon, a man Mike held in high esteem as a batsman and captain, made an impressive 139 in Worcestershire's first innings and 59 in the second. Set 290 to win, Mike scored 67 to accompany his 50 in the first innings. A dashing century from Jonathan 'Pom-Pom' Fellows-Smith, a South African who was to play four Test matches for his country in 1960, just failed to get Oxford over the line. He had scored 80 in the first innings and also took five wickets in the match.

The next match against Hampshire was to fortuitously produce a new opening partner for Mike. Hampshire, having declared at 367/8 with a fine 158 from Desmond Eagar, their captain and a former Oxford blue, left Oxford half an hour to bat at the end of the day. Mike, having lost his opening partner with only 14 on the board, was joined by tailender Jimmy Allan[7] as nightwatchman. The following day, after Mike departed for 53, Jimmy surprised everybody by making 118 and featuring in a partnership of 176 with Charles Williams, who made 139. After declaring their second innings with a lead of over 200, Hampshire bowled out Oxford in the final over of the match to win by 22 runs. Allan was to finish up as an opener for the rest of his time at Oxford.

The next match was against the Free Foresters, a nomadic, amateur club established in 1856. The 1954 Free Foresters' side contained five former England captains: Nigel Howard, Gubby Allen, Bob Wyatt, Freddie Brown and Errol Holmes. The Free Foresters, batting first, made 268/6 declared, Nigel Howard scoring 81 and Bob Wyatt, then aged 52, making 63 not out. Oxford's reply was a rather feeble 120/8. Allen, bowling with a lot less pace than in his heyday, took 3-12 in seven overs, including the wickets of Cowdrey and Williams. Rain prevented any play on the final day and the match ended in a draw with the veterans taking the honours.

---

7 Jimmy Allan (1932–2005) was born in Leeds and educated at Edinburgh Academy and Worcester College, Oxford, where he studied classics. He played in the university side from 1953–56, gaining his blue each year. Originally a left-arm slow bowler, he progressed from being a tailender to an opening batsman after scoring a century as a nightwatchman. Between 1954 and 1957 he also played several matches for Kent. After leaving university and moving to Scotland he was a regular member of the Scottish team and in 1966 was persuaded by his former Oxford captain Mike Smith to play for Warwickshire. In his first-class career he took 435 wickets and scored 4,988 runs. Later he worked as an investment analyst and stockbroker in Edinburgh, spending much of his free time as a volunteer cricket coach.

A non-first-class match against the Army followed. This also ended in a draw with Lance Corporal Doug Padgett, a future Yorkshire stalwart, making 73 not out and fellow Lance Corporal Peter Richardson 103 not out. The Army had the better of the match, Oxford finishing 52 runs short with eight wickets down.

Oxford completed their season of home games at the Parks with a drawn game against Sussex. Hubert Doggart, Sussex's captain, excelled with a century in each innings, with Allan and Cowdrey making centuries in Oxford's first innings and Harry Birrell[8] 64 in the second.

Oxford now had four away games to play: Gloucestershire at Bristol, Surrey at Guildford, Warwickshire at Edgbaston and MCC at Lord's. The game at Bristol was drawn after Gloucestershire racked up 358/8 declared with Arthur Milton making 142, Tom Graveney 61 and Jack Crapp 66 before retiring hurt after a blow on the hand. Oxford made 288 in reply, Cowdrey and Jonathan Fellows-Smith scoring half-centuries. Gloucestershire only made 134 in their second innings. Left to score 205 in two and a half hours, Oxford started strongly and were well placed at 105/1 after an hour. However, the off-spin of John Mortimore (4-54) reduced this to 170/9, after which Oxford managed to hang on for a draw, the last pair surviving for half an hour.

---

8 Harry Birrell (1927–2003) was a South African who was educated at St Andrew's College, Grahamstown and Rhodes University before coming to Lincoln College, Oxford in 1952. The following year he finished second in the batting averages to Colin Cowdrey with 812 runs at 32.48. He also won a blue for rugby at Oxford. He had played cricket for Eastern Province for several years before coming to Oxford and played for them again on his return to South Africa. He pursued a career in teaching and, after moving to Bulawayo, played several games for Rhodesia. The Harry Birrell Scholarship Trust, founded in 1996, helps African children from underprivileged backgrounds to receive a quality secondary education. Harry's son Adrian, at the time of writing, is head coach at Hampshire Cricket Club.

The match against Surrey was also drawn, Oxford making 161 in their first innings, Peter Loader taking 7-28 in 20 overs. Only Allan (50) and Williams (52) offered any real resistance. Loader accounted for four batsmen for a duck, including Cowdrey, and Mike only made scores of 5 and 11 against him. Surrey's total of 422/8 (Bernie Constable 121, David Fletcher 63, Eric Bedser 61) made it unlikely they would need to bat again and only a fighting second-innings 79 from Cowdrey saved the day, Oxford ending on 160/8.

In the match against Warwickshire at Edgbaston honours were almost even on first innings, both sides scoring just under 300. Fred Gardner, on whom Mike was later to rely heavily for providing a solid foundation to Warwickshire's innings when he became captain, top-scored with 67 and also made 75 in their second-innings total of 282/9. Cowdrey had sportingly declared Oxford's second innings closed at 288/5 (Mike 75, Geoffrey Marsland 60), but in spite of Allan picking up five wickets for 87, Warwickshire got home with a few minutes to spare to win by one wicket in an exciting finish. Roly Thompson held his end up without scoring while Philip Bromley (38 not out) scored the remaining 13 runs required. This was the closest Oxford came to winning all season.

Oxford's last game before the Varsity match was a two-day non-first-class game against MCC at Lord's, which MCC won by 37 runs.

The culmination of the season was the Varsity match, which Oxford were unlucky not to win. After Cowdrey won the toss and chose to bat, Mike and his opening partner Allan put on 145 for the first wicket, giving Oxford the perfect start. Mike was lucky to survive the first over, having edged a ball from Colin

Smith[9] between the wicketkeeper Michael Melluish and Dennis Silk at first slip, which these two future presidents of MCC left for each other to Mike's astonished relief. According to Mike, it was the wicketkeeper's catch, and it proved to be a very expensive error. The ball went to the boundary, getting Mike off the mark. After Allan's dismissal for an aggressive 86, Mike was joined by Harry Birrell, who was now in his final year. The pair put on 76 runs for the second wicket before Birrell fell to Smith for his only wicket of the match. Mike was joined by Cowdrey and the two proceeded to put on 180 for the third wicket in two hours, Cowdrey finally being dismissed by Gamini Goonesena,[10] the Sinhalese Nottinghamshire leg-break bowler, for 66. Thereupon Cowdrey declared at the handsome total of 401/3 with Mike on 201 not out. Mike's practically faultless display had dominated the partnership.

If the first day had been Oxford's, the second was clearly Cambridge's, with a century from Dennis Silk and a cultured 73 from John Pretlove helping Cambridge to within 57 of Oxford's

---

9 Colin Smith, later Sir Colin Stansfield Smith (1932–2013), was a celebrated architect and academic. He apparently decided to add the 'Stansfield' to his name after a banking error confused him with another 'Smith'. He was educated at William Hulme's Grammar School, Manchester and Christ's College, Cambridge, where he studied architecture from 1953–58. He played in the Cambridge XI for four years as a right-handed batsman and bowler, gaining his blue in 1954 and taking 50 wickets in each of his last two years. He also scored a century against Warwickshire in 1957. He was capped by Lancashire in 1957, but only played a few games for them. After a career with Cheshire and Hampshire local authorities, he became Professor of Architecture at Portsmouth University and later Emeritus Professor. He was appointed a CBE in 1988 and knighted in 1993 for services to architecture.

10 Gamini Goonesena (1931–2011) was born in Colombo, Ceylon (now Sri Lanka), and was educated at Royal College, Colombo and Cambridge University. He played in the university team from 1954–57, winning a blue each year, captaining the team in his final year and scoring 211 in the 1957 Varsity match, which Cambridge won. He was a right-handed batsman and a right-arm leg-spin bowler. He joined Nottinghamshire the year before attending university and played for them until 1964. He also played several matches for New South Wales. After Sri Lanka were awarded Test match status in 1982 he managed the Sri Lanka Test team on a tour of India. In 2004 he moved to Australia and died in Canberra in 2011, aged 80.

score. Pretlove was an outstanding natural athlete who also won blues for football and rugby fives. Oxford, in their second innings batted until 3.55pm on the final day, declaring at 148/9, Birrell making 64 and Goonesena taking 6-71. With the captains agreeing to dispense with the tea interval, Cambridge were set a target of 206 in 145 minutes. They were never up with the rate though and lost wickets steadily to Birrell, who finished with 5-20. When Cowdrey claimed the extra half hour the total stood at 132/6 but, after losing two further wickets, Melluish and Brian Parsons hung on to foil Oxford. Cowdrey even gave Mike two overs near the end in the hope of producing a false stroke. Earlier, a hard-hit 47 from the Jamaican Vincent Lumsden had held up Oxford's progress.

So Oxford finished their season with yet another draw, ten in all, no victories and four defeats. In fairness, a lot of the matches had been affected by rain and, had they been completed, Oxford would probably have lost most of them. Mike had a very successful season with 1,065 runs at an average of 48.40, above Cowdrey (983 at 42.73) and Charles Williams (774 at 36.85). It was Cowdrey's final year at Oxford, and a few months later he was on the boat to Australia in the elevated company of Len Hutton, Denis Compton, Bill Edrich, Peter May and Tom Graveney. Mike maintains that he learned more from batting at the other end with Cowdrey than from any other player. 'His technique was immaculate', enthuses Mike, 'and his strokeplay exquisite.' After they both left Oxford they were to share many moments on the field together, sometimes in subordinate captaincy roles to each other and sometimes in opposition. Although some have questioned Cowdrey's captaincy ability, Mike has always retained his esteem for Colin as a highly talented batsman, an exceptional slip fielder and a good friend.

The season was not over for Mike, though, and he went on to play ten matches for Leicestershire during the summer vacation with mixed success. He finished fourth in the Leicestershire batting averages with 475 runs at 27.94, three half-centuries and a top score of 72 made in his second game against Essex. Leicester used him as an opening batsman, partnering either Gerry Lester or Maurice Hallam, normally their regular opening pair. In the match against Hampshire he was out caught off Derek Shackleton for 0 and bowled by Vic Cannings for 4, although he made 65 in the return match at Leicester. He fared little better against Surrey, falling victim to Jim Laker for 1 and to Alec Bedser for 21. At Northampton he was bowled by Frank Tyson for 22 and caught off Vince Broderick for 49 in the second innings. Mike reckons Tyson was the fastest bowler he ever played against. 'He was the only bowler to hit me on the head,' he reflected. 'Fortunately it was a glancing blow; otherwise I probably wouldn't be talking to you now.' Against Warwickshire, in a match in which only one and a half hours' play was possible, Mike was dismissed cheaply by Jack Bannister, who was later to become one of his principal opening bowlers when he took over the captaincy of Warwickshire.

Leicestershire were a pretty weak side in 1954, winning only three of their 30 matches and finishing next to bottom in the County Championship table.

CHAPTER 4

Second Year at Oxford

THE 1955 season began under the captaincy of Charles Williams with Mike as the secretary, a role which ensured his succession as the following year's captain.

Oxford's first match against Gloucestershire ended in a high-scoring draw, Oxford declaring at 383/8, Williams making 120, Peter Delisle 113, Jimmy Allan 54 and freshman Chris Walton 52.[11] Gloucestershire replied with 368/8, Martin Young making 170 and John Mortimore 120. Once again Mike did not get to see Tom Graveney bat as he had to leave the match on hearing of the death of his father-in-law. Williams added 64 not out to his first-innings century out of a total of 111/2 when time ran out.

Mike's poor form continued against Lancashire when he gained his first 'pair of spectacles', bowled both times by Brian Statham, who was to claim his wicket 17 times in his career. Oxford struggled to 111 before dismissing Lancashire for 159, Allan taking 5-60. Oxford had reached 126/3 in their second innings before rain wiped out most of the last day. Low scores

---

11 Chris Walton (1933–2006) was born in Georgetown, British Guiana (now Guyana). He played in the Oxford XI from 1955–57, winning a blue in all three seasons and captaining the side in his final year. He scored 2,254 runs in those three seasons at an average of 28.90, his best season being 1956 when he scored 1,128 runs at 41.77, including three centuries. He also played 35 matches for Middlesex between 1957 and 1959. He later emigrated to Australia and died in New South Wales, aged 72.

of 23 and 10 against Yorkshire, a side of almost Test match strength, prolonged Mike's 'bad trot'; he was dismissed on both occasions by Bob Appleyard, who ended the season top of the national averages. Oxford lost by an innings and 23 runs, having failed to reach Yorkshire's 317 after two attempts. For Yorkshire, Frank Lowson made 72, as did Norman Yardley in his last season as Yorkshire's captain. Fred Trueman was the main architect of Oxford's downfall with the impressive match figures of 10-32 off 34.3 overs. He was clearly too good for the students.

The match against Warwickshire was drawn, with no play possible on the final day. Inserted by Williams, Warwickshire were dismissed for 149 on a difficult wicket, with only New Zealander Ray Hitchcock[12] making a half-century. Oxford, all out for 134, fared no better, Mike making a modest 17. In their curtailed second innings, Bert Wolton and 20-year-old Jim Stewart, in his first first-class match, put Oxford to the sword with 105 not out and 33 not out respectively, putting on 131 by the end of day two. Jim was to become a long-standing member of Mike's Warwickshire side and a good friend.

The game against Middlesex also ended in a draw, proceedings not starting until 4.45pm on the first day and being brought to a halt by a storm on the last day. In the interim Oxford made 124

12 Ray Hitchcock (1929–2019) was born in Christchurch, New Zealand and joined Warwickshire in 1949 after a two-week trial, having worked his passage to England on a Liberty cargo boat to fulfil his ambition. He spent the voyage helping to paint the ship. He was a left-handed batsman who scored 12,229 runs at an average of 27.82 and was the last survivor of Warwickshire's 1951 Championship-winning side, retiring in 1964 to become Second XI captain. He also took 182 wickets at 28.56 as a leg-break bowler. He was one of the main driving forces behind the Warwickshire Pool, the phenomenal success of which assured Warwickshire's financial future. He opened a sports outfitters shop in his home town of Solihull and later, together with his wife Anne, formed Messenger Stud, where they bred many winners. Mike remembers him as a free-scoring middle-order batsman, a fine fielder with a good arm, a useful partnership breaker with his bowling and a great team player.

and 231/9 (Williams 80, Peter Walshe[13] 77). Middlesex made 145 in their only innings. Fred Titmus had match figures of 6-33. Mike failed again with 0 and 17, being bowled by John Warr on both occasions. Warr, whilst still at Cambridge, had toured Australia with MCC under Freddie Brown in 1950/51, preferred perhaps because of his pedigree to superior county pros like Les Jackson and Derek Shackleton, who had both taken more wickets and finished higher in the first-class averages. He played in two Test matches, taking 1-281 and was never selected for England again, although he gave his county sterling service with 956 wickets at 22.79.

Next to visit the Parks were the Free Foresters, who again included Bob Wyatt and Freddie Brown. Colin Ingleby-Mackenzie was also in the team. Having played a full season for Hampshire in 1954, he had turned down a place at Trinity College, Oxford to work for Slazenger and only played one game for Hampshire that year. The Free Foresters won by five wickets in spite of the loss of the first day to rain. Oxford's first-innings total of 228 was largely due to John Baker, a freshman from Taunton School who had already represented Somerset several times, making 91 not out, including three sixes off Brown. In the Free Foresters innings, wicketkeeper David Blake, an amateur and dentist by profession, who played 79 matches for Hampshire between 1949 and 1958 when work permitted, made 81 and a hard-hit 70 from Brown took their score to 283. Oxford declared their second innings at 241/6, leaving Free Foresters to make 187 in 105 minutes. They

13 Peter Walshe (1934–) was born in Salisbury, Southern Rhodesia and educated there before entering Wadham College, Oxford in 1953. He spent four years at Oxford and played in the university team as a wicketkeeper each year, gaining his first blue as a freshman. During this time he scored 900 runs at an average of 14.75, took 48 catches and made 12 stumpings. On his return to South Africa he lectured at the University of Lesotho for three years before moving to the United States where he became Professor of Political Science at Notre Dame University. He has written a number of books on African politics.

accomplished this feat with eight minutes to spare, largely thanks to a rapid second-wicket partnership of 88 between Blake (60) and Ingleby-Mackenzie (68). With a total of 59 runs in his two innings, Mike's form was improving slightly. The next game against the Army, ranked as non-first-class, was drawn with only three innings completed.

The first two days of the following match against Mike's county club Leicestershire were lost to rain but for 15 minutes on the first day. On the final day Oxford made 154, Mike and Jimmy Allan putting on 87 for the first wicket. The highlight of the innings in this dead game was Allan taking 27 off one over from the Australian Vic Jackson with two sixes and three fours. Leicestershire's other Australian Jack Walsh took 4-9 in five overs and Vic Munden 4-30. Leicestershire made 87/5 in reply, Gerry Lester scoring 45 not out. Jackson and Walsh had been recruited by Sir Julien Cahn in the 1930s to play for his private XI, which toured New Zealand and Ceylon, after which they joined Leicestershire. Vic Jackson was a right-handed all-rounder who did the double in 1955. After his career with Leicestershire ended, he returned to Australia, where he died in a road accident aged 48. Walsh was a left-arm wrist-spinner and a left-handed batsman who did the double in 1952 and took over 100 wickets seven times. Mike's recollection of Jackson from his time with Leicestershire is of a fairly typical tough Aussie and not much of a mixer, whereas Walsh was a sociable individual and a good team man who later became an assistant coach at Leicestershire and captain of the Second XI.

Oxford went down to Worcestershire by five wickets in their final home game. The match started badly for Mike when he was bowled by Jack Flavell for a duck, but he redeemed himself in the second innings with a confident 73. Oxford's totals of 181 and 242 proved to be well within Worcestershire's reach, and with 194 required to win in two and three-quarter hours, 83 runs from Bob Broadbent with four sixes and six fours saw Worcestershire home by five wickets in the nick of time.

With the home matches over, it was now time for Oxford to hit the road again with their first match against MCC at Lord's. MCC, batting first, posted 274. At last Mike's form blossomed and he and Jimmy Allan put on 167 for the first wicket in reply, Mike making a stylish 118 and Allan 47. Jonathan Fellows-Smith with 52 helped the total to 271. MCC declared at 272/8 in their second innings, which was dominated by a superb century from Colin Cowdrey in his first appearance of the season. Oxford were left with just under four hours to make the 276 needed for victory but were never up with the rate and finished a disappointing 38 runs short with four wickets in hand. Mike was bowled by Don Bennett for 14 and thereafter, although several batsmen got starts, only Allan with 59 and Ian Gibson,[14] 52 not out, showed sufficient enterprise.

Oxford lost the next two games to Hampshire and Surrey. At Bournemouth, Oxford posted a decent total of 282/9 declared, Allan making 62 and Williams 42. Derek Shackleton bowled tightly to take 4-53. Hampshire declared 33 runs behind, with the veteran Neville Rogers making 121 not out. In the second innings only Mike was able to deal with the off-spin of Mervyn Burden, who took 7-53. For the first time in his career Mike carried his bat for 76 not out. Hampshire easily secured victory by six wickets, West Indian Roy Marshall making a typically dashing century.

14 Born in Glossop, Derbyshire in 1936, Ian Gibson was educated at Manchester Grammar School, where he captained the First XI in his last two years, and at Brasenose College, Oxford. He played in the university team from 1955–58, gaining his blue in all four years and scoring a total of 1,404 runs at an average of 20.65 with one century in 1957. He played several games for Derbyshire first and Second XIs in 1957. He was also a useful leg-break bowler who took 51 first-class wickets. After qualifying as a doctor, he developed mental health problems and sadly took his own life in 1963 at the age of 26.

He played in four Test matches for the West Indies and was a key member of Hampshire's 1961 Championship-winning side.

Oxford were soundly thrashed by Surrey at Guildford, losing by an innings and 12 runs. Only Peter Delisle and Fellows-Smith with half-centuries prospered against the hostile bowling of Peter Loader, who took 4-44 and bowled Mike for low scores in both innings. With fifties from Bernie Constable and Dennis Cox, and 113 from Tom Clark, Surrey amassed 399, which proved enough for them not to have to bat again. Oxford were only able to manage 149 in their second innings, Fellows-Smith with 48 the only one to put up any real resistance.

The match against Sussex was drawn on a pitch which gave the bowlers little help. Oxford scored 363/5, Mike making 89 and Allan 69 in a first-wicket partnership of 133. Chris Walton and Charles Williams continued the good work with scores of 68 and 95 respectively. Sussex also found the pitch benevolent and were able to declare 15 runs ahead for the loss of five wickets. John Langridge made a masterful 153, Arthur Lawrence 62 and David Sheppard 58 not out. Mike scored his second century of the season, making exactly 100 with two sixes and 11 fours. Nearly all the other batsmen reached double figures on this increasingly benign pitch. Needing 264 to win, Sussex finished 118 runs short when time was called, Lawrence making another half-century.

Oxford had the best of the match against DR Jardine's XI at Eastbourne, a side which included Cowdrey, Bob Wyatt and Errol Holmes. They dismissed their opponents for 95 after having made 215, of which Mike was the main contributor with 64. It was Fellows-Smith who brought about the Jardine XI's downfall with 7-26. Oxford scored 233 in their second innings by the end of the second day. Set 354 to win, Jardine's XI were saved by the rain, which wiped out the whole of the final day.

The day of the eagerly awaited Varsity match had now arrived, a game prized by both sides above all other encounters. Selection for it meant obtaining the permanent honour of a blue and this year's captain Charles Williams deliberated long and hard before announcing his choice. One player who must have been particularly disappointed to be omitted was John Baker, who had already represented Somerset and who, in only five matches, was topping the university batting averages, marginally ahead of Mike.

On winning the toss, Dennis Silk, that year's Cambridge captain, opted to bat, dropping himself down the order to number eight because of an injured thumb. He had made centuries in his previous two Varsity matches but had little chance of repeating the feat in that position. Although in pain, he featured gamely in an important seventh-wicket partnership of 70 with John Pretlove, who made an attractive 114. A first-wicket stand of 56 between Robin O'Brien and Brian Parsons had given Cambridge a good start, and they ultimately reached 304 all out. Fellows-Smith performed tirelessly for Oxford to finish with figures of 5-83 off 37 overs.

In reply, Oxford struggled against the bowling of the turbaned Swaranjit Singh, a future team-mate of Mike's at Warwickshire, and Goonesena, who took four wickets apiece. Walton was the only player to offer any serious resistance with 57, and Oxford were all out for 170. Silk declared Cambridge's second innings closed at 178/6 at one o'clock on the final day, setting Oxford the task of making 313 to win in four and a quarter hours. David Fasken, in his last match for Oxford, took 4-38 in 18 lively overs. Fasken was a right-arm medium-fast bowler who made 27 appearances between 1953 and 1955. His most notable performance was against the 1953 touring Australians when he took 5-108, including the wickets of Graeme Hole, Arthur Morris and Richie Benaud. He later became the director of the Earls Court and Olympia exhibition centres, playing a major role in their growth and development.

After the loss of two early wickets, Mike and Williams made a bold effort to go for the target with a partnership of 103 in 90 minutes, but after Mike was out, caught at long on by Singh off Goonesena for 104, the chance of a win evaporated. With six wickets down, Williams was happy to bat out time for a well-made 47 not out. An earlier declaration by Cambridge could have produced a result in either team's favour, but the stakes are too high in these matches to risk the ignominy of defeat.

Mike's achievement of scoring a double century in his first year at Oxford and a century in his second equalled the feat of Alan Ratcliffe, who had made 201 for Cambridge in the 1931 Varsity match and 124 the following year. Ratcliffe later played a few games for Surrey without much success. Mike was to go one better in 1956, as we shall see.

For the first time in his burgeoning career Mike was selected to play for the Gentlemen versus the Players, a match which had its origins in the early part of the 19th century, when bowling was still of the underarm variety. It was contested between the amateurs and the professionals, and continued to be played right up to 1962, when this outmoded distinction was abolished. Charles Williams, Oxford's captain in 1956, who later played for Essex as an amateur, wrote in 2012 of the demise of this tradition in an excellent book entitled *Gentlemen and Players: The Death of Amateurism in Cricket.* The relegation of this fixture to the scrapbook of history was only lamented by a few die-hards, but the matches had produced some exciting, hard-fought contests, the majority won by the professionals.

Before this fixture at Lord's, Mike was due to play again for Leicestershire against Derbyshire at Ashby-de-la-Zouch. Leicestershire opted to bat first and Mike, resuming his previous year's opening partnership with Gerry Lester, scored 29 in Leicestershire's first innings but only seven in the second. Maurice Tompkin[15] top-scored with 67. A superb 146 from Derbyshire's captain Donald Carr gave Derbyshire a substantial first-innings lead, but Leicestershire made a good recovery in their second innings thanks to a century from Vic Jackson and 71 from Tony Diment. Carr used all 11 of his side as bowlers, including one over from George Dawkes, who took off his pads in an attempt to winkle Leicestershire out, but it wouldn't have made any difference as Leicestershire were already 180 ahead when the match ended in a draw.

The Gentlemen v Players match was due to start the following day. Mike travelled to London from Ashby-de-la-Zouch. He would have almost certainly gone down by car with his captain Charles Palmer,[16] who was also playing for the Gentlemen, and Maurice Tompkin, who was in the Players' team. The Players batted first, making 316, of which Tompkin made 115. John Warr took 4-54 and Robin Marlar 3-61. The Players' total was exceeded by the Gentlemen, Palmer making a chanceless 154 and Doug Insole 72 in a total of 336/8 declared. Goonesena with 6-83 restricted the

15 Maurice Tompkin (1919–56) was from Countesthorpe, a village no more than four miles from Broughton Astley and was a friend of Mike's father. He played for Leicestershire from 1938–56, scoring 19,927 runs at an average of 31.83 with 31 centuries. He also played professional football for Bury, Leicester City and Huddersfield Town. He died of pancreatic cancer in 1956, aged 37, after returning from an MCC tour of Pakistan.

16 Charles Palmer (1919–2005) was an amateur who joined Leicestershire as captain and secretary in 1950, having previously played for Worcestershire in 1938 and a few games for them in 1948. For Leicestershire he scored over 1,000 runs in six successive seasons and during his career took 315 wickets at 25.15 apiece with his slow-medium bowling. In May 1955, in Jack Walsh's benefit match against Surrey, he had the remarkable figures of 8-7 from 14 overs in the first innings and 0-1 from 13 overs in the second. It could have been 9-0 in the first innings as Laker was dropped off his bowling. He was appointed player/manager for the 1953/54 England tour of West Indies, an ill-tempered series in which he made his only Test appearance. After retirement he became chairman of Leicestershire, was president of MCC in 1978, and chairman of the TCCB between 1983 and 1985. He was awarded the CBE for services to cricket in 1984.

Players to 220 in their second innings, with Tom Dollery, in his final year as Warwickshire captain, making 82. This proved to be enough, however, as the Gentlemen, after a first-wicket stand of 63 between Mike and Gerry Tordoff, could only manage 180 in their second innings, with Fellows-Smith making a fighting 51 with eight fours and a six. Cowdrey, although injured, came in at number 11, but was out caught for a duck, leaving Pretlove stranded on 3 not out. The Players were thus victorious by 20 runs with five minutes to spare.

As soon as the match was over, the Leicestershire trio had to dash up to Manchester for their game against Lancashire starting the next day. Mike must have wondered afterwards whether it had been worth the effort as, batting at number four, he was lbw to Brian Statham for 4 and caught off the bowling of Roy Tattersall for 1 in the second innings. Leicestershire were soundly beaten by an innings and 59 runs, Lancashire declaring at 389/9 with Cyril Washbrook, Jack Ikin, Ken Grieves and even Statham scoring half-centuries.

Leicestershire followed this disappointment with an exciting two-wicket win against Hampshire at Leicester, Mike making 70 in Leicestershire's first innings, batting at number four. He remained in this position for the game against Essex at Brentwood, top-scoring in each innings with 60 and 63, Leicestershire finishing victorious by 20 runs. They lost the next game against Hampshire at Bournemouth by ten wickets, Mike being dismissed cheaply by Derek Shackleton in both innings. They then suffered another humiliating defeat at the hands of Northamptonshire, losing by nine wickets in spite of a fighting second-innings century by Palmer. Mike was bowled by Frank Tyson in the first innings but it was the Australian left-arm spinner George Tribe[17] who did most of the damage with match figures of 12-91. The next game against Yorkshire was a keenly contested, close-run affair which Yorkshire ended up winning by two wickets thanks to a vital second-innings partnership by those two great Yorkshire stalwarts, Brian Close and Ray Illingworth. Trueman, who dismissed Mike 14 times in his career, accounted for him on this occasion in both innings, bowled and lbw.

The following match against Warwickshire at Edgbaston, which was soon to become Mike's second home, was a rain-affected draw, enlivened only by centuries by Palmer for Leicestershire and Dick Spooner for Warwickshire. Gerry Lester also made a tedious five-hour one for Leicestershire and Maurice Hallam an attractive half-century before having to retire with what *Wisden* described as a 'chill'. Of his two opening partners during Mike's time with Leicestershire, Hallam was clearly the better batsman who, according to Mike, was 'a very nice bloke'. In a career running from 1950 to 1970 he scored 24,488 runs at an average of just under 30 and captained the side for four seasons. Gerry Lester, however, was a slow scorer, whose career ran from 1937–58. *Wisden* described him rather unflatteringly as one of the circuit's stodgiest players. He captained the Second XI for several years and later became the county's coach.

In mid-August Leicestershire entertained Sussex, winning convincingly by 143 runs, Vic Jackson taking 13 wickets in the

17 George Tribe was an Australian who played three Tests for Australia against England in the 1946/47 Ashes series in Australia. Discarded by Australia, he came over to England to play in the Lancashire League, where he enjoyed considerable success before being taken on by Northamptonshire in 1951. A left-arm wrist-spin bowler and left-handed batsman, he played for Northants for nine seasons, doing the double in seven of them. He took 1,378 wickets at 20.55 in his career and scored over 10,000 first-class runs. He was one of *Wisden*'s five Cricketers of the Year in 1955. He, probably more than anyone else, was responsible for Northants becoming a force to be reckoned with and Keith Andrew thought he was the best cricketer he had ever played with. In his younger days he was a prominent Australian Rules footballer for Footscray in Melbourne.

match. Mike went back to opening the innings in place of Hallam, who was still unwell, but he did not prosper, being run out for 1 in the first innings and caught by David Sheppard in the second for 2. Following this, Leicestershire achieved their first double of the season when they beat Essex by 59 runs in the return fixture at home, Jackson scoring a century in Leicestershire's first innings. They achieved another victory at Cardiff against Glamorgan, winning by ten wickets after making 305 in reply to Glamorgan's 209, Mike making 61 and Jackson 105. In the second innings Mike made 39 not out of the 51 needed to win. Leicestershire's roller-coaster ride continued with a defeat by Middlesex at Lord's by 40 runs. Required to make 219 to win in 165 minutes, their last few wickets fell to Jack Young and Fred Titmus in failing light.

Leicestershire's final game of the season was against Worcestershire, who, batting first, declared at 292/7 with Don Kenyon and Martin Horton both scoring centuries. Leicestershire's reply of 194 did not augur well but, after bowling Worcestershire out for 123, they made the 222 runs needed for the loss of only five wickets largely thanks to a stand of 166 between Jackson (114) and Palmer (63). Mike had made a useful 46 in Leicestershire's first innings, but was out for only 4 in the second, bowled by Reg Perks.[18] This was Leicestershire's 11th Championship victory and it moved them up to sixth in the table, a big improvement on the previous season. Mike finished fourth in the Leicestershire batting averages with 688 runs at 26.46, behind Tompkin, Jackson

18 This was Perks' (1911–77) penultimate game for Worcestershire, as he retired at the end of the season at the remarkable age, for a pace bowler, of 43. He had given fine service to the county since joining them on the ground staff in 1928 as a 16-year-old. He made his first-class debut two years later and during his career took 2,226 first-class wickets, a number bettered only by Wilfred Rhodes and Tich Freeman until overtaken later by Eric Hollies. He played two Test matches for England, one of them the 'Timeless Test' in South Africa in 1939, when the team had to abandon the run chase to catch the train for their journey to Cape Town before the boat back to England departed.

and Palmer. Unbeknown to his Leicestershire team-mates and to himself at the time, this was Mike's last game for the county of his birth, as he was to be offered the captaincy of Warwickshire combined with the duties of assistant secretary, which would enable him to continue playing as an amateur. In spite of a natural loyalty to Leicestershire, this was an opportunity too good to refuse. 'I saw my future at that time in cricket administration', says Mike, 'and I felt this job would provide a route to it while still allowing me to play for several seasons.' Leicestershire were obviously very sorry to lose him and were prepared to offer him administrative employment but were not able to come up with anything sufficiently tempting. 'We cannot, and do not, grumble at his decision,' said a spokesman at the time.

CHAPTER 5

Captain of the XI

IN KEEPING with the traditional policy of succession, Mike was duly appointed captain of the university for 1956 with Chris Walton, the captain for 1957, serving as secretary. Williams, Fellows-Smith and Fasken were missing from the previous year's line-up, but with Jack Bailey, a future secretary of MCC, and Esmond Kentish, a 39-year-old West Indian with two Test caps, they had gained in the fast bowling department. Freshman Mike Eagar[19] was a valuable addition to the batting resources. The season began with a team strong enough to reverse the history of several barren seasons.

Fortunes did not change immediately as Oxford lost their first match by an innings and ten runs against Gloucestershire. An excellent opening partnership of 119 between Mike (56) and Stanley Metcalfe[20] (63) had laid a good foundation, but after their

19 Mike Eagar (1934–2019) was educated at Rugby School and Worcester College, Oxford. He played in 87 first-class matches during his four years there, scoring 2,288 runs at an average of 26.30, gaining his blue every season. He also won a hockey blue. His best year was 1956 when, as a freshman, he scored his first first-class century and topped the batting averages with 41.95. He played several games for Gloucestershire and was apparently being groomed for the captaincy but ultimately opted for a teaching career at Eton.

20 Stanley Metcalfe (1932–2017) was born in Horsforth and was educated at Leeds Grammar School and Pembroke College, Oxford. He played in the university team in each of the three years he was there but didn't do much of note until his final year when he was awarded his blue. After university he played for the Free Foresters and joined Rank Hovis McDougall, later becoming their chairman.

departure the innings folded for a mere 65 additional runs. Mike's regular opening partner Jimmy Allan had decided to concentrate on his studies in his final year and only played after his exams. Oxford did even worse in their second innings, collapsing to 105 all out. Gloucestershire did not need to bat again after their first-innings total of 299.

The following day Middlesex were the visitors and on this occasion Oxford got the better of a drawn game. In spite of being 37 behind in the first innings in which Mike made 69 and Chris Walton 48, they did better in the second, a century from Mike and 43 from Walton enabling them to declare 257 runs ahead. At one point, going for victory, Middlesex were 135/7, but Peter Parfitt and John Warr put on 74 for the eighth wicket to prevent defeat.

Against Yorkshire the following day Oxford did not fare so well. After Doug Padgett had departed for 10, a record unbroken second-wicket partnership of 343 between Frank Lowson (183 not out) and Vic Wilson (165 not out) allowed Yorkshire to declare at 360/2. Oxford's response of 125 all out in the first innings was the forerunner of an abysmal effort in the second when they were bowled out for 46 to lose in a day and a half. The Oxford batsmen could not cope with the guile of Johnny Wardle, who had match figures of 9-41.

In the following match against a strong Lancashire side, Oxford, batting first, made 221/7 declared, Chris Walton making 63 and Peter Delisle 56. However, a maiden century by Peter Marner, 89 from Alan Wharton and 56 not out from Cyril Washbrook enabled Lancashire to declare at 336/8. Oxford knocked up a good total of 262/3 in their second innings with a maiden century from Chris Walton, 52 from Ian Gibson and 47 not out from Peter Delisle before the match petered out into a draw.

The next game against Hampshire was probably the most exciting of the season and the nearest Oxford had come to winning a match during Mike's time in the team. Both sides were dismissed for meagre totals in the first innings, but in the second Hampshire reached 330 all out, Colin Ingleby-Mackenzie making 124 and Peter Sainsbury 76. This left Oxford 305 to win at the not uncomfortable rate of 50 an hour. Oxford kept up with the clock with contributions from Walton (45), John Kumleben (56) and Mike Eagar (80) taking them to the position of needing two to win off the last two balls with two wickets standing. Vic Cannings was Hampshire's saviour, however, bowling Jack Bailey for 18 and Esmond Kentish first ball to give Hampshire victory by one run.

No doubt acutely disappointed by this narrow defeat but encouraged by having come so agonisingly close, Oxford proceeded to win their next game against the Free Foresters, their first victory since the 1951 Varsity match. Mike was unable to share in this triumph, as he was taking his finals. Freddie Brown and Bob Wyatt again played for Free Foresters, as did Ingleby-Mackenzie, Fellows-Smith and the future High Court judge Oliver Popplewell. John Currie, the future England rugby international, made his debut for the university, scoring 6 and 15. Gibson made 74 in Oxford's first innings, but the star of the show was Eagar, who scored a flawless maiden century in the second innings. Set to score 383 to win, Free Foresters could only manage 289 to lose by 93 runs in spite of Freddie Brown's 11 wickets in the match.

Mike returned to the side for the game against Nottinghamshire, no doubt pleased about what had been achieved without him, but still without a win as captain. 'Maybe I should stay away more often,' was the sort of dry comment Mike would have made to his team-mates. The university made their best total of the season, 309/9 declared, Walton making 98, Mike 60, Eagar 58 and Roy Woodcock 52. Nottinghamshire easily overtook Oxford's total, declaring at 359/7, and with minimal time left for a third innings, an inevitable draw ensued.

Oxford's next fixture was the eagerly awaited match against the visiting Australian touring team, which included legendary players such as Neil Harvey, Keith Miller, Richie Benaud, Ken Mackay, Ian Craig and Ray Lindwall. Oxford, batting first, were all out by tea for 157, with only Metcalfe, Eagar, Walton and John Phillips reaching double figures. Kentish and Phillips bowled with hostility at the start of Australia's innings, having them 33/4 at one point with John Rutherford, Harvey, Mackay and Miller all back in the pavilion, the latter two for ducks. Mackay was actually given out after being caught at gully by Metcalfe off a full toss he hit into the ground. It was clearly a bump ball, and in spite of Mike saying to the umpire 'Sir, but nobody appealed', the umpire refused to change his decision. Mackay remembers Mike's sportsmanship and mentioned it in his book *Quest for the Ashes* written ten years later. Any hopes of dismissing Australia cheaply were dispelled by a fifth-wicket stand of 73 between Peter Burge and Colin McDonald, who went on to make a century the following day, albeit with the help of a runner. The wicketkeeper Gil Langley shored up the innings with a lusty 41 to help Australia to a first-innings lead of 77. Oxford did somewhat better in their second innings of 191, with Metcalfe and Eagar both making half-centuries before Miller, taking the new ball, quickly cleaned up the tail with 4-30. Needing 115 to win, the Australians accomplished the task without much difficulty, losing only two wickets. Mike bowled his only two balls of the season, perhaps to give the Australians the satisfaction of delivering the *coup de grace* from the captain.

After a drawn non-first-class game against the Army, for whom Corporal Phil Sharpe made 68 and Walton 113 and Kumleben 70 for Oxford, Sussex were the next visitors. With no play possible on the first day, both captains tried to engineer a result with three declarations. With Mike again absent on account of exams, the efforts were almost successful, Oxford hanging on at 145/9 when play ended. Alan Oakman, who was much later to coach at Warwickshire, made 56 and 110 for Sussex. For Oxford, Walton's 116 not out in 61 minutes was the season's fastest century. Kumleben continued his good form with 20 not out and 67. Robin Marlar, with 6-17 from his off-breaks, nearly pulled off the win for Sussex.

Oxford's final match at the Parks was against Derbyshire. Allan, back in the side after his exams, made 89 in Oxford's first innings, Walton 71 and Mike 66 not out, enabling Oxford to declare at 243/3. Kentish, bowling with pace and fire, soon had Derbyshire in trouble and only a middle-order partnership of 66 between Derek Morgan and wicketkeeper George Dawkes salvaged some respectability. The Derbyshire innings closed on a modest 148 with Kentish taking 5-49. Oxford declared again in their second innings at 182/5 (Walton 63, Mike 40) but Derbyshire, without their captain Donald Carr who had injured a hand, never made any real attempt to go for the 278 required, finishing up at 172/3. It was during this match that, according to Mike Eagar, Mike was recalled to university for a viva. He had been asked to define 'relative humidity' and had struggled to find an answer. The examiners evidently took pity on him, as they re-phrased the question in terms he would understand: 'Would you be more likely to put on a swing bowler when it was overcast or when the sun was shining?'[21]

Six away matches remained. The first at the Oval resulted in a win for Surrey by 54 runs. Oxford took a slender first-innings lead, Walton and Mike both making 75. Alec Bedser, captaining in the absence of Peter May, declared Surrey's second innings closed at 237/2, David Fletcher making 112 not out and Micky Stewart 63. Left to make 214 to win, Oxford succumbed to Eric Bedser's off-breaks. He finished with 5-54 to accompany his first-innings analysis of 4-60.

---

21 *The Way it Was: Glimpses of English Cricket's Past*, Stephen Chalke.

Moving on to Bristol, Oxford achieved their first victory against a county since 1950 when, under the captaincy of Donald Carr, they had beaten Yorkshire, Warwickshire, Leicestershire and the joint champions Surrey. Allan and Gibson gave Oxford a good start with a partnership of 79 for the first wicket but it was a partnership of 205 between Mike (126) and Delisle (76) which gave Oxford the commanding total of 336/8 declared. Gloucestershire's reply of 199 owed a lot to Arthur Milton's 84. Kentish took 5-63 and Gibson 3-8. Oxford were bowled out for 143 in their second innings, Eagar top-scoring with 49. Gloucestershire, needing 281 to win, were fairly well placed at 162/3 but they had no answer to Gibson's leg-breaks after he was rather belatedly brought into the attack. He broke the 110-run partnership between Ron Nichols (61) and Derek Hawkins (63), dismissing both batsmen, and then took three of the remaining four wickets to give him a final analysis of 5-63. Gloucestershire's last five wickets fell for 19 runs to leave a delighted Oxford winners by 78 runs.

Next up were Warwickshire at Edgbaston. Continuing their good form with the bat, Oxford declared at 336/8, mainly thanks to a superb 152 from Walton, who figured in partnerships of 110 with Allan (63) and 117 with Mike (37). Warwickshire's young side capitulated easily, being dismissed for 155 and 159 to give Oxford victory by an innings and 22 runs on the third morning. Kentish, Jack Bailey and the off-spinner Victor Clube[22]

22 Victor Clube (1934–) was educated at St John's School, Leatherhead and Christ Church, Oxford. He appeared 17 times for the university between 1956 and 1959 as an off-spin bowler, taking 47 wickets at 32.21, winning his only blue in 1956 when he claimed the wicket of Ted Dexter. Among his international victims were Ian Johnson and Peter Burge against the Austrailians in 1956 and Walcott and Weekes against the 1957 West Indians. Against the counties his victims included Micky Stewart, Peter Parfitt, Bob Gale and Jack Robertson. After obtaining his doctorate in 1959 he became one of the world's leading astrophysicists and astronomers. He is a former dean of the astrophysics department at Oxford University and is one of the few people to have the rare distinction of having an asteroid, 6523 Clube, named after him. He has lived in France for over 30 years and the author recently received an interesting letter from him saying that, in spite of all his scientific achievements, one of his best memories is the moment when Mike awarded him his blue.

each took six wickets in the match. Kentish finished the season with 44 wickets at 25.77. After leaving university he went on to become deputy governor of the Bank of Jamaica and died in 2011, aged 94.

After these two convincing victories Oxford had high hopes when they visited Worcester. But they were unfulfilled as they were well beaten, failing utterly in their second innings and being bowled out for 95 to lose by 131 runs. With 64 not out from Eagar, 71 from Delisle and 49 from Mike, they had made a respectable reply of 252/5 declared to Worcestershire's 294 all out (George Dews 94, Peter Richardson 58 and leg-spinner Roly Jenkins 45 not out), but set 227 to win after Worcestershire's declaration of 184/5, only Walshe, Delisle and Mike reached double figures, off-spinner Martin Horton taking 4-19 and pace bowler Len Coldwell 3-33.

Oxford's last two games were at Lord's, where Mike always loved playing. The first match was against MCC, who the previous month had lost to Cambridge by nine wickets. Oxford, batting first, started well with a second-wicket partnership of 116 between Gibson (85) and Metcalfe (70) setting them well on their way to a declared total of 257/4. Mike put himself down the order to number six, perhaps to give others some batting practice in preparation for the Varsity match, and he was only at the crease for a few minutes before declaring. Soon after passing Oxford's total, MCC declared. In Oxford's second innings Metcalfe was again successful, making 75 before disaster struck. With the score on 146/4, Don Smith performed the hat-trick, Mike being the first of his victims, followed by Metcalfe and Clube. The innings was soon wrapped up for 190, Smith taking 7-40 with his left-arm medium-pace seamers. He then went on to cap his bowling performance by putting on 104 in 50 minutes with Alan Oakman, an opening stand which set MCC well on the way to victory. Thereafter, however, a collapse followed and at 149/8 the game had swung in

Oxford's favour. In the end though MCC scored the remaining 24 runs needed without the loss of any more wickets thanks to one of Mike's team members of the previous year, David Fasken, who, although not renowned for his batting, steered MCC home with a judicious 28 not out. Last year's Oxford captain Charles Williams also played for MCC but did little of note in the match. Clube (3-27) and Allan (4-50) had nearly pulled it off for Oxford and it must have been galling to have been deprived of victory by a former one of their own.

The highlight of the season for the Oxford team had now arrived and Mike, as captain, had the difficult decision of who to leave out. The South African John Kumleben was particularly unlucky to miss out on a blue, as he had put in some good recent performances, although he did win one for hockey.

Cambridge had a particularly strong side in 1956. Their batting included Bob Barber, Ted Dexter, John Pretlove and Michael James, the centurion against the touring Australians earlier in the season. Their bowling was also strong with Nottinghamshire player Gamini Goonesena, Swaranjit Singh, later with Warwickshire, Colin Smith and Don Smith, who played Minor Counties cricket for Cheshire from 1967–71. Cambridge, winning the toss and batting first, had made 303/7 when captain Michael Melluish declared, mainly thanks to a fine 146 from Robin O'Brien.[23] O'Brien was well supported by someone Mike was to come to have the highest regard for, Ted Dexter, who made 46.

Oxford, in reply, were in serious trouble at 76/5, finding Goonesena and Singh very difficult to play. It was only when

23 Robin O'Brien (1932–59) was an Irishman born in India in 1932 and was educated at Wellington College. After entering Cambridge in 1953, he played in the First XI from 1954–56, making 35 appearances with 1,418 runs at an average of 22.87. His best season was in 1956 when he made 796 runs, second only to Ted Dexter. He also won blues for hockey and golf. This multi-talented sportsman fell ill with leukaemia in 1959 and died in the same year at the age of 26.

OXFORD v CAMBRIDGE – 1956

Cambridge University

RW Barber (Ruthin and Magdalene) c and b Allan	35	– c Smith b Allan	7
R O'Brien (Wellington and Corpus Christi) c Clube b Kentish	146	– c Delisle b Kentish	0
BCG Wilenkin (Harrow and Trinity) b Bailey	7	– c Eagar b Allan	20
ER Dexter (Radley and Jesus) c Walton b Clube	46	– st Walshe b Gibson	17
JF Pretlove (Alleyn's and Caius) run out	16	– not out	34
RM James (St John's Leatherhead and Trinity) c Walshe b Kentish	8	– not out	24
S Singh (Khalsa College, Punjab University and Christ's) run out	1	– c and b Kentish	26
CS Smith (Wm Hulme's GS and Christ's) not out	13		
G Goonesena (Colombo and Queen's) not out	18		
B 3, l-b 8, w 1, n-b 1	13	B 2, l-b 1, n-b 3	6
1/53 2/66 3/176 4/241 (7 wkts, dec)	303	1/1 2/25 3/48 (5 wkts, dec)	134
5/266 6/270 7/271		4/51 5/100	

DJ Smith (Stockport GS and St John's) and MEL Melluish (Rossall and Caius) did not bat.

Bowling		
Bailey	24-2-76-1	3-1-6-0
Kentish	24-6-83-2	12-6-15-2
Allan	34-10-82-1	18-7-36-2
Clube	12-0-49-1	11-2-20-0
Gibson		11-2-51-1

Oxford University

JM Allan (Edinburgh Academy and Worcester) b C Smith	6	– not out	14
IM Gibson (Manchester GS and Brasenose) c Melluish b Goonesena	19	– b C Smith	5
AC Walton (Radley and Lincoln) lbw b Singh	13	– lbw b C Smith	0
MJK Smith (Stamford and St Edmund Hall) c Melluish b Goonesena	117	– c Pretlove b Goonesena	10
GPS Delisle (Stonyhurst and Lincoln) b Singh	7	– c D Smith b Goonesena	2
SG Metcalfe (Leeds GS and Pembroke) st Melluish b Goonesena	7	– b C Smith	16
MA Eagar (Rugby and Worcester) not out	55	– not out	7
AP Walshe (Milton, Rhodesia and Wadham) c D Smith b Goonesena	5		
SVM Clube (St John's, Leatherhead and Christ Church) b Goonesena	0		
JA Bailey (Christ's Hospital and University) run out	5		
B 6, l-b 6, n-b 1	13	B 4	4
1/25 2/35 3/47 4/66 (9 wkts dec)	247	1/12 2/12 3/31 (5 wkts)	58
5/76 6/217 7/225 8/225 9/247		4/31 5/33	

ESM Kentish (Cornwall College, Jamaica and St John's) did not bat.

Bowling		
C Smith	29-5-83-1	13-6-22-3
D Smith	20-6-34-0	3-0-7-0
G Goonesena	31-8-77-5	14-9-21-2
S Singh	18-6-40-2	3-3-0-0
Barber		2-1-4-0
Pretlove		1-1-0-0

Umpires: P Corrall and E Davies
Match drawn

Mike was joined by Mike Eagar that the innings recovered and the follow-on was averted. They put on 141 together, Eagar making 55 not out and Mike 117, thereby creating a record by scoring centuries in each of his three Varsity matches. The morning's play on the second day had been lost to rain and when Mike declared 56 runs behind shortly before one o'clock on the final day, there were only two sessions left to complete the match. Cambridge, batting again, showed little initiative and did not declare until 4.30, leaving Oxford to make 191 to win in an hour and three-quarters – a tall order. After being reduced to 33/5 by Goonesena and Colin Smith, Allan and Eagar shut up shop and played out the last 45 minutes for a draw.

Thus ended Mike's illustrious career at Oxford. In 43 matches over three years he had scored more than 3,000 runs for the university at an average of 41.22 against county sides containing many England players. He had also played against some of the world's best international players and had witnessed some remarkable performances. With an aggregate of 477 runs in the three Varsity matches, Mike had beaten the previous highest aggregate of 457 runs established by the Nawab of Pataudi Senior some 30 years earlier. In his final year he had captained the side to two victories against county sides for the first time since 1950. Six matches had been drawn and seven lost.

If cricket had been Mike's only game, his name would have been registered forever in the annals of Oxford sport, but he was also a rugby player of outstanding calibre who, in partnership with Welsh scrum-half Onllwyn Brace, brought a new dimension to half-back play. Mike had captained the Stamford School rugby team playing at fly-half and had also played for Hinckley from the age of 16. He did not win a blue for rugby until his second year when, after playing the whole season at fly-half, he was put at full-back for the Varsity match by the captain in a reshuffle.

Oxford lost the match 3-0. The following year Brace arrived at Oxford and the half-back partnership he established with Mike produced some of the most exciting rugby seen in England for a long time.

Brace was a highly unorthodox scrum-half who would confuse the opposition with jinking lateral runs which created openings for the other three-quarters. This time Oxford triumphed in the Varsity match, beating a strong Cambridge side 9-3. The success Mike enjoyed in his final year led to his selection for England for the international against Wales at Twickenham. In a closely fought contest with Wales leading 5-3, Mike attempted a drop goal, which was charged down and from which Wales went on to score and win 8-3. Although there was a suspicion of a knock-on by the Welsh player who gathered the ball and the extra three points didn't affect the result, the error cost Mike his place and he was never selected again. 'It was fair enough,' says Mike without bitterness. 'I had a bad game.' This book is about Mike's cricket career, though, and his success on the rugby field has been well documented elsewhere, not least in Douglas Miller's excellent biography of him, *MJK Smith: No Ordinary Man*.

On account of his overall sporting prowess, in his final year Mike was elected president of Vincent's, a club founded in 1863 by the Oxford rower Walter Bradford Woodgate, who stated in its constitution that it 'should consist of the picked hundred of the university, selected for all-round qualities; social, physical and intellectual qualities being duly considered'. This was the crowning glory of Mike's time at university and he joined a long list of famous sportsmen who had been accorded this honour, including 'Shrimp' Leveson-Gower in 1896, who co-managed England's notorious 'Bodyline' tour in 1933/34, Roger Bannister in 1950 and Donald Carr in 1951. I say 'sportsmen' because the club did not admit female members until 2016, when this long overdue change was voted in by an 85 per cent majority, the motion having been rejected the previous year.

Having cut his teeth on the Championship circuit with Leicestershire, Mike was now looking forward to the challenge of captaining Warwickshire. Having been offered the job of captain and assistant secretary earlier in the season on a five-year contract, he obviously had mixed feelings about leaving the county of his birth, but the opportunity to captain a county side was too great to refuse. Also, Edgbaston was being developed and would soon become a Test match venue.

Leicestershire were obviously sorry to see such a fine prospect leave, but graciously accepted his departure. If Mike had thought he would be able to take up the job immediately though, he was to be disappointed as MCC made players changing counties take a year out before becoming qualified to play in Championship matches. Tom Graveney and Peter Richardson were later to suffer the same fate. Accordingly, after the university matches finished, Mike played only three more games in 1956, the Gentlemen v Players match at Lord's and twice for Warwickshire, one against Scotland and the other against the touring Australians. For the 150th anniversary of the Gentlemen v Players match, the Players side had the formidable bowling attack of Frank Tyson, Fred Trueman, Tony Lock and Jim Laker, effectively an England line-up. The Players had made 236 all out and the Gentlemen 179/6 before the weather prevented any further play.

Mike was given the opportunity to captain a young Warwickshire side in the game against Scotland, which ended in a draw, Warwickshire finishing 100 runs short with six wickets down when play ended. Mike top-scored in Warwickshire's first innings with a careful 72, thus helping to avoid the follow-on after Scotland had made 315. Scotland were all out for 153 in their second knock and, in Warwickshire's second, Tom Cartwright,

'Billy' Ibadulla and Swaranjit Singh all made half-centuries. Warwickshire's best bowler in the match was 17-year-old left-arm spinner Michael Youll, who took 5-99 and 2-26.

Mike was due to go on a combined Oxford and Cambridge rugby tour to South America at the end of the summer with a team that contained eight internationals. Their departure coincided with Warwickshire's match against the touring Australians and the opportunity to play against them again was one he did not want to miss. He therefore arranged to take a later flight out to join the rugby team.

Batting first against the Australians, Warwickshire could only realise 194 in their first innings, the batsmen finding Benaud a handful. He took 5-44 and the only players to counter him were Mike with 55 and Singh, the Cambridge blue, who scored 41 not out. When Australia batted, a massive second-wicket partnership of 280 between Jim Burke (194) and Neil Harvey (145), followed by 46 not out from Keith Miller, put the tourists in an invulnerable position at 424/4 declared. Eric Hollies, who in 1948 by bowling Don Bradman for a duck in his final Test innings had prevented him from averaging 100, bowled 49 overs for no wickets and 149 runs. Warwickshire fared even worse in their second innings, Benaud cleaning them up again with 6-31. Australia won by an innings and 127 runs. Miller accounted for Mike in the first innings and Benaud dismissed him in the second.

After the match Mike took a flight to 'The Argentine', as he still calls it, to join the rugby tour and in transit got into conversation with a fellow passenger who arranged for him to spend the night at his house in the affluent Hurlingham district of Buenos Aires. They were met at the airport by one of his new friend's female relatives, who chauffeured them home. The chauffeur, Diana, was to become Mike's wife four years later.

CHAPTER 6

Captain of Warwickshire

WARWICKSHIRE HAD been captained in 1956 by Eric Hollies, who took over from Tom Dollery,[24] who had retired after seven years as captain to become the second team captain and coach. Hollies was his reluctant successor in his penultimate year in county cricket and it was not a responsibility he enjoyed. He was only too happy to hand over to Mike.

Back from Argentina, Mike assumed his job as an assistant to the Warwickshire secretary Leslie Deakins, which, if truth be told, was little more than a sinecure. Deakins was a highly competent administrator and the principal driving force behind Warwickshire developing a football pool run by the supporters' club, which was the envy of other counties and ensured Warwickshire's future financial security. Initially charging its members one shilling a week, it had grown from a membership of 42,000 in 1956 to 650,000 in 1963. It was so successful they were even able to give

---

24 Tom Dollery (1914–87) joined Warwickshire in 1934 and became the country's first professional captain in 1949. He took Warwickshire to the top of the Championship table in 1951 for the first time since 1911, using only 13 players. He was the mainstay of Warwickshire's batting, scoring over 1,000 runs in 15 consecutive seasons from 1935–55 with 24,414 career runs and an average of 37.50. He played four times for England and was one of *Wisden*'s five Cricketers of the Year in 1952. Jack Bannister rated him as an exceptional captain who helped his development enormously in his early days as a Warwickshire bowler. *Wisden* described him as the most skilful of all the county captains.

other counties financial assistance and Essex were able to build their new ground at Chelmsford with a substantial interest-free loan from it. When asked what his actual duties were, Mike replies, 'I'd have to think deeply about that.'[25] Suffice it to say that during the summer months his time was solely occupied with cricket and in his first winter there he continued to play rugby for Hinckley and Leicestershire.

Mike's first season as captain of Warwickshire started with three drawn games and a thrashing by Lancashire at Coventry by an innings in a match in which Brian Statham took 8-34 in Warwickshire's first innings and 7-55 in the second, including Mike's wicket twice for 5 and 2. Their fortunes changed in the next match when they beat Somerset by six wickets, Mike making 97 not out to help steer Warwickshire home. This was the start of an unbeaten run of 18 matches, of which they won 11. By the end of July they lay second in the Championship to Surrey, but by failing to win any of their last 11 Championship games they finished in 11th place. From a personal point of view, Mike had made a bad start, making double figures only once in his first eight innings before his 97 not out revived his fortunes. He went on to score over 2,000 runs with three centuries. He had inherited a mostly young side with a few seasoned professionals – Dick Spooner, the wicketkeeper, Ray Weeks, Alan Townsend, Fred Gardner, Bert Wolton and Eric Hollies. 'None of them gave me any trouble,' says Mike. In fact, the senior players responded to Mike's style of leadership and Alan Townsend, who had come down from Durham in 1948, regarded him as a very good skipper who wasn't afraid to ask for advice.

Mike was particularly pleased to have the services of Hollies, if only for one year. In his final season he bowled over 1,000 overs,

25 *MJK Smith: No Ordinary Man*, Douglas Miller.

more than anyone else in the country, and took over 100 wickets for the 14th time. During a career stretching with Warwickshire from 1932 to 1957 he took 2,323 wickets. His economy rate was one of the lowest for a leg-spinner, such was his control of line and length. He was not a big spinner of the ball, according to Mike, and he got a lot of wickets against batsmen playing for turn that wasn't there. 'Eric was a joy to have in the team,' says Mike. 'Everybody loved him – his team-mates, the opposition and especially the crowd. He had a wicked sense of humour and was great for morale.'

Mike had only two regrets over Eric – first that he had only one season playing with him, and second, a regret that Eric shared, that he didn't have the opportunity to play limited-overs cricket. Dennis Amiss recalls an incident before Mike joined the club where, having already sent down around 40 overs, Eric was asked to bowl again by Tom Dollery and rode on to the square on a bike borrowed from the groundsman, to the amusement and delight of the crowd.[26] Mike says that he wasn't the most nimble of fielders and there is a story in Eric's autobiography, *I'll Spin You a Tale*, that when playing for England in Australia, he was beaten several times lumbering after the ball to the boundary. 'Don't they bury their dead in Birmingham these days, Eric?' shouted an English fan in a Brummie accent.[27] 'Nah, they stuff 'em and send 'em out to Australia,' retorted Eric. Everyone appreciated his dry Black Country sense of humour. Commenting once on Tom Dollery's driving, he quipped, 'I'm not saying he drives fast. It's just that the telegraph poles look like a sheet of corrugated fencing.'[28] He could also be quite mischievous, on occasion slipping unnoticed into the opposition dressing room to eavesdrop on their tactics

26 Conversation with Dennis Amiss.

27 *I'll Spin You a Tale,* Eric Hollies.

28 *The History of Warwickshire County Cricket Club,* Jack Bannister.

before teasingly revealing his presence with, 'Talk as much as you like – you won't win!'[29]

In his final match at Edgbaston against Surrey when he went out to bat at number 11, the players formed a guard of honour for Warwickshire's finest ever spin bowler. He had helped to avoid an innings defeat but with Surrey needing only 13 for victory, Mike asked him and Fred Gardner to bowl. Hollies bowled two overs which went for two runs, the remainder coming off Gardner. Warwickshire's annual report said this of him: 'We shall always recall his enthusiastic approach to the game, which never dimmed with the passing years, his good fellowship, his gentle repartee and his constant desire to help his colleagues to enjoy it all to the full as much as he was doing. No cricketer ever had a greater love for the game than Eric.'[30]

It was the turn of the West Indies to visit England in 1957 and they played two games at Edgbaston, the first Test and one against Warwickshire later in the season. The Test at Edgbaston was the first one on that ground for 28 years and it turned out to be a remarkable match. After being dismissed for 186, principally by Sonny Ramadhin with 7-49, England faced a first-innings deficit of 282 after West Indies had posted a total of 474, Collie Smith making 161, Clyde Walcott 90 and Frank Worrell 81. England were saved from defeat by a record fourth wicket partnership of 411 between Peter May (285 not out) and Colin Cowdrey (154). They almost went on to win the game, having the West Indies 72/7 with fielders clustered round the bat when time ran out, and nearly pulling off one of the most sensational turnarounds in Test cricket history.

---

29 *The History of Warwickshire County Cricket Club*, Jack Bannister.

30 *The History of Warwickshire County Cricket Club*, Jack Bannister.

Ramadhin bowled a record 98 overs in England's second innings to return 2-179. An earlier declaration by May after Cowdrey was out may have produced an England victory, but the press found it hard to criticise a man who had just scored 285 not out. The restored venue was universally approved and the claims for Edgbaston to become a permanent Test match ground considerably strengthened. Mike was only able to read about this historic match as he was away with Warwickshire against Hampshire and Gloucestershire for its duration.

The West Indies' return to Edgbaston in August resulted in a drawn game, rain preventing any play on the final day. Warwickshire acquitted themselves well though, bowling West Indies out for 212 (Hollies 5-55), Horner just missing out on a century in Warwickshire's first innings and Mike and Jim Stewart making half-centuries in Warwickshire's second innings. It would have been Mike's first sight of 21-year-old Rohan Kanhai, who top-scored with 74 in West Indies' only innings. He was to see much more of him 11 years later after he joined the county, when, in Mike's opinion, he was for several years the finest batsman in world cricket.

Mike topped the Warwickshire batting averages in 1957 with Norman Horner, Fred Gardner and Alan Townsend all passing 1,000 runs. The Pakistani 'Billy' Ibadulla topped the bowling averages with 53 wickets at 17.20, Eric Hollies took 123 at 19.35, Jack Bannister 64 at 24.15 and Ray Carter 67 at 27.29. A system of bonus points was introduced for the Championship as well as a limitation to five fielders on the leg side with no more than two behind square leg. Alan Townsend took 35 catches.

At the end of the season Mike was invited to go on a short tour of East Africa with an MCC amateur side under the captaincy of Freddie Brown and the management of Billy Griffith, who played in the matches as wicketkeeper. This provided Mike with an experience that has stayed long in his memory because of the spectacular beauty of the scenery. The team played nine matches, all on matting wickets, winning three, drawing five and losing one. Mike came second in the batting averages to Hubert Doggart, who scored two centuries on the tour. Also in the party were Peter Richardson, Colin Ingleby-Mackenzie, Dennis Silk, Charles Robins, Jack Bailey and John Warr. Robins, Brown, Warr and Bailey shared the wickets. The matches against Tanganyika and Kenya were drawn and MCC beat Uganda by ten wickets.

CHAPTER 7

Test Match Debut

MIKE'S SECOND season as captain of Warwickshire was a disappointing one. The team won five matches out of 32, only three of which were in the Championship, and they finished the season one place from the foot of the table. In England's continued search for an opener to partner Peter Richardson (Trevor Bailey had been tried in South Africa in the 1956/57 series and Don Smith against the West Indies in 1957), Mike was asked by MCC to try his hand in that position and was willing to comply. It was not a successful experiment, however, and, in addition to setting back his career development, it also entailed the break-up of the successful pairing of Gardner and Horner as Warwickshire's openers. It was not a complete disaster but, suffice it to say, once restored to his preferred position at number four, he did much better. He still managed to be one of only three players in the country to score 2,000 runs, finishing fourth in the first-class averages and top of the Warwickshire ones. For Warwickshire only Gardner and Horner managed more than 1,000.

In the bowling department they badly missed Hollies and, with Bannister struggling with back problems, Carter shouldered most of the burden with a mixture of medium pace and off-spin, taking 71 wickets. Geoffrey Hill, who took 59 wickets with his left-arm slow bowling, looked to be a possible solution to the departure of

Hollies but after one good season his bowling deteriorated, and he was later released. Eddie Leadbeater, who had joined from Yorkshire the previous season as a potential successor to Hollies, took 25 Championship wickets, but at too great a cost and his contract was not renewed. The way of finding out whether your services had been retained for the coming season was quite crude and insensitive in those times, according to Jim Stewart. At the end of the season individual envelopes were pinned on a notice board, the contents either enclosing a new contract or telling you that you would not be coming back. On opening them, players left to seek winter employment either with smiles on their faces or in tears.

For MCC's match against the champion county, Surrey, Mike was selected to open with Don Smith of Sussex. Both did exceptionally well against an attack which included Peter Loader, Jim Laker and Eric Bedser. They put on 299 for the first wicket, Mike making 160 and Don 173. Arthur Milton and Micky Stewart were selected as openers for MCC in the match against the touring New Zealanders with Mike at number three. Milton made 12 and 22 in his two innings and Stewart 6 and 46. An attractive 70 from Mike in MCC's second innings and 48 from Roy Swetman took MCC to the brink of victory at 253/5 with only 40 needed, but John Hayes polished off the tail to finish with 7-49, leaving New Zealand winners by 13 runs with two minutes to spare.

Half-centuries in the next three county matches against Gloucestershire, Derbyshire and Northants, albeit batting at number four, clinched Mike's place as an opener to partner Peter Richardson in the first Test on his home ground at Edgbaston. Unfortunately, Mike disappointed in both innings, being dismissed for 0 and 7, both times by Tony MacGibbon. He was lbw in the first innings and caught at the wicket after an uncharacteristic flash outside the off stump after he had been struggling to score runs on a wet wicket for almost an hour. Richardson consolidated his hold on the opening spot by scoring 100 in England's second innings in a match England won by 205 runs.

In spite of these failures, Mike was selected for the second Test at Lord's in an unchanged England team. On the opening day the flags were lowered at half-mast in memory of Douglas Jardine, news of whose death in Switzerland after a long illness had just come through. Mike, opening again with Peter Richardson and well aware that he was playing for his place, took almost half an hour to get off the mark and his laborious 47, described by John Arlott as 'joyless', took almost four hours. As *Wisden* commented, 'One could sympathise with him in his anxiety to do himself justice, but he looked a vastly different cricketer from the one who had set a university record by hitting three hundreds for Oxford against Cambridge on this same ground.'[31] England finished with 269 (Cowdrey 65) before dismissing New Zealand twice for totals of 47 and 94 on the third day. The New Zealanders had no answer to Lock and Laker on a pitch which had become treacherous with overnight rain, Laker finishing with match figures of 5-37 and Lock 9-29. To entertain the crowd of 25,000, a light-hearted 20-overs match was hastily arranged, Richardson keeping wicket and Godfrey Evans having a bowl!

England kept faith with Mike for the third Test at Headingley, resting Richardson to give Arthur Milton a chance to make a claim, perhaps the only time in history two double internationals have walked out together. When the match finally started on the third day New Zealand were quickly bowled out for a paltry 67, again none of the batsmen having an answer to Lock (4-14) and Laker (5-17). Milton staked his claim to the opening slot in

31 *Wisden Cricketers' Almanack 1959 edition.*

no uncertain terms, scoring 104 not out on his Test debut and sharing an unbroken partnership of 194 with Peter May, although he might have been out without scoring had Eric Petrie held on to a difficult chance. Such are the fine margins between success and failure. Mike had no such luck, caught by New Zealand's captain John Reid at slip off MacGibbon for 3. He must have realised then that his chance had gone and he was not selected for the final two Tests, Willie Watson being given a shot as an opener in the fourth Test and at number three in the fifth. Watson did well, his 66 in the fourth Test getting him on the boat for Australia along with Milton, but there was no place for Mike, his four Test innings having produced a mere 57 runs. In the event, Watson and Milton only featured in two Tests, Trevor Bailey being reverted to an opener in four of them, again with limited success.

Mike was philosophical about the opening issue. His view was that, although it was not his preferred position, if you are asked by the England selectors to do it, you really have no choice but to comply. Mike was to have further Test match chances, as we shall see. As a consolation prize, Mike was asked to join a strong MCC team of amateurs to tour South America in December 1958 and January 1959, captained by Hubert Doggart. Four matches were to be played in Brazil and seven in Argentina. They went on to win nine of their 11 matches against opposition of no more than club standard. Thanks to an innings of 216 not out in the final match against the Argentine Cricket Association, Mike was the tour's leading run-scorer with 498 at 62.25, which put him third in the batting averages behind tour manager Donald Carr (415 runs at 103.75) and Dennis Silk (457 runs at 76.16).

CHAPTER 8

Annus Mirabilis

THE SEASON of 1959, for the first time played on covered pitches, was one in which Warwickshire's fortunes were transformed from being also-rans into title contenders. This was partly due to several useful additions to the squad, the development of some of the younger players and a more attacking approach to run-scoring – and, by no means least, to the incredible season that Mike had with the bat. For the first time since Len Hutton had achieved the feat in 1949, Mike scored over 3,000 runs (3,245 to be exact at an average of 57.94), topping the national averages. He also set a club record with 43 catches. One of the highlights of his season came in a match against Gloucestershire at Stroud. Set 318 to win, he played an unbelievable innings of 182 not out to bring Warwickshire home by four wickets. He hit five sixes and 28 fours, making 147 of the last 174 runs required. The Gloucestershire team had three fine spinners in David Allen, John Mortimore and Sam Cook, but Mike took them all apart. Jim Stewart and Tom Cartwright both maintained it was the finest innings they had ever seen[32] and Mike himself thought it was one of his best, although he, with typical modesty, admits the boundaries square of the wicket were on the short side.

32 *MJK Smith: No Ordinary Man*, Douglas Miller.

GLOUCESTERSHIRE v WARWICKSHIRE
At Stroud, 30 May, 1–2 June 1959

Gloucestershire

DM Young b Thompson	13	– c Cartwright b Bridge	17
CA Milton lbw b Thompson	2	– b Bridge	27
RB Nichols c Thompson b Wheatley	35	– c Smith b Bridge	3
TW Graveney b Cartwright	53	– absent hurt	
DG Hawkins c Fox b Cartwright	13	– c Thompson b Ibadulla	52
JB Mortimore c Fox b Ibadulla	28	– c Cartwright b Bridge	13
DA Allen c Fox b Thompson	39	– c Ibadulla b Bridge	21
AS Brown b Thompson	28	– b Bridge	0
DR Smith c Fox b Thompson	29	– c Wolton b Bridge	12
BJ Meyer c Cartwright b Thompson	0	– not out	6
C Cook not out	4	– b Bridge	14
B 9, l-b 2, n-b 2	13	B 1, l-b 9	10
1/12 2/17 3/83 4/116 5/123 6/159	257	1/25 2/37 3/65 4/95	175
7/210 8/240 9/240 (2.43 an over)		5/123 6/123 7/137 8/161 9/175	

Bowling:

Wheatley	34-7-75-1	10-2-17-0;
Thompson	29.4-7-74-6	12-3-15-0;
Townsend	9-2-19-0	
Cartwright	23-6-61-2	1-0-6-0
Ibadulla	10-4-15-1	20-7-61-1
Bridge		30-9-66-8

Warwickshire

NF Horner c Nicholls b Brown	1	– b Mortimore	20
WJ Stewart c Brown b Cook	43	– b Smith	30
TW Cartwright b Smith	3	– lbw b Cook	40
MJK Smith c Milton b Smith	3	– not out	182
K Ibadulla c Meyer b Cook	28	– c and b Mortimore	2
AV Wolton c Brown b Cook	4	– c Milton b Mortimore	4
A Townsend b Cook	0	– c Milton b Mortimore	24
WB Bridge lbw b Mortimore	3	– not out	3
JG Fox c Brown b Mortimore	6		
RG Thompson c Graveney b Cook	4		
OS Wheatley not out	4		
B 6	6	B 10, l-b, w 2	13
1/3 2/22 3/26 4/80 5/96 7/100	115	1/43 2/66 3/131 (6 wkts)	318
8/100 9/107 (1.75 an over)		5/144 5/278 6/288	

Bowling:

Smith	23-8-44-2	25-9-61-1
Brown	15-5-36-1	15-2-46-0
Cook	17.3-13-13-5	31-11-89-1
Mortimore	10-5-16-2	29-12-64-4
Allen		13-4-45-0

Warwickshire won by 4 wickets

This innings was one of several high scores Mike made in 1959. He had a fantastic run in July with 184 not out against Leicestershire, 200 not out against Worcestershire, 166 for the Gentlemen against a strong Players side and a superb 142 against Derbyshire in successive games. He was chosen as one of *Wisden*'s five Cricketers of the Year along with Donald Carr, Ken Barrington, Geoff Pullar and Ray Illingworth. In addition to his prodigious batting feats, Mike also took 49 catches, most of them at forward short leg, and captained a very happy side with a consistently attacking approach.

Twenty-four-year-old Jim Stewart came of age, replacing the steady Fred Gardner as an opening batsman and finishing second to Mike in the Warwickshire averages with 1,444 runs at 40.11. Strongly built, Jim played rugby in the backs for Coventry and, but for an untimely injury, might have been capped by Wales. He was at one point offered terms in rugby league with Leigh, but decided to remain as a player with Coventry until Warwickshire asked him to stop. Jim was a renowned big hitter, who in 1959 struck 17 sixes in a match against Lancashire at Blackpool, then a record. As Leslie Duckworth in his *Story of Warwickshire Cricket* wittily put it, 'He provided his own illuminations with a pyrotechnical display that is never likely to be equalled.'[33] He scored centuries in each innings, 155 in the first and 125 in the second – this after making 155 against Glamorgan and 156 against Essex the previous week.

Wilf Wooller, then an England selector, wanted England to give him a chance but was overruled by Gubby Allen on the basis that he was 'just a slogger'. 'Well, he's slogged 2,000 runs this season,' said Wilf, but Gubby was intransigent, preferring a more cultured style of player. Jim relates his first encounter with Wooller, which came the week after the Oxford match when he

33 *The Story of Warwickshire Cricket*, Leslie Duckworth.

was picked to make his Championship debut against Glamorgan. When he came out to bat at number seven in his first match against a county side, Wooller, not one to have any sympathy for a rookie, shouted to slow left-armer Willie Jones, 'If you give him one to get off the mark, you'll be on the next train back to Cardiff.' Willie disobeyed the instruction and gave the grateful 20-year-old debutant a single. According to Jim, Wooller carried out his threat, although this is somewhat at odds with the scorecard, which shows Jones top-scoring with 41 in Glamorgan's second innings, although he didn't bowl in Warwickshire's second. Maybe Wooller couldn't afford to dispense with his batting but could do without his bowling.

Later in his innings of 27, Jim remembers hitting Wooller on the shoulder with a powerful on-drive which went like a tracer bullet before Wooller could get his hands on it. 'I made the mistake of asking him if he was alright,' chuckles Jim. 'Of course I'm bloody alright,' said Wooller. 'If you hit another bugger like that, I'll catch it.' 'I think Wooller actually had a soft spot for me, though', says Jim, 'probably because I was Welsh by birth. In fact, later on, he tried to persuade me to leave Warwickshire for Glamorgan, telling me I should be wearing the daffodil, but I enjoyed the atmosphere at Warwickshire and had a benefit coming up, so I decided to stay.'[34]

Norman Horner also had one of his best seasons ever, scoring 1,773 runs at 36.18 with four centuries. He was also an outstanding fielder in the covers, always quick to swoop on the ball and take a shy at the wicket at the bowler's end. Three other players, Bert Wolton, Alan Townsend and Tom Cartwright, also got 1,000 runs. Roly Thompson took 93 wickets with his fast-medium bowling at 17.90 apiece and Basil Bridge 63 wickets at

34 Conversation with Jim Stewart.

23.41 with his consistently accurate off-spin. Jack Bannister took 40 wickets, having missed a large part of the season through injury but, even after taking all ten wickets in an innings against Combined Services, could not immediately get back into the side. Ossie Wheatley, playing full-time as an amateur after leaving Cambridge, where he had set a record for the number of wickets in a university season with 80 the previous year, augmented the fast-bowling attack and took 91 scalps at 24.82. He was only to play for Warwickshire for one more season before he was recruited by Glamorgan to succeed Wilf Wooller. The Glamorgan committee had been firmly against the appointment of a professional captain, which ruled out Allan Watkins, the only other potential amateur candidate being Tony Lewis, but he was still at university.[35] 'I got a call from John Arlott, one day,' Ossie said, 'asking me if I would like to captain a county side, and I said I would. Most county sides were captained by amateurs in those days and Warwickshire did not want to stand in my way. I don't know why, but unlike Mike, I didn't have to take a year out to qualify.'[36] Tom Cartwright also reinvented himself as a bowler that season, taking 75 wickets at 25.90.

According to Jim Stewart, Tom developed his tight, economical style by bowling at the members in the nets, where, as junior players, you had to fetch the ball yourself if you got hit. He was to become one of the most successful seam bowlers in the country over the next ten years. 'Tom hardly ever bowled a bad ball,' says Mike. 'He was so accurate, I could dispense with fine leg and third man and have more fielders in close catching and run-saving positions in front of the wicket. His length was so accurate that after a spell from him even on a good wicket there would be a

35 *The Story of Warwickshire Cricket*, Leslie Duckworth.

36 Conversation with Ossie Wheatley.

worn patch about a square foot in size where the ball had been landing. And, of course, this helped him to move the ball more off the seam.' Alan Smith concurs: 'He was quite exceptional. He didn't have bad days. It was almost unthinkable for him to bowl badly or to be out of sorts. And he was capable of bowling a lot of overs.'[37] 'I hated batting against him,' said Tom Graveney. 'I could never see how I was going to score a run.'[38]

Overall Warwickshire had a very good season and the future looked bright. They won 13 matches, lost ten and drew five. They were title contenders until the last two matches of the season when they contrived to lose to both lowly-placed Essex and Sussex, handing the honours on a plate to Yorkshire, who ended Surrey's seven-year winning run. Mike was on Test match duty for the game against Essex and, deprived of him, Warwickshire made less than 200 in each innings. The Second XI also did well that season under Tom Dollery, winning the Minor Counties Championship.

With Mike in such tremendous form with the bat, it was inevitable that he would get a Test recall. India were the visitors that year and Mike had attracted the selectors' attention again with 82 and 64 not out for MCC against them at Lord's in May. He was not recalled until the fourth Test, however, his prolific run-scoring by then being impossible to ignore. He fully justified the selectors' decision by making 100 in the first innings, batting in his accustomed position at number four. John Arlott, in his *Cricket Journal* for that year, described his innings thus:

> 'Smith is, without any possible doubt, a highly accomplished batsman. Most of his runs in this match have been made on the on-side and, while he is unmistakably strong there, he

37 *Tom Cartwright: The Flame Still Burns*, Stephen Chalke.

38 *Tom Cartwright: The Flame Still Burns*, Stephen Chalke.

> is so capable that it would be unfair to label him solely as an on-side player. Indeed, several of his drives through the off field were as fine as any strokes he made. He exerted an unobtrusive and unhurried dominance over the bowlers and his runs came fluently out of a poised and well-balanced variety of strokes.'[39]

England went on to win the match by 171 runs in spite of second-innings centuries from Abbas Ali Baig and Polly Umrigar.

On the strength of this performance Mike was retained for the final Test, where he just missed a hundred after being bowled by Ramakant Desai for 98 in England's only innings. Raman Subba Row opened the batting and he and Mike put on 169 for the third wicket out of a total of 361. India were dismissed for 140 and 194 mainly by Trueman and Statham, who between them took 12 of the wickets. England won the series 5-0 against what was in truth a very weak Indian side.

---

39 *John Arlott's Cricket Journal 2.*

CHAPTER 9

In the Caribbean with Peter May's Team, 1959/60

AFTER HIS phenomenal performances during the summer of 1959 Mike was an automatic choice for the tour of West Indies. Under the management of Walter Robins and the captaincy of Peter May, the squad selected was generally considered rather weak and the media did not give them much hope of a series victory. There was no Tom Graveney, Peter Richardson, Trevor Bailey, Tony Lock, Jim Laker or Godfrey Evans and when the team left England there was no player aged over 30. The batting consisted of Colin Cowdrey, Ken Barrington, Ted Dexter, Geoff Pullar, Raman Subba Row and Mike, wicketkeepers Roy Swetman and Keith Andrew, pace bowlers Brian Statham, Fred Trueman and Alan Moss and spinners Tommy Greenhough, Ray Illingworth and David Allen. Pullar was to open with Cowdrey, who was willing to perform the role. Jim Parks joined the team when Statham had to return home before the final Test. In the view of journalist Alan Ross, Parks would have been a better bet from the start instead of Andrew on account of his batting and England should have taken Johnny Wardle instead of one of the other three spinners on the basis that his dispute with Yorkshire was a local affair and should not have ruled him out.

The West Indies had lost Clyde Walcott and Everton Weekes, but they still had Frank Worrell, Rohan Kanhai, Garry Sobers and a crop of up-and-coming batsmen such as Conrad Hunte and Basil Butcher, who flourished on placid West Indian pitches. They also had Sonny Ramadhin, who had caused England so much trouble ten years earlier, albeit less so in 1957, Wes Hall and one or two emerging fast bowlers. The captain Gerry Alexander, a close friend of Peter May's at Cambridge, had barred Roy Gilchrist from the series because of his 'inflammable temperament'. Gilchrist had been sent home from the West Indies' previous tour of the Indian subcontinent on account of his conduct on and off the field.

To cut down on travel expenses a decision had been made for England to go by boat and the team embarked from Avonmouth on the *Camito*,[40] an Elders and Fyffes banana boat making its homeward journey. Several of the players had taken a supply of seasickness pills with them, although Alan Moss's preventive remedy was a mixture of port and brandy! By all accounts it was a pretty rough crossing initially, with most of the players, including Mike, suffering from seasickness. According to Mike, they didn't see much of Fred as he shut himself in his cabin for most of the journey. Ray Illingworth spent a day naively exploring the vessel for the snooker room, after being mischievously challenged to a game by Moss.[41] According to Robert Louis Stevenson, 'to travel hopefully is better than to arrive', but it is doubtful if you could have got much agreement among the players about that and there must have been audible sighs of relief on arrival at Bridgetown, Barbados. The team kept fit during the calmer final stages of the voyage by embarking on

40 The *Camito* had been built in 1956 and was scrapped in 1973. It was the second company boat of this name, the first having been torpedoed and sunk by a German U-boat in the North Atlantic in 1941.

41 *MJK Smith: No Ordinary Man*, Douglas Miller.

two sessions of circuit training per day, under a plan adopted by MCC on the advice of the Amateur Athletic Association chief coach Geoffrey Dyson.

The players received the warmest of welcomes on arrival and enjoyed a lavish reception at the Marine Hotel together with the probable West Indian team who had flown in from the various islands. Two days later they were off to Grenada for a flag-flying three-day match against the Windward Islands played on a matting wicket. Feeble totals of 89 and 69 by Windward Islands resulted in a ten-wicket win for MCC. The local batsmen were unable to cope with the leg-breaks and googlies of Greenhough (6-32) in the first innings and the pace of Trueman (5-22) and Moss (3-21) in the second. MCC also struggled, with only May (38) making a decent score. On their return to Barbados MCC played a two-day match against Barbados Colts, which ended in a draw. Mike made a century and Cowdrey and Barrington half-centuries out of an MCC total of 323/7 declared. Barbados Colts replied with 222 all out. There was time for only nine overs in MCC's second innings.

With only a day in between, MCC, woefully short of match practice, took on a strong Barbados side containing several Test players. On winning the toss, Weekes elected to bat. They were still at the crease after tea on the second day, Seymour Nurse (213) and Sobers (154) having put on 306 for the third wicket. Conrad Hunte had earlier created a sound platform with a well-struck 69. Weekes declared with the score at 533/5, leaving MCC an hour and a half to survive before the close. The captain had not needed to bat. The hero of the hour for Barbados was 21-year-old Charlie Griffith who in the space of two overs dismissed Cowdrey, Mike and May, leaving MCC reeling at 23/3. Cowdrey was lbw, Mike was yorked first ball and May caught at gully from one that lifted. Pullar and Barrington held out until the close and on the following day took the score to 113 before Pullar fell for a stubborn 46. Dexter joined Barrington and for a while batting looked a lot easier until Dexter was run out for 33 responding to Barrington's call for a leg bye. Barrington finally fell for a patient 79 in just under four hours in Griffith's first over with the new ball. Swetman proved his worth with 33 before MCC were all out for 238. Asked to follow on, MCC batted better in the second innings, May making 69, Barrington another 79 and Illingworth 72. With time running out and a draw looking likely, Weekes, an occasional bowler, brought himself on and his leg-spin accounted for Barrington, Illingworth, Swetman and Statham to render MCC all out for 352 and leave Barbados needing 58 to win in 28 minutes. Hunte and Cammie Smith, promoted to open, remarkably achieved this in 6.2 overs from Trueman and Statham, Smith making 40 not out with some amazing strokeplay as the rain started to fall. MCC earned much praise for staying out in the wet and slippery conditions and for eschewing any negative tactics. This was a historic victory for Barbados, the first time they had beaten an MCC team for 33 years. Unfortunately, by persevering in the rain, Statham had slipped on delivery and pulled a hamstring muscle. He had hoped to be fit for the first Test starting four days later but had to pull out on the morning of the match.

The first Test was held at Bridgetown, Barbados, the third consecutive match that England played on this ground. They had already become painfully aware of its unresponsive wicket and were handicapped by the loss of Statham. England brought in Moss to replace him and Allen was preferred to Greenhough, whose one wicket in the previous match had cost 125 runs. It was to be hoped that Dexter would bowl better this time, as his one wicket against Barbados had cost over 100 runs. Having said that, Trueman had also gone for 110 and finished wicketless. Mike, who had complained that he was not seeing the ball well because of the brightness of the light combined with the glare from the glassy surface of the wicket, was moved from number three to five, swapping places with Barrington.

For West Indies, England had not yet seen Easton McMorris, Basil Butcher, Reg Scarlett, an off-spinner, or Chester Watson, a fast bowler with, some said, a rather suspect action. Otherwise the team consisted of experienced, talented Test players. There was criticism in some circles about the omission of Seymour Nurse and Charlie Griffith, but West Indies had an embarrassment of riches and these two would eventually get their chance in the series.

May was no doubt delighted to win the toss this time and had no hesitation in deciding to bat. By the end of the first day England's score stood at 188/3. After a solid start between Cowdrey and Pullar which yielded 50 before Cowdrey fell to Watson for 30, Pullar and Barrington put on 103 for the second wicket before Pullar was run out by a smart piece of fielding by Kanhai. He was clearly at fault and was slow in responding to a call from Barrington for what should have been a fairly comfortable single. May didn't last long, falling to a very good catch by Alexander from a fine leg-side tickle. Mike was 9 not out at the close and took his score to 39 the next day before nicking a ball to Alexander which jumped a bit. Barrington's innings ended on 128 when he was given out caught down the leg side by Alexander off Ramadhin. He was clearly unhappy about the decision and was unable to conceal his disbelief. Thereafter Dexter assumed majestic control, as only he was able. He received excellent support from Swetman, who rode his luck for an enterprising 45 before he was out just before the close.

They put on a much-needed 123 for the seventh wicket, steering England to relative safety at 430/7 at the end of the second day. England added a further 52 runs the following morning, Dexter ending up with 136 not out in the presence of his proud parents, to boot. Watson and Ramadhin took three wickets each.

But now it was West Indies' turn. English hopes would have been raised when the third day ended with the home side on 114/3. They had an unexpected success when McMorris was run out off a Trueman no-ball after a neat piece of work by Allen, who broke the wicket at the non-striker's end with an accurate underhand throw. Barrington accounted for Hunte and Trueman for Kanhai, leaving Sobers and Worrell at the crease when play ended. These two great batsmen consolidated West Indies' position on the fourth day, playing with restraint and were unparted, having put on 177 when rain curtailed proceedings. At the end of the fifth day West Indies were four runs ahead. Sobers and Worrell were still at the wicket with Sobers on 216 and Worrell on 177.

On the morning of the final day Sobers was bowled by Trueman after adding a further ten runs. Worrell took his score to 197 not out. Worrell had taken over two hours to add his last 20 runs. When Alexander closed the innings at 563/8, Worrell and Sobers had put on 399 together, but at a pace so slow it effectively killed the game. Sobers batted for almost 11 hours and Worrell for slightly more in spite of signals from his captain towards the end to get a move on. There was some speculation that the timing of his declaration, which prevented Worrell's double century was a rebuke for his slow scoring as another ten minutes would not have made any difference to the result. Trueman stuck to his task manfully and was rewarded with the wickets of Butcher, who had been padded up for two days, and Hall and Alexander, to finish with 4-93 from 47 overs. Allen, Moss and Illingworth were wicketless, the latter two going for over 100 apiece, although, to be fair, there were several missed catches, two by Trueman. Pullar and Cowdrey batted out the remaining time in a subdued manner, disdaining the temptation of going after Hunte and Kanhai, who bowled the final eight overs. If the wickets in the remaining Tests were all going to be like this, a dull series beckoned.

England's next stop was Trinidad for a four-day match against the island side at Port-of-Spain, which did not contain any current Test players, as Ramadhin was omitted, probably to hide him from view. Trinidad made steady progress to a total of 301/9 declared, 22-year-old left-hander Joey Carew demonstrating his future promise with an attractive 102 not out. He was to go on to captain Trinidad and to play in 19 Tests. MCC's reply was most unconvincing and after a first-wicket stand of 53 between Subba Row and Pullar, they had no answer to the well-flighted left-arm spin of 21-year-old Charran Singh, who took 5-57, and the right-arm off-spin of Ollie Corbie, who took 3-34. MCC narrowly avoided having to follow on thanks to the efforts of Trueman and Statham. A sporting declaration by Trinidad's captain at 131/7 left England needing 262 to win in 210 minutes. MCC accepted the challenge and were given a good start by Subba Row, who made 73. Mike (47 not out) and Dexter (69 not out) knocked off the last hundred runs in fine style in just over an hour.

A second match against Trinidad, this time at Pointe-a-Pierre, started two days later. Ramadhin was again left out, as was Singh, who had created havoc in the first innings of the previous match. He was due to make his debut in the second Test and perhaps the West Indian selectors did not want to give the England batsmen the opportunity to work him out. May won the toss, and Cowdrey and Pullar had 174 on the board before Pullar was out for 68. Cowdrey dominated the remaining proceedings, going on to score an impressive 173 in just over two hours. MCC declared at 337/9. Mike made only one run and Peter May was not at his best, skying one to cover for 25. Corbie's off-spin brought him a return of 4-107 from 38 tidy overs. Allen, with figures of 7-33 on a deteriorating pitch, was the main architect of Trinidad's demise and they were all out for 166, Carew failing this time. He did better in the second innings with 70, out hit wicket to Statham, but no one else did and Trinidad were all out for 172. Allen got another three wickets for 30, as did Barrington for 42 runs. With two runs needed to win, it mattered little who went out to get them. A light-hearted 18-over a side match followed to give the crowd their money's worth.

It was back to Port-of-Spain for the second Test starting five days later, where the West Indies team had been holding a two-day trial match while MCC were beating Trinidad. On the strength of this, the Jamaicans, Scarlett and McMorris, were dropped from the Test team, immediately raising arguments about inter-island rivalries, particularly since the Trinidadian Charran Singh took Scarlett's place and Joe Solomon from British Guiana replaced McMorris. Seymour Nurse was in the 12 but would have to wait until the third Test for his debut. The only change for England was a fully recovered Statham for Moss.

May happily won the toss again and chose to bat. Both Cowdrey and Pullar were subjected to hostile spells from Hall and Watson with a plentiful supply of short-pitched bowling. They coped well for the first three-quarters of an hour until Pullar feathered one from Watson to Alexander. Cowdrey did not last much longer, getting an inside edge on to his stumps from a rising ball from Hall. May never looked comfortable and was caught at second slip off Watson without scoring just before lunch. At 57/3 things looked bleak but a marvellous fourth-wicket stand of 142 between Barrington and Dexter, promoted to number five above Mike, put England firmly back in control. After Dexter went for an imperious 77, caught and bowled by Singh for his first Test wicket, Mike and Barrington batted the day out cautiously to take England to 220/4 at the close. It was a particularly gutsy performance from Barrington, who had taken several painful blows in his 93 not out, including one on the head from a Hall bouncer. On the following morning Barrington and Mike carried on where they had left off, taking the total to 265 by lunchtime. Barrington finally fell to Hall for 121, brilliantly caught off an inside edge by Alexander diving to his left. Thereafter Mike proceeded in his determined way to the second Test match century of his career, 108, until superbly caught by Worrell at short midwicket from a full-blooded drive off Ramadhin. He owed a lot to Trueman and Allen, who with long stays at the wicket had ensured he reached this milestone, as when the seventh wicket fell he had only just reached his half-century. An indication of his unselfishness as a team player was apparent from the fact that, when on 99, he refused easy singles if it left Allen exposed. England's ultimate total of 382 was more than satisfactory given their bad start. Ramadhin and Watson each took three wickets and Hall two.

If England's start had been bad, that of the West Indies was nothing short of disastrous. Resuming on the morning of the third day at 22/0, by lunchtime they were 45/5 with the cream of their batting back in the pavilion. Trueman had accounted for Kanhai, Sobers and Worrell, Statham for Hunte, and Solomon was run out after being sent back by Worrell after a smart piece of work by Allen. Sobers was caught off a loose shot by Barrington at slip after May had parried the speeding ball. After lunch a most tedious passage of play ensued as West Indies tried to recover. Barrington bowled 12 overs for three runs and Illingworth seven overs for eight. Never have a West Indies team scored so slowly. It was as if they were too shell-shocked to score runs and their only thought was survival. Butcher took almost two hours to make nine runs before falling lbw to Statham, and only the captain Alexander offered any real resistance until he shouldered arms to a Trueman delivery and was adjudged lbw. After Butcher was out, Ramadhin, who normally batted at number 11, was unaccountably sent in at number eight and was on 13 and enjoying his promotion until he contrived to run out his partner Singh in a vain attempt to keep the strike. At this point, with the West Indies score standing at a scarcely believable 98/8 on a perfect batting wicket, all hell broke loose as a section of the crowd invaded the pitch, causing mayhem.

100 INJURED IN TEST RIOT

From Brian Chapman, Port of Spain, Saturday.

RIOT stopped play! That is the fantastic news here tonight.

On the third day of the second Test between England and the West Indies this happened:—

THE UGLIEST battle that ever disgraced a sports ground flared, and left:

ONE HUNDRED people injured—thirty had to be taken to hospital.

BOTTLES, beer crates and missiles were hurled.

THE CROWD invaded the pitch from three sides.

FIRE HOSES were turned on.

SIRENS screamed.

A RIOT SQUAD moved in, batons drawn, and fought with the demonstrators.

And then, across the bottle-strewn grass, walked three men appealing—in vain—for the mob to disperse.

Famed Test cricketer Learie Constantine strode out from the pavilion.

Battle of the bottles

The Spark

The End

West Indies fans riot at Port-of-Spain.

The 15 policemen on duty at the ground were understandably unable to prevent this and, as the riot developed, the players made their way as best they could to the safety of the pavilion amid a hail of bottles and even bricks, one of which struck Pullar painfully on the arm. Mike recollects Statham telling him to grab a stump for self-defence, a piece of advice he wisely declined. He remembers a chap running past him saying, 'We're not after you, we're after that umpire.'[42] Presumably he meant Lee Kow, who had given the local boy, Charran Singh, run out. According to the players and Singh himself, it was a perfectly correct call, evidenced by the fact that Singh continued running to the pavilion without waiting for the decision, which in the light of subsequent events proved to be a sensible choice. It would appear to have been the fuse that led to the pitch invasion and the riot, although the crowd's dissatisfaction with a couple of umpiring decisions, disappointment at the West Indies' abysmal performance, the slow rate of scoring, the passionate nature of the West Indian temperament and liberal intakes of rum

42 *MJK Smith: No Ordinary Man,* Douglas Miller.

were no doubt all contributory factors. It took some time for order to be restored in spite of appeals from the good and the great, including Sir Learie Constantine, one of Trinidad's heroes.

Peter May's genteel plea, 'Kindly get off the ground. If only you chaps would go and sit down we could get on with the game and you would see some decent cricket,' also had little effect. The riot was not without its moments of comedy, one of the recently arrived riot squad being drenched by his own hosepipe when the water from it arrived unexpectedly, causing great hilarity in the crowd. Rex Alston, who was commentating, was concerned about his wife who was in the grandstand watching, but he need not have worried, as she said it was one of the most exciting day's cricket she had ever seen. The match was abandoned for the day, but England were happy to resume and play the match out. The umpires were willing to continue to stand and it was agreed that the time lost was to be added on by lengthening each day's play. The following day was thankfully a rest day which allowed the shock and emotions to subside, and after play resumed there was no further crowd trouble. Trueman and Statham finished off the innings quickly and West Indies were all out for 112. Trueman had the excellent figures of 5-35 and Statham 3-42.

Instead of enforcing the follow-on, which, with Trueman and Statham refreshed after the rest day, would almost certainly have been the better option, May decided to bat again. England made heavy weather of their second innings and at close of play on the fourth day had scored 196/7, having been 133/7 at one stage. Barrington had contributed 49 and May and Pullar 28 each. It was thanks to the two Yorkshiremen, Illingworth (41 not out) and Trueman (37) that England were able to declare at 230/9 after an hour on the fifth morning of this six-day Test, leaving West Indies ten hours to make 501 to win. Hall and Watson both picked up three wickets, Singh two and Ramadhin one. By the end of the day West Indies were 134/2 with Hunte having gone for 47 and Kanhai on 55 not out. Allen had taken the wickets, both caught by Swetman. With 367 still required, a West Indies win was highly improbable and it now became a question of whether they could hold out for a draw. In the end it proved beyond them in spite of some rather strange captaincy decisions by May, who turned to Barrington after Trueman had removed Sobers and Statham had dismissed Worrell. Statham had had Butcher playing and missing frequently. After lunch the pace bowlers were recalled and Statham finally got his man lbw.

Kanhai gave the crowd something to celebrate when he reached his century with a flurry of strokes off Trueman. Dexter then came into the attack and, true to the adage that it's often the bad ball which gets the wicket, had Kanhai neatly caught off a full toss at midwicket by Mike. He then promptly had Ramadhin lbw for the fourth one of the innings. No one could accuse the umpires of patriotic bias! The writing was now on the wall and Allen and Barrington polished off the tail despite Singh holding out for nearly an hour. The West Indies were all out for 244, leaving England victors by 256 runs with just under two hours to spare. Allen, who was proving to be a real asset, took 3-57, Dexter 2-7, Barrington 2-34, Statham 2-44 and Trueman 1-44. It was a fine team performance, but the honours must go to Trueman and Statham for achieving the unlikely feat of bowling West Indies out on a near-perfect batting pitch in the first innings for just over a hundred runs. The crowd were fulsome in their applause when England left the field, no doubt in part to compensate for the embarrassment right-minded spectators must have felt about the riot. Anyway, England were now in the enviable position of being one up with three to play. An offer to play the final Test elsewhere was firmly rejected. 'We intend to play it here as arranged unless prevented by the West Indies Board,' said Robins.

The next stop was Jamaica and England were able to enjoy several days to bask in their glory and take to the beach before playing again. In a two-day match against Jamaica Colts at Sabina Park where honours finished even after each side had completed only one innings, MCC gained some useful batting practice on the ground for the third Test, Swetman making 100 and Pullar 84 in a total of 306/9 declared. The Colts, not to be outdone, replied with 295 all out, 22-year-old Teddy Griffith making 177. He was the son of the legendary fast bowler Herman Griffith who played in West Indies' first tour of England in 1928, taking 11 wickets in the three Tests, including 6-103 in the final one at the Oval. For MCC, Greenhough took 5-91 and Barrington, frequently among the wickets in the lesser games, 4-72.

Two days later, this time on Kingston's other first-class ground, Melbourne Park, MCC took on the full Jamaica side, which included Griffith after his earlier showing. Batting first Jamaica made 374, a century from McMorris giving him a good chance of regaining his Test place. Worrell made 75 and Scarlett 72 not out at number seven, but Griffith failed to impress, being bowled in each innings in his teens. Trueman was the pick of the bowlers with 4-54 and Greenhough took 3-58. In reply, MCC's batting prospered and their 525/6 declared was their highest ever total against Jamaica. It was pleasing to see May recover his form with 124, Subba Row at his best with 92 and Dexter (75), Mike (111) and Illingworth (60 not out) all scoring at a rapid rate. With four hours remaining to try and force a win, MCC came close and had it not been for McMorris (74) and Scarlett (59), they might well have done, Jamaica finishing on 202/7.

West Indies made a couple of changes for the third Test, one of them enforced, for Worrell had sprained an ankle missing a step on a visit to MCC's hotel. McMorris and Scarlett were recalled to replace Solomon and Singh, and Nurse was brought in for his debut to replace Worrell. England were unchanged, although apparently Cowdrey had unselfishly offered to give up his place to Subba Row because of his poor form. As things turned out, it was well that his offer was declined. May won his third successive toss and again opted to bat. Things went reasonably well until Pullar edged Hall to Sobers at second slip just before the first hour. From then on the cricket was attritional with Watson and Hall bowling fast and short, making strokeplay difficult and survival hazardous.

Barrington was next to go, caught off his gloves trying to pull away from a Watson bouncer, and May perished after a brief, uncomfortable stay, fending off a rising delivery from Hall, which Hunte caught smartly at short leg. Dexter and Cowdrey, who had ridden several painful blows stoically, then dug in and at tea the score stood at 113/3 with Dexter having batted 80 minutes for 25 and Cowdrey 210 brave minutes for 42. It soon became 113/5 when Dexter edged Hall to Alexander and Mike was yorked off Hall's next ball. By the close England had limped to 165/6 with Illingworth also out to the last ball of the day after doggedly resisting for an hour and a half. A bruised and battered Cowdrey was still there on 75 not out. In mid-afternoon play had been interrupted when the roof of a stand collapsed under the weight of a number of spectators who had made an illegal entry to the ground via scaffolding from the garden of a neighbouring house, causing a number of minor injuries but happily none too serious, more by luck than good stewardship.

On the following morning 165/6 quickly became 170/7 when Swetman was removed for a duck by Hall, putting England in dire trouble. Fortunately the tail wagged and Trueman, Allen and Statham all made valuable contributions to help Cowdrey add over 100 runs for the last three wickets. Cowdrey's valiant innings came to an end when he was well caught by Scarlett off Ramadhin for one of the hardest-earned centuries of his career in an innings which had lasted almost seven hours. Hall, whose pace had never flagged in the 31 overs he sent down, finished with the excellent figures of 7-69.

When West Indies batted, Trueman and Statham proved just as difficult as Hall and Watson had been and it was not long before Statham had Hunte back in the pavilion, caught at backward short leg by Illingworth. The next wicket to fall was that of Kanhai, crazily run out when both batsmen finished alongside each other at one end. Going for a three, Kanhai made his ground at the danger end, only to find McMorris also there with his back turned. Swetman quickly relayed Cowdrey's return to Statham, who took off the bails at the end where McMorris should have been. Such poor communication does not make for good team morale. These were to be England's only successes of the day unless one counts McMorris having had to retire hurt after being struck under the heart by a rising ball from Statham. He had batted almost five hours for his 65 runs. Sobers, who had completely dominated the partnership and was playing with sublime freedom, was now joined by Nurse, and by the end of the day West Indies' score had progressed to 291/2 with Sobers not out on 142 and Nurse on 46.

At this stage it looked as if West Indies had England at their mercy. Strange things can happen in cricket matches, though, and how West Indies only managed to increase their score by 62 runs from such a commanding position is hard to fathom. Although credit must be given to all the England bowlers, to a large extent the West Indian batsmen were the architects of their own downfall. After Sobers fell lbw to Trueman, having added only five to his score, a wave of uncertainty seemed to wash over the team. Once Nurse and Solomon had both perished trying to take the attack to England, a pessimistic torpor seemed to overcome the remaining batsmen and one by one they got themselves out by indecision. McMorris and Scarlett, the saviours of Jamaica the previous week, were unrecognisable and played like condemned men for a time until losing their wickets attacking the wrong ball. Unlike England's, the West Indies' tail remained limp and none of the last six batsmen attained double figures. The West Indies innings closed at 353, Statham having taken three wickets and Trueman and Illingworth two each. Incredibly, the last seven wickets had fallen for just 24 runs. It was a fine recovery by England, aided by good fielding and catching, but they were 76 behind in the first innings with a lot of work still to do.

Re-enter Cowdrey, England's first-innings hero, and the doughty Pullar. By the end of the fourth day they had almost wiped out the deficit and on day five they took their opening partnership to 177, the highest England first-wicket stand for ten years. Sadly, both fell at the same total, Pullar caught off Hall for 66 and Cowdrey off Ramadhin for 97. He had surely deserved to join the short list of players who had made a century in each innings of a Test match (only Denis Compton since the war) but it was not to be. Barrington was out lbw for 4 a few overs later and May was joined by Dexter. The latter started well but was unlucky to be undone by a shooter from Watson, no doubt it having pitched on one of the cracks which were starting to widen. May and Mike batted resolutely until tea but on the resumption Mike was adjudged lbw to Watson. At the end of the fifth day England were 280/9, 207 ahead, May having been dismissed for a patient 45 on a difficult wicket with Illingworth, Swetman and Trueman all going cheaply. Since lunch England had lost nine wickets for 114 runs. As Alan Ross wrote of England's collapse, 'It was like watching money pouring out of a hole in a wealthy man's pocket.'[43] On the final day Allen and Statham held out for three-quarters of an hour, adding a further 25 priceless runs.

43 *Through the Caribbean*, Alan Ross.

West Indies now needed 230 to win in just over four hours. Under normal circumstances this should not have been beyond them but, with the wicket misbehaving, batting had become something of a lottery. McMorris, with his chest well padded, was soon bowled by Trueman by one that cut from leg to off and kept a bit low. Hunte was next to go, bowled by Trueman by one that cut back. He had batted aggressively for 40 out of 48/2. Sobers joined Kanhai and they were progressing nicely until disaster struck when Sobers was needlessly run out by several feet at the non-striker's end by a quick underarm throw from Dexter to Statham after having been sent back by Kanhai. One could not fault Kanhai here as he had given no indication to run. This was undoubtedly a key turning point in the match, for West Indies had now lost their best player. The next to go was Nurse, who had started well but lost his off stump to Trueman, who now had three wickets for not very many, all bowled. Ninety runs were now needed with five wickets standing and 80 minutes left. Alexander then sent in Scarlett ahead of himself and Solomon as someone who could score at the rate required. Scarlett and Kanhai proceeded to put on 25 quickly, swinging the game back in West Indies' favour. After Illingworth's last two overs had gone for 16, May brought back Statham, who in his first over had Scarlett lbw from one which kept low. The game could now go either way. Alexander joined Kanhai. At this point a controversy arose which did England no credit. Kanhai had succumbed to cramp and had asked for a runner. May incorrectly refused the request and Kanhai was reduced to having to limp to the other end for his runs, potential twos being turned into singles. Clearly, the umpires should have overruled May, but it would appear that one of them, as well as May, was ignorant of the law. Soon afterwards Kanhai was bowled by a Trueman yorker from a rash stroke. Thereafter, with 78 runs needed in 45 minutes, West Indies decided to shut up shop and Alexander and Solomon safely batted out time.

This was a match which West Indies really should have won and surely would have done but for Cowdrey's heroic batting, Trueman's tireless bowling, Statham and Allen's late-order resistance and Sobers' suicidal run-out. Trueman returned the excellent figures of 4-54. After the match both Robins and May apologised to Alexander and Kanhai for their mistake. Umpire Lee Kow said he knew Kanhai was entitled to a runner, but his co-umpire Perry Burke had disagreed and in such situations the status quo had to be preserved.

At the end of this exciting, incident-packed Test, MCC travelled to Antigua for a three-day match against the Leeward Islands. The home side batted first, making 296 against an attack without Trueman and Statham. MCC's innings turned into a run-fest, Cowdrey, Subba Row and Dexter all making centuries in MCC's total of 456/5 declared. Leeward Islands scored 199/3 in their unfinished second innings, as the match ended in a draw.

It was then on to British Guiana, who boasted six Test players in Walcott, Kanhai, Solomon, Butcher, Glendon Gibbs and Lance Gibbs. On an easy-paced pitch British Guiana made 375/6 declared, Butcher scoring a century, Walcott 83 and Glendon Gibbs a rather slow 78. Pullar and Cowdrey put on 281 for MCC's first wicket, Cowdrey making 141, Pullar 139 and Mike 97 in MCC's final total of 494 all out. There was just time for Dexter to take two wickets in British Guiana's second innings. May was down to play but did not bat, as complications from an abdominal operation a year earlier had ruled him out. He had been having some secret treatment since arriving in the Caribbean, but had kept the problem largely to himself, although he had confided in his wife and Cowdrey but not his team manager. In Mike's view, he was not well enough to tour and should never have made the trip.

The fourth Test started on the same ground four days later. For West Indies Walcott was brought out of retirement and Singh replaced Ramadhin, who had shoulder trouble. Cowdrey, now in charge after May was considered unfit, continued the toss-winning sequence and elected to bat. Rain delayed the start of the game by an hour and, when it did commence, scoring proceeded at a gentle pace. At the close England were 152/2 with Cowdrey 65 not out. On the resumption Cowdrey was out caught behind off Hall's second ball of the day without adding to his score. Barrington retired hurt a few balls later, in some discomfort after having been hit on the elbow by Hall the previous evening. Mike came in to replace him but only lasted two balls, bowled by a fast yorker, as in the first innings of the previous Test. Illingworth and Swetman then perished, Illingworth to a Sobers googly and Swetman lbw to Watson. England had now lost four wickets for 23 runs in just over an hour and the score stood at a dismal 175/6. Once again Allen rode to the rescue. In partnership with Dexter, many of whose best shots were going straight to fielders, they put on 44 runs before Dexter was caught off a mis-timed hook from a Hall bouncer. Barrington re-entered the fray, clearly in some pain and gave Allen good support by holding up his end. Allen reached his maiden Test fifty but departed soon after, caught at the wicket off Hall. Barrington soldiered bravely on, but was only able to add five runs to his score and went for 27, caught at slip off another Sobers googly. Statham showed once again that he could bat with 20 not out and he and Trueman put on 27 for the last wicket to give England the reasonably respectable total of 295. Hall once again was the mainstay of the West Indies attack with 6-90.

England's innings had lasted into the third day and at the close, on a day interrupted by rain, West Indies had countered with 139/2. The openers, Hunte and McMorris, were out and Kanhai and Sobers were at the crease, ominously on 31 and 33, having already put on 62 together, albeit at a slow rate. Their partnership was eventually worth 115 when Trueman dismissed Kanhai for 55. Walcott was sent in next in an attempt to quicken the scoring rate but to no avail, as his leg stump was soon uprooted by an inswinging yorker from Trueman. At the end of the fourth day West Indies were 332/4 and, barring disasters, in an unbeatable position but, having scored less than 200 runs in the day, the draw was a strong possibility. Sobers added only three runs to his overnight total and Worrell none, Allen, who had started with Illingworth, dismissing them both. At this point, with a lead of over 40 and four wickets standing, West Indies needed to accelerate to stand a chance of winning the match. But they didn't and the next partnership between Alexander and Scarlett only produced 45 runs in 75 minutes. Alexander was finally run out for 33 at the bowler's end by a direct throw from Mike. When Singh, who had been brought in to replace an unfit Ramadhin, was bowled by Trueman for a duck, Alexander declared at 402/8.

West Indies had a first-innings lead of 107 and there was eight hours of playing time left. By the close England had knocked off the deficit and the score stood at 110/2 with Cowdrey gone for 29, stumped off Singh. He had never looked in any trouble but missed a defensive push and raised his back foot long enough for Alexander to whip off the bails. Pullar was never completely at ease, but stubbornly held up his end for 47 until just before the end, being out lbw to Worrell off the last over of the day. Dexter, promoted to number three, was batting well and was on 30 not out.

The final day was played in front of a sparse crowd. Dexter and Subba Row were rightly taking no chances and waiting for the loose ball to punish. West Indies tried six bowlers but the only two to have any real success were Worrell and Singh. Watson was too injured to bowl and Hall, for once, finished wicketless. Dexter and Subba Row both progressed to centuries, putting on a match-saving 148 together. Barrington went for a duck and Mike made a careful 23 before being caught by Scarlett off a full toss. England ended up with 334/8. They had saved the match and were still one up with just one to play. As the match was drifting to a close, it was decided that Peter May would play no further part in the tour and would return home with his wife. Statham had also decided to go back to England because his five-year-old son was seriously ill in hospital. The need to return home would have been disappointing for such a dedicated cricketer, who would have wanted to help England see things through. Cowdrey was then appointed tour captain, Subba Row vice-captain and Trueman promoted to senior professional in place of Statham. Apparently, Trueman's first comment, on hearing of his elevation, was 'Well, they can cut out all that bloody swearing for a start.'

Before travelling to Trinidad for the final Test, MCC had one more match to play in British Guiana against Berbice, who had three Test players, Kanhai, Solomon and Butcher. Two of these, Solomon and Butcher, put on an unbroken 290 on a very placid batting wicket, Solomon making 201 and Butcher 131. Berbice declared at lunch on the second day at 387/2. In reply, England simply used the match for batting practice, compiling a massive 641/6 in their innings, which lasted until the end of the match. Parks made 183, Barrington 103, Illingworth 100 and Mike, Pullar, Dexter and Subba Row half-centuries. Parks, who had been coaching in the Caribbean, had been called in and given the wicketkeeper's gloves for this game to see if he was good enough to take over in the wicketkeeping duties in the final Test, as Keith Andrew had been unwell for most of the tour and Swetman had scored a mere 13 runs in his last six Test innings.

Solomon's and Butcher's innings were not sufficiently regarded to earn them a Test recall and West Indies went into the final Test with the same batting line-up as in the previous one. There were two bowling changes, though – Singh was dropped, Ramadhin, now fit, was recalled to replace Scarlett and Charlie Griffith given his first Test outing as an extra fast bowler. Parks, who had played only one Test previously for England against Pakistan in 1954 as a batsman, was entrusted with the gloves. Moss, who had enjoyed little success on the tour, was the only obvious replacement for Statham. Cowdrey won the toss, the fifth time it had gone England's way in the series, and batted. After Pullar went cheaply to Griffith, Cowdrey and Dexter put England back in command with a second-wicket partnership of 191 in three and a half hours. Sobers then dismissed both batsmen in the space of two overs and England finished the day on 256/3, Barrington having retired hurt for the fourth time in the series after being hit on the hand by Hall from the last ball of the day.

He was ready to resume the following morning, but the umpires correctly ruled that a new batsman had to go in as a batsman who had retired hurt could only return after the fall of a wicket. So Mike joined Subba Row at the crease. Runs flowed nicely until Subba Row was beautifully caught at slip by Hunte off Hall at backward short leg. Barrington returned and from the outset it was evident that he was out for revenge, playing shots with unaccustomed freedom against the quick bowlers, who seemed determined to rough him up again. Sometimes this approach works and it did on this occasion. Mike, who had been batting confidently, was the next to go, bowled off stump by a Ramadhin leg-break. Parks then entered the fray and fully justified his belated recall to Test cricket, immediately going on the attack. A big total beckoned but Ramadhin, bowling with his former guile, had other ideas and in short order dismissed Barrington for 69 with his quicker ball and then a mesmerised Illingworth for a duck. He had taken 3-14 in nine overs and put West Indies back in the game. Thereafter the innings folded quickly, Parks going for 43 and

Allen failing for once. England had made 393, the last six wickets going down for 85 runs. Ramadhin had taken 4-73, Sobers 3-75.

West Indies' innings started badly. Hunte had to retire hurt after receiving a sickening blow on the forehead when attempting to hook a Trueman bouncer and McMorris was run out after a fierce straight drive by Alexander was deflected on to the non-striker's wicket by Trueman's boot. Alexander had come in at number three in place of Kanhai, who had injured his hand fielding the previous day. Following rain on the third day, Alexander was next out, bringing Walcott in to join Sobers. The pair put on 87 before Walcott was stumped by Parks off Allen when jumping out to drive. After lunch on the fourth day, when the score stood at 216/3, the new ball was taken by Trueman and Moss. Worrell, who had not been in long, played on to Trueman's first delivery with it. Moss then dismissed Kanhai, who had come in at number seven, in the same manner. He then proceeded to bowl Sobers middle stump. These two wickets had been a long time in coming for Moss and he was clearly overjoyed. Sobers had batted over five hours for his 92 – not the rate of scoring needed to win the match and level the series. Ramadhin was in for an hour for 13, before Hall and a bandaged Hunte put on 65 for the eighth wicket, at which point Trueman bowled Hall for 29. A few runs later Alexander declared at 338/8, 55 runs behind.

With not much time left for play on the fourth day England lost Cowdrey, caught by Sobers off Hall at backward short leg for nought, a misfortune they could have done without. Allen came in as the nightwatchman and he and Pullar warily saw out time. The next morning Allen once again more than played his part and the score moved on at a comfortable rate. Hall had strained his side and was bowling at half pace until Watson took over. After half an hour's unsuccessful toil, Ramadhin came on, and the hopes of the West Indies now rested on him. The partnership was ended when Allen was run out for 25 after being a bit slow to set off for a single. Had he not taken evasive action to avoid Griffith's throw he might have made his ground. Sobers was now introduced into the attack and the move led to him dismissing Pullar for a well-made, valuable 54. Worrell was brought on at the other end and he bowled 11 overs for 16 runs which, although tidy, in no way advanced West Indies' cause. It would have helped had he hung on to an easy caught and bowled chance from Dexter. Ramadhin then had Subba Row lbw for 13 and soon afterwards Barrington departed for 6, turning a Sobers chinaman into short leg's hands. Dexter was then brilliantly run out by Hunte in the covers after a half-stop which caused Dexter a fatal moment's hesitation. Hunte rapidly recovered and threw the wicket down with not much more than one stump to aim at. The score now stood at a precarious 148/6 (effectively 203/6 with England's first-innings lead). West Indies were now clear favourites and it would take something special for England to recover and save the series. The last of the recognised batsmen, Jim Parks and Mike, were now at the crease together with half an hour to go to tea. If either one of them were to fail West Indies would most likely have at least a full day to make around 250. They were not found wanting. The pair played out the rest of the day at first carefully and later with more freedom, and by the close they had put on 90 together. The following morning they added a further 100 runs. Mike was finally out for 96, caught behind off Hunte. Cowdrey had England bat on a few more minutes to allow Parks to reach a well-deserved century and declared half an hour after lunch at 350/7. This left West Indies with the virtually impossible task of making over 400 to win in less than two sessions.

The West Indies innings thus became something of a tedious formality. Moss got his third wicket of the series, an lbw, the first apparently after having had 26 turned down on the tour. Did he honour his boast to do a lap of honour round the ground if he was awarded one? Worrell made 61 and Sobers was undefeated on 49 out of a final total of 209/5. In the last half hour a carnival atmosphere developed with Cowdrey, Mike and Pullar all bowling for the crowd's entertainment. Pullar had Worrell well caught one-handed on the boundary by Trueman near the end to the spectators' delight; this was his only Test wicket.

And so England had achieved a draw and a series win, 1-0. Everyone was happy. Well, nearly everyone, that is. Walter Robins wasn't. He felt strongly that England should have declared earlier and gone for a win. At some point during England's second innings, while Mike and Parks were piling on the runs, he entered the England dressing room and tried to persuade Cowdrey to declare. Colin was having none of it. In the end he was frogmarched out of the dressing room by Trueman. Subba Row, one of only two living witnesses, prefers the word 'escorted'. This is one story about Fred which is not apocryphal! After the match Robins, a strong advocate of 'brighter cricket', publicly upbraided Cowdrey but he was clearly in a minority of one. 'He was from a different generation', says Subba Row, 'where the spirit of cricket was more important than the result.'[44] The spirit of cricket is indeed important but so is a series win and there was no way England were going to allow West Indies a way back in, especially when they had a player of the calibre of Sobers.

The Test batting averages were topped by Dexter with 526 runs at 65.75. Second was Cowdrey with 491 at 54.55, Barrington third with 420 at 46.66, Pullar fourth with 385 at 42.77 and Subba Row fifth with 162 at 40.50. Mike, with 308 at 34.22, had a disappointing series by his standards, but came good in the last Test when it mattered. David Allen was a great success as a later

44 Conversation with Raman Subba Row.

batsman and Jim Parks was a sensation with innings of 43 and 101 not out. For West Indies Sobers was head and shoulders above everyone else with 709 runs at 101.28. Worrell had 320 at 64.00, Hunte 291 at 41.57 and Kanhai 325 at 40.62.

Trueman was heroic with 21 wickets at 26.14 and Statham unfailingly accurate with ten at 28.60 – both remarkable performances in the context of the wickets on which the matches were played. For the West Indies, Hall was the most dangerous with 22 wickets at 30.86. Ramadhin took 17 at 28.88 and showed that he was still a force to be reckoned with. Watson took 16 at 37.04.

Before returning home MCC played two one-day matches in Belize, British Honduras, which, unsurprisingly, they won easily, the first by 218 runs and the second by 163.

The tour was an outstanding success overall. Apart from the riot, it was free from major incidents and a great learning experience for the young squad that went out and returned successful.

CHAPTER 10

The Visit of the South Africans, 1960

THE WARWICKSHIRE players arriving for training at the start of the 1960 season were greeted with the appearance of a new sight screen at the City end of the ground. In the match against Northants the previous season several players had complained that it had been difficult to pick up the ball from Frank Tyson's bowling against the background of the crowd.[45] In spite of this Mike had mastered him with a superb unbeaten 142 out of a first-innings total of 252. The last 68 of Mike's runs came in a last-wicket stand of 78 with Ossie Wheatley, who had no pretensions as a batsman. 'Mike made sure I didn't have to face Tyson during the partnership', says Ossie, 'but he got me in the end.'

For the 1960 Championship season, as part of a bizarre ruling, Warwickshire were one of eight counties designated to play 32 matches, the other nine playing 28. This obviously necessitated the restructuring of the points system to a percentage basis. This imperfect and potentially unfair arrangement was to endure for a further two years. Irrespective of this, Warwickshire had a poor season relative to the previous one. They won only four Championship matches, lost 12, drew 16 and slipped from fourth to 15th in the table. Yorkshire, one of the other teams to play 32

45 *The History of Warwickshire County Cricket Club,* Jack Bannister.

matches, finished as champions for the second year running by a clear margin. The reasons for Warwickshire's decline lay to some extent in the imbalance between the batting and bowling strength. Because of their powerful batting line-up composed of many quick scorers, opponents were wary of setting them achievable targets and many games finished either as draws or narrow defeats after the pursuit of a difficult target. Also, they were weak in the spin bowling department. It had been hoped that Basil Bridge, the off-spinner who had enjoyed a good season in 1959, would come good again but he faded and part way through the season lost his place in the team. They were also handicapped by injuries to Tom Cartwright and Roly Thompson. Ossie Wheatley, in his second full season, did well again and Jack Bannister emerged as an opening bowler of high quality. They both took 100 wickets. There was little back-up, however, and once these two had exhausted themselves, there was no one to contain the opponents' later-order batsmen.

Dick Spooner had retired at the end of the previous season and Bert Wolton only played one game in 1960. They had been stalwart Warwickshire professionals who had both played a principal part in their Championship win in 1951. Wolton, who joined the county in 1947, scored over 1,000 runs eight times and was a fielder with a powerful throw. Spooner, an agile wicketkeeper and left-handed batsman from Durham, whose first-class career had started one year later after being recommended to Tom Dollery by Alan Townsend, topped the Warwickshire batting averages in their Championship-winning season with 1,767 runs and four centuries. He was unlucky to be a contemporary of Godfrey Evans but made seven Test appearances when Evans was unavailable or injured. The journalist Alex Bannister described him as a great team man. Jim Stewart recalls the angry stare Spooner gave you if you ever sent in a poor return. Jim also recalls a game when he was wearing a pair of new boots which were killing him, and he went out to field in sandals. Spooner was captain and angrily ordered him off the field to put his boots back on.[46] Tom Cartwright also remembers getting a harsh telling-off from Spooner for not chasing the ball all the way to the boundary even though it was a lost cause.[47] It was a tough school for the junior players, but it bred disciplined professionals with good habits. Jim Stewart, Tom Cartwright, Fred Gardner and Clive Leach[48] all lived in Coventry and used to travel up to Birmingham by train together and then take a tram to Edgbaston. Woe betide them if they ever arrived late for training. At the end of the day they were required to bowl at the members in the nets before taking the train home. 'I hated bowling at the members,' says Jim Stewart. 'We never used to get home before nine o'clock.' After a couple of years, Clive Leach got a car which made things easier for them. Spooner was replaced by Jackie Fox, who then lost his place to Alan Smith when his Oxford University matches finished.

Mike topped the Warwickshire averages again with 1,867 runs at 47.87 and finished third behind Subba Row and Javed Burki in the national averages with 2,551 runs, more than any other player. Jim Stewart had his best season yet with 1,444 runs at 43.47 and Norman Horner, Ray Hitchcock and Billy Ibadulla all scored over 1,000.

The highlight of the season, though, was an unbroken opening partnership of 377 in five hours 20 minutes between Norman

46 Conversation with Jim Stewart

47 *Tom Cartwright: The Flame Still Burns*, Stephen Chalke

48 Clive Leach (1934–) was born in Bombay and grew up in Coventry. He made 39 first-class appearances for Warwickshire as a left-arm spin bowler and right-handed batsman between 1955 and 1958, when he was released. He went on to play Minor Counties cricket for Durham, primarily as a batsman, becoming their chairman in 2004. In 1961 he commenced a career in television with Tyne Tees Television, later becoming chairman and chief executive of Yorkshire-Tyne Tees Television. In 2000 he was awarded the CBE for services to education and training.

Horner and Ibadulla against Surrey at the Oval in early July. Mike was on Test match duty against South Africa and Ossie Wheatley skippered the side. Ossie clearly remembers this record partnership, Surrey's slow batting, and the reluctance of Surrey skipper Alec Bedser to make a game of it, maintaining that he had a weakened team. Rain on the final day washed out any chance of a result. Jack Bannister took the first wicket of the match, that of Micky Stewart, just before lunch on the second morning, claiming it to be a record for the longest time for a wicket to fall in a county match! Dennis Amiss made his debut in that match at the age of 17, but, at number six in the batting order, could only look on in admiration and perhaps with some disappointment that he was unlikely to get a bat. He didn't, as that was Warwickshire's only innings but he did get a bowl, dismissing Eric Bedser. He was very disappointed to be left out of the side a few weeks later when, just before the start of a home match, it was discovered that Warwickshire had 12 players on the field, a fact that had been brought to Mike's attention by Jim Stewart. He was the unlucky one told to leave to his great disappointment. As it was a Saturday, he went off to play for Smethwick in the Birmingham League instead, which he had been doing when there was no Second XI game.[49] He did not get many more chances in the first team until the end of the season, when he was selected for several away matches. Amiss had joined the club as a 15-year-old schoolboy and was coached under the strict, demanding eye of Tiger Smith and the Jamaican Derief Taylor, both of whom invested a lot of time in their young prodigy's development. Tiger was a tough taskmaster who was appointed as Warwickshire's coach in 1946 at the age of 60 and continued in the post until 1955. He had played for Warwickshire before the First World War

---

49 *Not Out at Close of Play*, Dennis Amiss.

and had been a successful wicketkeeper in Warwickshire's first Championship win in 1911 and in England's Ashes triumph over Australia in 1911/12 when he stood up to the bowling of Sidney Barnes and Frank Foster. His knowledge of the science of batting was legendary and many seasoned professionals came to him for advice. Jim Stewart, though, didn't respond at all well to Tiger's aggressive coaching style and Jim says Tiger handed him over to Derief,[50] whose gentler approach suited him much better.

Derief Taylor had come to Warwickshire through Tom Dollery, whom he had met in the Eighth Army in North Africa during the war after having given up his job as a London taxi driver to join up. After playing a few games for Warwickshire after the war, he became the county's junior coach and invested almost all his time either coaching or looking for potential talent. On one occasion, one of his charges came running excitedly across the field to tell him how many runs he had scored in a match. 'How many did the team get?' asked Derief. The boy didn't know and Derief sent him all the way back to find out. He wanted to instil the right values in his 'youts', as he called them in his broad Jamaican accent. According to Leslie Deakins, Warwickshire's long-serving secretary, Derief's virtues were a deep love of the game, his infinite patience and his unique understanding of the teenage mind.[51] He was awarded a testimonial in 1976 after 25 years with the club. He and Tiger made a great team and were responsible for Warwickshire developing a lot of home-grown talent in the 1960s. Dennis Amiss also benefitted from Tom Dollery's wise counsel and disciplined approach as captain of the Second XI. Dollery had served in the war under desert conditions and had no time for namby-pambies. 'Drinks? What do you want drinks for? In

50 Conversation with Jim Stewart.

51 *The Story of Warwickshire Cricket*, Leslie Duckworth.

the desert we had to make do with two pints of water a day – and that was for you and your vehicle.'[52]

The visit of the South African touring team to England in 1960 was not popular with everyone, in particular those who had strong views about the policy of apartheid in that country. On arrival at London airport the team was greeted with an army of demonstrators. The Reverend David Sheppard, a potential England captain, had taken a principled stance and had stated his unwillingness to play against the tourists either for England or for his county Sussex. There was also significant opposition to the tour at the universities of Oxford and Cambridge, sarcastically referred to by the veteran South African wicketkeeper John Waite in his book *Perchance To Bowl* as the 'enlightened Youth of Britain', and in the various mining communities scattered around the country. Waite was highly critical of Sheppard's views and genuinely believed that the British public were 'dangerously misinformed and uninformed about South Africa' because of the press. In the event, the tour proceeded with minimal disruption and it would take the Basil D'Oliveira affair and another ten years before links with South African cricket were cut. Waite's views, which were probably a fair reflection of the other members of the touring party, sprang from a generally held belief that 'the black and coloured public of South Africa is not equipped or ready for multi-racial sport any more than the black and coloured public of the Union is ready to govern South Africa or to manage its industries, primary and secondary'.[53] Sixty years on, this makes difficult reading but, sad to say, it was also the view of most members of English cricket's establishment, who genuinely believed politics and sport should be put in separate compartments. In a show of support, Billy Griffith

52 *Tom Cartwright: The Flame Still Burns,* Stephen Chalke.

53 *Perchance To Bowl,* John Waite.

rode in the team coach with the South Africans on their journey from the airport to their Piccadilly hotel, a more Christian gesture than Sheppard's in Waite's opinion.

Mike was selected for the first Test at Edgbaston in a team containing most of the side that had taken the field for the last game in the West Indies. There were a couple of new faces – Bob Barber, then captain of Lancashire, and Peter Walker of Glamorgan both made their Test debuts. Barber, with scores of 5 and 4, was unable to make the most of his opportunity and was not selected for the rest of the series. Brian Statham was back in the team instead of Alan Moss. Ken Barrington was omitted after a poor sequence of scores, as was David Allen, one can only assume in the case of the latter through injury or illness, as he missed several games for Gloucestershire during that period. Mike made 54 and 28 in a match which England won by 100 runs, Statham and Fred Trueman being the main wicket-takers, Statham with five and Trueman seven. The match was a rather tedious affair with slow scoring rates by both sides, overcast weather and poor attendances.

For the second Test, Barrington came in for the injured Geoff Pullar, who had cracked a bone in his wrist in the first Test fending off a Neil Adcock bouncer. Moss was brought in as a third pace bowler in place of Barber. Mike just missed out on a century, caught Waite, bowled Geoff Griffin for 99 in England's only innings. England made 362/8 declared, Raman Subba Row scoring a laborious 90 and Ted Dexter 56. They then dismissed South Africa for 152 and 137, Statham taking 11 wickets in the match for 97 runs, bowling, as John Arlott described it, with 'glorious and hostile precision'.[54] The day was memorable for the unhappy fate of 21-year-old Griffin, who, after taking a hat-trick

54 *John Arlott's Cricket Journal 3: Cricket on Trial.*

(Mike, Walker, Trueman), was no-balled several times by umpire Frank Lee. After England had won soon after lunch on the fourth day, an exhibition match was arranged, in the course of which Griffin was no-balled again twice, this time by umpire Syd Buller, after having allowed the first two balls of the over to pass as legitimate. Skipper Jackie McGlew then went into a discussion with Buller to ask him how Griffin might finish the over. Buller's reply was by bowling underarm. When Griffin did this, he was no-balled again for not informing him of his change of action. This, although strictly in accordance with the Laws of Cricket, by any standards of common sense seems unreasonable, especially as the change was at Buller's suggestion. McGlew made his feelings on the matter known to the press immediately after the game. Buller had asked Billy Griffith, MCC's assistant secretary, prior to the exhibition match, if the Laws of the game were to be strictly upheld, to which Griffith had said they should be. The whole matter was unfortunate and cast a shadow over England's win and it ended Griffin's Test match career. He retired from the game at the age of 23 but would forever hold the distinction of taking the first ever Test hat-trick at Lord's. The Queen and Prince Philip were in attendance that day and both teams were presented to them during the tea interval. Fortunately, they had arrived too late to witness the unedifying spectacle of Griffin's humiliation. Unlike the crowd, Mike's sympathies were clearly with Buller, who he felt had had the courage to uphold the Laws of the game. Sadly, Buller was to die of a heart attack at Edgbaston in August 1970 when standing in a county match between Warwickshire and Nottinghamshire.[55]

The throwing controversy of the early 1960s saw the end of several Test careers. Some bowlers, like Charlie Griffith and Peter

55 *Wisden Cricketers' Almanack 1971 edition.*

Charlie Griffith bowling against England in 1961. Some have questioned the legitimacy of his action.

Loader, whose actions many considered suspect, managed to escape unscathed and others, like Tony Lock, were forced to modify their action. The question of throwing is not a new one and, as far back as 1822 one of its earliest alleged practitioners, John Willes, an MCC member to boot, was no-balled at Lord's for his round-arm action and rode away from the ground in high dudgeon, vowing never to play again. The problem will probably always be with us, in spite of modern-day technology.

The third Test ended in an England win by eight wickets. England made 287 (Cowdrey 67, Barrington 80). On this occasion Mike failed to trouble the scorers, falling lbw to Trevor Goddard. South Africa were then bowled out for 88, Statham and Trueman each taking 3-27. South Africa did better in their second innings, making 247 (Sid O'Linn 98, Waite 60). It should have been more, as Jackie McGlew, responding to a call from O'Linn for a quick single, was run out for 45 by a throw from Statham after a collision with the bowler Moss, when he would otherwise almost certainly have made his ground. Statham appealed and he was given out by umpire Charlie Elliott. McGlew departed; Cowdrey called him back but Elliott, after a couple of minutes' discussion with his co-umpire Frank Lee, refused to change his decision on the basis that the collision was accidental. In terms of the Law, this was strictly correct, but not something that the English crowd appreciated and they made their disapproval of the decision known in no uncertain terms. Had Statham not appealed, no decision would have been made, but he had been focused on the run-out, not the collision.

Mike was left out for the fourth Test and Doug Padgett brought in for his debut. He only made single figures in each innings; he was selected again for the fifth Test but was unfortunate to be run out for 31 in the second innings and was never selected again. Pullar was brought back and Allen reinstated. The match was drawn following no play on the first two days and defensive play by both sides on the final day. Set to score 185 to win in just under two hours, South Africa made no attempt to go for the target and finished up with 46 for no wicket from 26 overs, the last four bowled by Pullar, Padgett and Cowdrey.

Mike was brought back for the final Test at the Oval but got a duck in the first innings, bowled by Adcock second ball, and he only made 11 in the second innings. Jim Stewart was made 12th man, in spite of Walter Robins having assured him he would be playing,[56] and that was, sadly for him, the nearest he ever came to Test selection; he did, however, tour New Zealand with a young England side in 1960/61, playing in all three unofficial Tests. Tommy Greenhough was given another chance in favour of Illingworth, who had been wicketless in the previous three Tests, although he hadn't been given many overs. South Africa brought in a left-arm spinner, the burly Athol McKinnon, for his debut. Athol was a larger than life character, one of John Arlott's favourites, who had represented Eastern Province at both rugby and cricket. 'Oh, Athol,' Arlott could be heard to exclaim in his rich Hampshire burr after one of McKinnon's optimistic appeals.

56 Conversation with Jim Stewart.

For the first time in the series South Africa made a better fist of things and, after bowling England out for 155 (Adcock 6-65), scored 419 to establish a commanding lead, Trevor Goddard making 99 and Waite 87. McKinnon, coming in at number 10, belted Trueman and Statham for 22 runs and on his return to the dressing room said to the earlier dismissed batsmen, 'I don't know why you've had so much trouble with these two fellows.' An opening partnership of 290 between Pullar (175) and Cowdrey (155) put paid to any hopes South Africa had of a victory and the match ended in another draw, leaving England 3-0 series winners.

Mike played in several other matches that season including Gentlemen v Players, which finished in a sensational manner when, off the last ball of the game, Dexter threw the wicket down from 35 yards to run out Moss who was going for a second run, leaving the scores level and the match drawn. He also played for TN Pearce's XI against South Africa in their last match of the tour, making 54 and 81. This match was captained by Trevor Bailey, who broke two fingers of his left hand in catching Peter Carlstein, whereupon Mike took over the captaincy. He came in for some scathing criticism in *Wisden* for giving Barrington 15 overs which went for 94 runs in South Africa's second innings and only nine overs to Harold Rhodes and Fred Trueman. South Africa won by four wickets, knocking off the 192 required in two hours. Mike presumably felt that spin was more likely to get wickets than pace but his strategy backfired on this occasion.

There was no overseas tour that winter and instead a Commonwealth XI known as The Cavaliers undertook a tour of Rhodesia and South Africa. Captained by Tom Graveney, they took eight English players – Graveney himself, Statham, Trueman, Moss, Barrington, Illingworth, Pullar and Mike – and four Australians, Richie Benaud, Norman O'Neill, Bobby Simpson and Len Maddocks – not a bad squad! They played two matches in Rhodesia, winning the first and drawing the second, and three in South Africa, winning two and drawing one. Mike had a good tour, making 93 in the drawn game against Rhodesia in Salisbury, 204 in the game against Natal in Durban and 54 not out in the final game against a Combined XI in Johannesburg. O'Neill, Simpson and Graveney all made centuries and Trueman was the most successful bowler.

On his return to England Mike had an important occasion awaiting him – his wedding to Diana Leach, whom he had first met in Argentina five years earlier on his rugby tour. Peter Robbins, an England international and rugby team-mate, was his best man. After their marriage Mike and Diana lived in a flat in Edgbaston, a convenient location for Mike's home games. This was to be the start of a long and happy partnership.

CHAPTER 11

The Visit of the Australians, 1961

WARWICKSHIRE ENJOYED a better season in 1961 than in the previous year and finished 12th in the Championship table, winning nine matches, losing ten and drawing 13. All-rounder Alan Townsend, who had joined the club in 1948, had retired, as had Fred Gardner, who had made his debut in 1947 and was a key member of the 1951 Championship-winning side. In Mike's opinion, good slip fielders are an essential ingredient of any side and there was no better slip fielder in the country than Townsend and, as far as Gardner was concerned, with his stocky frame and rock-solid technique, no braver nor more reliable opening batsman. He had played professional football for Birmingham City before joining Warwickshire and had moved to Coventry City by the time he joined Warwickshire. He was a tough character and on one occasion, after a peppering from Fred Trueman in a dogged, courageous innings which spanned two days, he was receiving treatment for his bruises from the Yorkshire physio. 'Don't bother with that one, it's one of yesterday's,' he said, reducing the dressing room to fits of laughter.[57] In 1956, the year before Mike's arrival, he had played for most of the season with a broken finger and later

57 *The History of Warwickshire County Cricket Club,* Jack Bannister.

suffered a fractured elbow.[58] He and Norman Horner opened for Warwickshire for almost a decade and were the perfect foil for each other, Horner always eager to attack and Gardner, although not pretty to watch, content to stay there all day. His career record of 19,705 runs at 33.71 and 29 centuries is impressive for an opening batsman in an era when there was no shortage of top-class fast bowlers. Mike was always happy to have him in the team as someone who could bat all day, if necessary. 'He would rather let the ball hit him than play a false shot,' says Mike. 'If the ball was flying around, there was no better man to have in your side.' He was also a canny player and Jim Stewart remembers him saying, 'Don't hit too many fours off him, we want them to keep him on.'[59]

Having graduated from Oxford, Alan Smith, who played as an amateur, was now available all season. The most significant development, though, was the further progress of Tom Cartwright as a genuine all-rounder. Tom had joined the club as a 16-year-old in 1952 as a batsman and had made 82 and 22 not out on his first-class debut that year in Warwickshire's final match of the season against Nottinghamshire. At that time he saw his future as an opening batsman and preferred to stay in the Second XI and go in first rather than down the order in the Championship side. His prowess as a bowler was discovered almost by accident when, in a Second XI Minor Counties match against Yorkshire at Scarborough, Tom Dollery asked him to come on as a change bowler and he took 7-19 in 26 overs. Over the years, as his bowling became more important, his batting declined in inverse proportion.

In the bowling department, Warwickshire had lost the services of Ossie Wheatley, who had been offered and accepted the

58 *The Story of Warwickshire Cricket*, Leslie Duckworth.

59 Conversation with Jim Stewart.

captaincy of Glamorgan. Jack Bannister was the leading wicket-taker and Basil Bridge had made a welcome return to form.

Mike again topped the Warwickshire batting averages with 2,009 runs at 41.85 and finished tenth in the national averages. Horner was second with 1,696 runs at 36.08 and Hitchcock, Stewart and Cartwright all scored over 1,000. Bannister headed the bowling averages with 131 wickets at 20.77, with Bridge second with 116 at 21.72, Thompson 77 at 23.89 and Cartwright 73 at 25.97. Mike also took 53 catches for Warwickshire, breaking his own 1959 record.

It was the turn of the Australians to visit England in 1961 and Mike was selected for the first Test along with the majority of players who had featured in the final Test against South Africa the previous year, although Subba Row was brought back to open with Geoff Pullar, Ray Illingworth replaced Tommy Greenhough and John Murray of Middlesex was preferred to Jim Parks and Keith Andrew. England, batting first on Mike's Edgbaston home ground, were bowled out for 195 by Richie Benaud and Ken Mackay, who got Mike for nought, caught off an apparent inside edge which flew to the debutant Bill Lawry off his pads. Mike swears he never hit it and says that afterwards the umpire apologised to him. Australia in reply scored 516/9 declared and only a second-innings partnership between Subba Row (112) and Dexter (180) saved the game for England. Mike's second innings score of 1 not out gave him no chance to reverse his bad luck and he took no further part in the series, which Australia won 2-1, clinching victory in the fourth Test at Old Trafford when Benaud spun England out with 6-70 in the second innings, famously bowling Peter May round his legs.

CHAPTER 12

In India and Pakistan with Ted Dexter's Team, 1961/62

ENGLAND HAD clearly not lost faith in Mike and he was selected as vice-captain to Ted Dexter for MCC's winter tour of Pakistan, India and Ceylon. Neither the current captain Cowdrey nor his predecessor May had declared themselves available, nor had Subba Row. Trueman and Statham also decided to pass on what was going to be a strenuous undertaking. Seven of the 15-man squad had no previous Test match experience and Barber had only played once.

The bowling attack consisted of opening bowlers 'Butch' White and Alan Brown; seamers Barry Knight and David Smith; spinners Lock and Allen; and Dexter, Barber and Barrington as all-rounders. Murray and Geoff Millman were selected as the wicketkeepers. Peter Richardson was back as an opener to partner Pullar. Even without Cowdrey and May, the batting looked fairly strong with Peter Parfitt and Eric Russell included, but a lot of work beckoned for the spinners.

The schedule was a highly unusual one, never to be repeated. Because India had committed to a tour of the West Indies in February, March and April 1962, the five Tests against India had to be sandwiched between the first Test against Pakistan and the last two. As a consequence a great deal of extra travelling was involved with minimal recovery time between matches, usually no more than one day.

The first match against the President's XI in Rawalpindi ended in a draw. The President's XI gained a small first-innings lead in a low-scoring game and, thanks to a fine second-innings century by Mushtaq Mohammad, set MCC 207 to win in four hours on the last day. Russell (72) and Richardson (30) gave England a good start but after they were out, MCC gave up the chase and finished on 154/7. Two days later MCC played the Governor's XI in Lyallpur. Having established a considerable first-innings lead, MCC were bowled out for 106 in the second, Antao D'Souza taking 7-33. Needing 237 to win, Allen with 7-67 was primarily instrumental in bowling the Governor's XI out for 210. Barrington and Pullar both scored half-centuries in the match but Mike made only 2 and 0, following his 4 and 5 in the first match.

England then travelled to Lahore, for the first Test which turned out to be a well-contested, exciting affair. Pakistan, batting first, put together the sizeable total of 397/9 declared, Javed Burki making a painstaking 138, his first Test century. Saeed Ahmed made 74 and Mushtaq Mohammad 76. White, who had given England a good start by dismissing both openers cheaply, finished with three wickets, as did Barber. England almost equalled Pakistan's score thanks to a fine stand of 192 between Barrington (139) and Mike (99). When on 99, Mike had said to Barrington, 'Don't go looking for it,' but in attempting a relatively easy single which would have given him his hundred, Barrington sent him back too late and he was run out.[60] Mike had invested in a pair of tinted spectacles to counteract the glare and they appear to have done the trick. Brown, Allen and Barber with three wickets each succeeded in dismissing Pakistan for 200 in their second innings,

60 *MJK Smith: No Ordinary Man*, Douglas Miller.

leaving England 209 to win. At 108/5 with Richardson, Pullar, Barrington, Mike and Russell all gone, the game looked in the balance, but a fine partnership of 101 between Dexter (66 not out) in his first match as England captain and Barber (39 not out) saw England home with time to spare.

With only a day intervening, MCC now travelled to Poona (now Pune) for a three-day match against Combined Universities to start their tour of India. On a very easy-paced wicket there was time for little more than one innings each. Combined Universities, a side containing several future Test players (Milkha Singh, Datta Gaekwad, Ajit Wadekar, Farokh Engineer and Erapalli Prasanna) made 346/9 declared. In reply, Pullar and Russell put on 100 for the first wicket, Barrington scored his second successive century, and Murray made 74 in MCC's total of 417. The game fizzled out with Combined Universities on 67/3.

MCC scored 272/7 in their next match against West Zone at Ahmedabad, Pullar making a century. West Zone were dismissed for 211, David Smith taking 5-58. Pullar had made 58 out of MCC's second-innings total of 167/5 when Dexter declared. The 229 required to win was beyond West Zone's capabilities and they finished 70 runs short for the loss of five wickets.

The next match against Bombay (now Mumbai) also ended in a draw. MCC declared on 286/5 before the end of the first day. Barber, opening with Pullar, scored 71, Mike made 56 and Murray 51 not out. Tony Lock was MCC's most successful bowler with 4-49. With a lead of 62 on first innings, Mike, captaining MCC in Dexter's absence, declared again at 125/1. The task of scoring 188 in 150 minutes proved too much for Bombay and when time was called they had scored 137/7.

Happily there was no travelling involved for the first Test which started two days later, as Bombay was the venue. England played Alan Brown and David Smith as opening bowlers and Lock and Allen as spinners. On a good batting wicket the two left-handers, Pullar and Richardson, got England off to an excellent start, putting on 159 for the first wicket. Dexter made 85 and Barrington continued his splendid form with 151 not out when England declared at 500/8, their highest total in India. India scored 390 in reply with Motganhalli Jaisimha, Vijay Manjrekar, Chandu Borde and Salim Durani all scoring half-centuries. As Pullar had gone down with a throat infection, Barber opened in his place in England's second innings and he and Richardson put on 74 for the first wicket. Barrington followed up his first-innings century with 52 not out before England declared at 184/5, setting India the not unreasonable target of 295 in just over four hours. India made no real attempt to go for the runs and ended up with 180/5, Jaisimha and Manjrekar making half-centuries again. Everybody had a couple of overs except the wicketkeeper and Pullar, who was absent. Mike even got his only Test match wicket, Jaisimha, caught by Barber. 'I'd half a mind to drop it, I didn't think he deserved a Test wicket,' laughs Bob.[61]

There were three matches to be played before the second Test, all in different locations. The first was a match against the President's XI at Hyderabad, captained by the 20-year-old Nawab of Pataudi, who later became the national team's youngest captain. The honours were more or less even after the first innings, Mike finding some form with 89 and Barber making 54. A sporting declaration from Pataudi gave MCC a chance of victory, which they took, mainly thanks to Parfitt, who steered the team home in the last over with an excellent 84 not out after they had been 112/5.

The next game against Rajasthan at Jaipur ended in a draw after both sides had made declarations to try and produce a result. Salim Durani made a century for Rajasthan, and the

61 *MJK Smith: No Ordinary Man*, Douglas Miller.

opening bowlers David Smith and Butch White took all ten first-innings wickets. This was the only game on the tour played on matting which gave little help to the bowlers and, apart from 91 from the ever-prolific Barrington, who took 26 off one over from Durani, there was little to get excited about. After Dexter had declared MCC's first innings 44 behind, Rajasthan showed no sense of urgency and their second-innings declaration left MCC the well nigh impossible task of scoring 202 in under two hours.

With only one further day's respite, it was on to Nagpur for the game against Central Zone. Centuries from Parfitt and Russell set MCC up well and their total of 405/3 declared was enough to make Central Zone follow on. They themselves declared, setting MCC a target of 65 in 20 minutes which they only just failed to achieve. Mike and Knight nearly did it by throwing the bat at everything, but came up seven runs short.

India put together a potentially match-winning total of 467/8 in the second Test at Kanpur, Polly Umrigar being their top scorer with 147 not out. Jaisimha (70) and Manjrekar (96) had earlier put on 109 for the second wicket against an England opening attack of David Smith and Knight, on his debut, which had proved innocuous. Farokh Engineer, another debutant, made 33 at number nine. The rate of scoring was slow, though, and England bowled nearly 200 overs.

When England batted, they struggled against the leg-breaks and googlies of Subhash Gupte, who took the first five wickets including Mike's for nought, and by the end of the third day they were 168/8. A ninth-wicket stand between Barber and Lock produced 81 valuable runs but was not enough to stave off the follow-on which India enforced. India had little success with the ball second time round and England had amassed 497/5 in their second innings when time ran out. Pullar, Barrington and Dexter all made centuries but Mike got his first 'pair' in Test cricket, falling lbw to Gupte off a ball that came straight on.

North Zone in Jullundur were next on the agenda and, batting first, the home team made 152, having struggled against the spin of Lock (4-17) and Barrington (2-18). Dexter made 72 when England batted but Mike could only manage 13, being dismissed by Venkatappa Muddiah, an off-spinner who took six England wickets. North Zone collapsed again to Barber (4-66) and Lock (3-31) and MCC knocked off the 42 required for the loss of one wicket.

The third Test in New Delhi ended in another draw, each side having time for only one innings after heavy rain washed out the last two days. India, winning the toss for the third consecutive time, amassed 466 all out in just under two days, Jaisimha scoring his maiden Test century and Manjrekar making 189 not out in seven and a half hours. Pataudi made his Test debut but only scored 13. Allen took 4-87. At the end of the third day England's total stood at 256/3, Barrington having made his fourth Test century in a row. Mike failed again, bowled by a Gupte googly for 2. He was having a terrible time, his last four Test innings producing a mere 2 runs. 'He was like a rich man suddenly brought to impoverishment,' wrote *The Times'* special correspondent.

The third Test was followed by a match against East Zone at Cuttack, some 200 miles south of Calcutta (now Kolkata). This turned out to be another boring draw in spite of MCC's effort to score rapidly on the first day. They declared at tea on 261/4, Barrington making 80 not out, Richardson 59 and Mike 40 not out. By contrast, East Zone took seven hours to overhaul MCC's total, leaving only one day's play, which MCC used for batting practice, Richardson making his only century of the tour.

The party then moved to Calcutta for a match against a Services XI captained by Venkatappa Muddiah and containing one other former Test player, the medium-pace bowler Surendra Nath. MCC batted first, scoring 339/9 declared before dismissing the Services XI twice for 172 and 130 to win by an innings. Mike was left out for this one to give Parfitt a chance to establish his credentials, which he did with a well-made century. Barber and Dexter also made attractive half-centuries. White took five wickets in the Services' XI first innings and Knight 4-7 in the second.

Mike was omitted from the team for the fourth Test in Calcutta and was replaced by Parfitt, for whom it was his first opportunity at Test level. Millman also made his Test debut as wicketkeeper to replace Murray, who had not done well in the previous three Tests and had had to return to England for an operation. Jimmy Binks was flown out as a replacement back-up wicketkeeper. Pullar was suffering from dysentery and was replaced by Russell. England stuck with David Smith and Knight as the opening bowlers. India left out Kripal Singh and Gupte for disciplinary reasons resulting from an incident in the previous Test in Delhi when, sharing a room, a hotel receptionist complained about having been invited, according to Gupte, by Kripal to join him in their room for a drink. In spite of protesting his innocence, Gupte, as the senior player and a married man, was accredited with most of the blame and was never to play Test cricket again.[62] Vijay Mehra and Vasant Ranjane were brought in, Mehra to open the batting in place of Jaisimha, who dropped down the order.

India won the toss again and posted 380, Mehra, Pataudi and Chandu Borde all making half-centuries. Apart from Richardson (62) and Dexter (57), no other batsmen made significant runs, most falling to Borde and Durani on a wicket now taking a lot of spin. England were all out for 212, a deficit of 168. Borde made another half-century and India's second innings closed for 252 just

62 *Indian Cricket Controversies*, KR Wadhwaney.

before tea on the fourth day. Allen and Lock bowled splendidly for England in both innings, Allen taking nine wickets in the match and Lock six. Set to make 421 to win in just over eight hours, England never looked like getting the runs and were all out for 233 midway through the afternoon on the final day, only Dexter (62), Parfitt (46) and Richardson (42) offering any serious resistance to the spin of Durani and Umrigar. This was only India's second victory over England and their first in India.

MCC won their next game against South Zone in Bangalore. Having gained a first-innings lead of 61, they declared their second innings at 192/2, Pullar making 52, Mike, having found a bit of form, 67 not out and Dexter 41 not out. David Smith, Brown, White and Barber shared MCC's first-innings wickets and Brown with 4-13 and Parfitt with 3-50 were responsible for dismissing South Zone for 216 to give MCC victory by 37 runs with 40 minutes to spare.

Only one more game now remained before England's return to Pakistan, the final Test against India and a chance to square the series. India again for the fourth time in the series had the luck of the toss and batted on a good pitch. Pullar had to drop out again through illness and Barber moved up to open. Mike was recalled and Parfitt retained his place. Brown would have played with a cut finger had not India objected to his wearing a plaster on it and David Smith kept his place. After losing two early wickets, Nari Contractor and Pataudi put on 104 for the third wicket, Contractor making 86 and Pataudi going on to complete a maiden century. India scored at a much faster pace than in previous matches and at the end of the day had reached 296/7 with Bapu Nadkarni and Farokh Engineer at the crease. They proved difficult to remove on the following morning, Engineer hitting Knight for 16 off his first over: the pair went on to establish a record Indian eighth-wicket partnership of 101, Nadkarni making 63 and Engineer 65.

This was to prove decisive, particularly as England made a poor start, losing their first four wickets for 54 runs. Mike came to the rescue with 73, receiving good support from the later batsmen. In spite of this England still finished 157 runs in arrears on first innings. India were all out for 190 in their second innings on a wicket now ominously taking spin, Manjrekar making a patient 85 and Lock taking 6-65. England now needed 338 to win. Time was not a problem but the pitch was, and England had problems coping with Durani and Borde. With Richardson, Barber and Dexter gone with only 41 on the board, things looked bleak and although Barrington made 48 and Knight and Parfitt 33 each, these modest contributions were not enough to save England from defeat by 128 runs.

The Indian leg of the tour had not been a great success. Travel arrangements had been hectic and at times disorganised with an insufficient period for rest between games. There had been too many official functions to attend under tour manager TN Pearce who, according to Bob Barber, was a poor organiser, put too high a value on the ambassadorial side of the tour and was more concerned with looking after himself than the players. Bob made little effort to hide his contempt for Pearce's managerial abilities and he suspects he may have played a part in his non-selection for the Australia tour of 1962/63.[63] The general standards of hygiene had been below expectations and had been the cause of much sickness and unavailability. Barber maintains he cleaned his teeth with Coca-Cola for the duration of the tour to avoid drinking the water.[64] In spite of all this, morale within the team had remained high and everyone had done their best, often under difficult circumstances. Mike had a very poor tour and admits

63 *Bob Barber: The Professional Amateur,* Colin Schindler.

64 *MJK Smith: No Ordinary Man,* Douglas Miller.

he did not play well there, although he was one of the few who suffered no illness. Having said all this, full credit must be given to the Indian team, who were clearly superior in the last two Tests and were rewarded by playing positive cricket in the final one. It was a weary, dispirited crew that travelled to Dacca for the second Test in the series against Pakistan due to start four days later.

England were glad to see the return of Pullar, whose batting they had missed in the last two Tests. To accommodate him they left out David Smith, risking Knight and Dexter to open the bowling. Having lost the toss again, England were in the field on the first day which, because of over-cautious batting, produced a mere 173 runs from 111 overs. Hanif Mohammad was particularly slow, his 111 taking over eight hours. Burki's 140 was made in much better time but it still took the best part of two days for Pakistan to score 393. England adopted a much more attacking approach with Pullar and Barber opening instead of Richardson and putting on 57 in even time by the close. The following day they continued their partnership, which realised 198. After Barber went for 86, Pullar (165) and Barrington (84) put on 145 for the second wicket to leave England nicely placed at 345/2. The game died, though, through slow scoring by both teams on the fourth day. England added only 106 and Pakistan took two hours to make 28 without loss. Another marathon innings from Hanif Mohammad, 104 in six and a half hours, saved the game for Pakistan and when their innings closed for 216, only 35 minutes remained. At one point in the afternoon Pakistan had been 159/6 but there was no shifting Hanif.

Two days later, after a gruelling 20-hour air and train journey, MCC took on a Combined XI at Bahawalpur. The first day of this three-day match was lost to rain but with no chance of a result MCC were skittled on a difficult wicket by the legendary pace bowler Fazal Mahmood, a former captain of Pakistan. Barrington,

Mike and Knight all made ducks and MCC were all out for 114, Mahmood taking 6-28. The ever-reliable David Allen was the only one to withstand the onslaught with 31. The Combined XI replied with 162, White taking 4-33 and Allen 3-39. MCC scored 69 without the loss of a wicket in the time remaining, Mahmood not bothering to put himself on again.

England's final Test in Pakistan was at Karachi. Barrington was unfit and Mike would otherwise probably not have played. Dexter lost the toss again and Pakistan batted. In spite of White breaking down after three overs, England bowled well to restrict them to 253 and were held up by just two players, Hanif Mohammad, who made 67 and Alim-ud-Din, who made 109. England then built up a commanding lead. Given a good start with 77 for the first wicket by Pullar (60) and Richardson (26), Dexter and Mike (56) proceeded to put on 143 for the third wicket and then Dexter and Parfitt 188 for the fourth. England finished on 507, Dexter making his first Test double-century (205) and Parfitt 111. Fazal Mahmood bowled 63 overs for Pakistan, finishing with 0-98, a far cry from his figures in the previous match. England could not get Pakistan out a second time and their total stood at 404/8 at the end of the match, Hanif Mohammad having spent five and a half hours over 89, and Imtiaz Ahmed having made 86 and Alim-ud-Din 53. Dexter and Barber each took three wickets. The match ended in another draw but England had won this interrupted series 1-0 with two matches drawn. It was now on to Ceylon for what must have been a welcome last lap.

MCC played two warm-up games before taking on Ceylon, the first against the Ceylon Cricket Association at Colombo which ended in a draw. The first morning of this two-day match was lost because the plane bringing the MCC team from Karachi was delayed and the remaining five sessions hardly allowed enough time for four innings. In the event, only three full innings were possible, MCC making 257 and 159 and Ceylon 235 and 20/0. Dexter, Parfitt and Richardson made half-centuries in MCC's first innings and Dexter took five wickets in Ceylon's.

The second two-day game was at Radella in the heart of Ceylon's tea country against an Up-Country XI. Gamini Goonesena made 68 out of the home side's total of 202. Brown took 6-38, including four wickets in four balls. MCC replied with 290, of which Mike made 85 and Lock 74. MCC bowled out the Up-Country XI for 93 in their second innings, Lock taking 5-22. MCC knocked off the 10 runs needed without loss.

Two days later MCC took on All Ceylon at Colombo, who gave a reasonable account of themselves on a sporting wicket with a first-innings total of 210, Abdul Lafir top-scoring with 84. Knight and Dexter took four wickets apiece. With Mike either sitting this one out, or not selected, Barrington made 93 and Parfitt 50 in a partnership of 129, but after they were dismissed, the innings collapsed to 284 all out. All Ceylon made a poor show in their second innings, plummeting to 80/7 at one stage before Goonesena with 44 staged a minor recovery. The second innings total of 144 left MCC needing only 71 for victory, which they accomplished easily before lunch on the final day.

And so, of the eight Tests played on the tour, England won one and drew two against Pakistan and lost two and drew three against India, giving India a series victory against England for the first time in their history. Even making excuses for the fact that several of England's leading players were missing, the absence of Pullar through illness for the last two Tests and the loss of the toss four times out of five, full credit has to be given to India for playing positive cricket in the last two Tests. Barrington, Dexter and Pullar all performed well with the bat and Allen and Lock were the pick of the bowlers. The pace bowlers were largely innocuous on unresponsive pitches. Mike had a disappointing tour, scoring only 126 runs in seven completed innings against India, and found life particularly difficult against the spinners Gupte and Durani, who each dismissed him three times. Leslie Smith, in his summary of the tour for *Wisden*, expressed his regret at some of England's best players being allowed to pick their tours; although this tour was harder and less comfortable than other tours, out of respect for the enormous interest in cricket on the subcontinent and the quality of the opposition, more effort was needed to be made by the authorities to ensure that full-strength teams were sent out in the future.

Mike leading in the hurdles at Stamford School.

Mike (front centre) in the Stamford School first XI at the age of 12.

Walking out to bat in 1954 with Jimmy Allan, his new opening partner.

The Leicestershire team of 1955. Back row: J Firth, EF Phillips, J Goodwin, LA Spense, MJK Smith, RA Diment, VS Munden; Front row: JE Walsh, M Tompkin, CH Palmer, G Lester, VE Jackson.

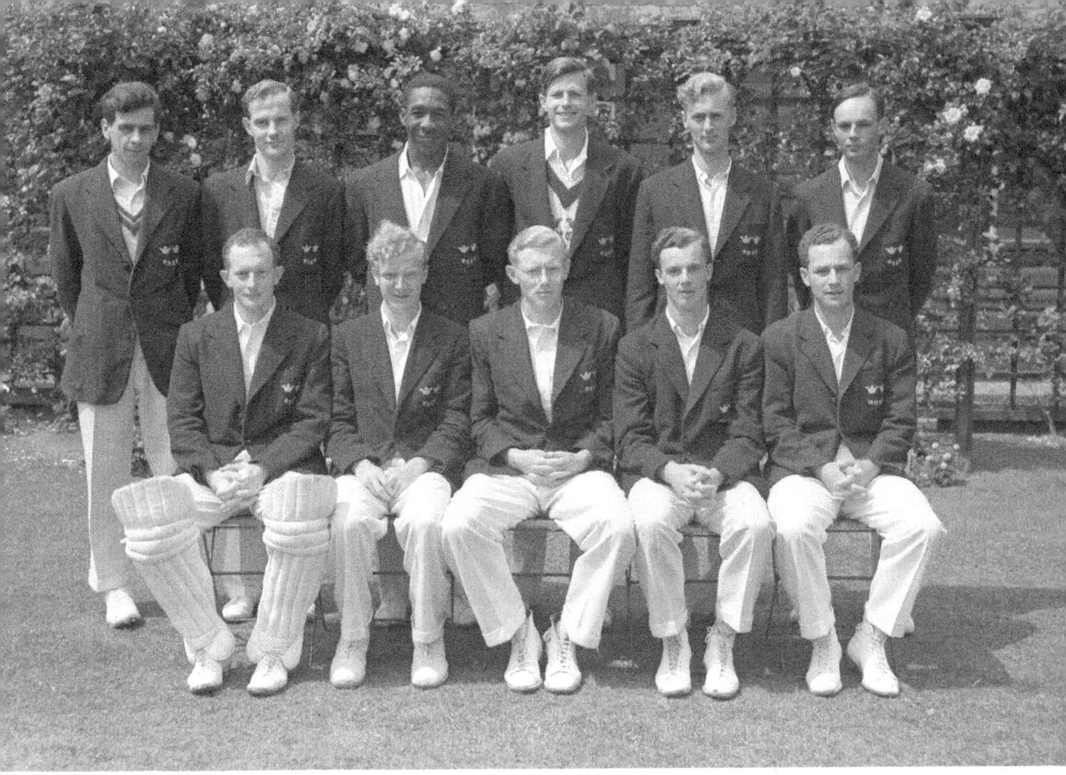

The Oxford University team of 1956. Standing: SVM Clube, SG Metcalfe, ES Kentish, JA Bailey, I Gibson, MA Eagar. Seated: AP Walshe, JM Allan, MJK Smith (Captain), AC Walton, GPS Delisle.

The Cambridge University team of 1956. Standing: RP O'Brien, RM James, ER Dexter, RW Barber, BCG Wilenkin, DJ Smith. Seated: JF Pretlove, G Goonesena, MEL Melluish (Captain), CS Smith, S Singh.

Hitting Compton for four – Warwickshire v. Middlesex, 1957.

Two double internationals, Mike and Arthur Milton, walking out to open for England v. New Zealand in the third Test at Headingley.

Warwickshire team, 1958. Back row: Jack Bannister, Geoffrey Hill, Ray Carter, Ossie Wheatley, Tom Cartwright, Barry Fletcher, Norman Horner; Front row: Bert Wolton, Fred Gardner, Mike Smith, Dick Spooner, Alan Townsend.

Walking out to bat with Fred Gardner at the Courtaulds Ground, Coventry, 1958.

MCC tour of South America in 1958. Back row: Charles Robins, Chris Howland, Ossie Wheatley, Ian Bedford, David Sayer, Jack Bailey, Mike Bushby, Dennis Silk; Front row: Colin Ingleby-Mackenzie, Donald Carr, Hubert Doggart, Mike Smith.

Sweeping Nadkarni for four in the fourth Test against India at Old Trafford in July 1959, for Mike's maiden Test century.

Mike receiving the Denis Compton Cup at the Sportsview studio in 1959 for his achievement of scoring over 3,000 runs.

MCC team in West Indies in 1960.

Mike batting in the fifth Test in the West Indies, 30 March 1960. He made 96. Gerry Alexander looks on.

CHAPTER 13

An Improving Warwickshire

THE 1962 season was a very good one for Warwickshire, who finished third in the County Championship, 22 points behind the winners Yorkshire, a significant improvement on the previous season. They won 12 of their 32 matches, lost five and drew 15, having led the table on several occasions. This was the final year of the 32-match experiment. Mike, Jim Stewart and 'Billy' Ibadulla scored over 2,000 runs in all matches and four players, Cartwright, Hitchcock, Horner and Alan Smith, all scored over 1,000. Mike scored five centuries, Stewart seven and Ibadulla five. Cartwright did the double, the first time since Frank Foster had achieved it for Warwickshire in 1914. He also scored a maiden double-century against Middlesex in a remarkable 244-run partnership with Alan Smith after Warwickshire had been 67/6. Horner, now 36, lost his place as an opener to Alan Smith later in the season and his thousand runs were made at a much lower average than previously.

The season of 1962 also saw the arrival of John Jameson in the first team. Three bowlers, Cartwright, Bannister and Albert Wright, took 100 wickets, Wright being the most improved with 111 at an average of 21.55 compared with 36 at 33.58 the previous year. Sadly, this was to be Wright's only good season and he gradually drifted out of the game.

Basil Bridge, the previous season's success story, was restricted to six matches through illness and never regained his form. Roly Thompson also retired from the game at the age of 30 after 12 seasons with the club. He had had a somewhat chequered career, never being able to command a settled place in the team. According to Jim Stewart, he was an extremely accurate bowler who Ted Dexter could never get away. He made his debut for Warwickshire at the age of 16 and the following year took 5-16 against Gloucestershire including the wickets of Tom Graveney and Jack Crapp. His bowling record is quite impressive – 479 wickets at an average of 22.75. Roly was a quiet, rather shy chap', says Mike, 'but a very reliable bowler who you knew was never going to spray it around. Although he was only fast-medium, he had such a long run-up that Alan Revill of Derbyshire used to joke that he was out of form by the time he arrived at the crease.[65] The lack of a top-class spin bowler, though, was a serious handicap to Warwickshire's chance of winning the Championship.

With Graveney now restored to the England team after his enforced sabbatical on changing counties, there was no room for Mike in England's middle order and he was not selected for any of the five Tests against the Pakistani touring team nor for the England team to tour Australia and New Zealand. One Warwickshire player who did make the trip, however, was wicketkeeper AC (Alan) Smith, who had made significant progress as a batsman as well as being a sound gloveman. Although probably taken initially as the reserve wicketkeeper to John Murray, he was to play in four of the five Tests in Australia and two out of three in New Zealand. He took 13 catches against Australia and seven against New Zealand. He didn't score many runs against Australia but

---

65 Conversation with Jim Stewart.

featured in an unbroken ninth-wicket partnership of 163 with Colin Cowdrey in the second Test against New Zealand.

Mike also played in the last Gentlemen v Players match at Lord's, MCC having decided in January 1963 after much soul-searching and debate that this fixture, which had been held almost continuously for the last 150 years, was now an anachronism. The previous autumn the Advisory County Cricket Committee had passed by 12 votes to 7 a proposal by Glamorgan that the status of amateur be abolished.[66] All were now simply players and there were no longer separate dressing rooms to the relief of many of the amateurs, such as Bob Barber, who had always found this arrangement embarrassing and divisive. When captain of Lancashire, he had been instructed by the committee to stay in a separate hotel from the professionals during away matches. Micky Stewart, Surrey's first professional captain, was even asked, ridiculous as it now sounds, to change in the amateurs' dressing room in the first year of his appointment. He was reluctant to do this, but agreed only because it would otherwise have meant that a long-serving attendant close to retirement would have been made redundant.[67]

There were, of course, die-hards like Gubby Allen, Billy Griffith and Jim Swanton who argued fiercely for the fixture's retention for the sake of tradition and in 1957 a sub-committee had been set up at Lord's to examine ways in which the status of the amateur could be preserved. In fact, it even resulted in amateurs receiving more favourable financial terms for overseas tours, leading the outspoken Jim Laker to ask Gubby Allen if he could be treated as an amateur on the 1958/59 winter tour of Australia, a request which did not go down too well.[68] However,

---

66 *Bob Barber: The Professional Amateur*, Colin Schindler.

67 *Micky Stewart and the Changing Face of Cricket*, Stephen Chalke.

68 *Bob Barber: The Professional Amateur*, Colin Schindler.

common sense ultimately prevailed and the change was welcomed by professionals and former amateurs alike. Charles Williams in his book *Gentlemen and Players: The Death of Amateurism in Cricket* gives an excellent description of the arguments leading up to the decision. *Wisden*, however, was not to be denied the last word, by lamenting in its centenary issue: 'By doing away with the amateur, cricket is in danger of losing the spirit of freedom and gaiety which the best amateur players brought to the game.'[69] There would be, though, no going back.

There was, in fact, one final Gentlemen v Players match which took place at the Scarborough Festival in September. Dexter was appointed as captain for the Gentlemen but was forced to withdraw due to illness, Mike taking over. Trueman again captained the Players. The Players won by seven wickets, Ken Barrington scoring a century in the Players' first innings and Bob Gale 88 in the second. Trueman's figures of 4-11 were decisive in restricting the Gentlemen to a modest second-innings total.

The scorecard is of the last match at Lord's in this fixture. Cowdrey was originally appointed captain of the Gentlemen, which was seen as a Test trial, but had to withdraw because of illness; so Dexter took over. The Players were captained by Fred Trueman. David Sheppard's classy century led to the newspapers acclaiming him as MCC captain elect, only for it to be revealed that Dexter had already been offered and accepted the role. Set to make 236 to win in three hours, the Players were up with the clock thanks to Peter Parfitt and John Edrich but the Gentlemen were saved by the rain, which curtailed proceedings with the Players needing only 29 more with half an hour left.

69 *Wisden Cricketers' Almanack 1963 edition.*

GENTLEMEN v PLAYERS

Gentlemen

Rev DS Sheppard c and b Titmus	112	– b Titmus	34
EJ Craig b Trueman	4	– c Titmus b Trueman	0
*ER Dexter c Trueman b Shackleton	55	– run out	1
MJK Smith run out	44	– not out	15
RM Prideaux b Trueman	14	– b Shackleton	109
AR Lewis lbw b Shackleton	2	– c Andrew b Titmus	10
RW Barber run out	0	– not out	3
DB Pithey run out	30		
TE Bailey c Walker b Shackleton	5		
AC Smith c Sharpe b Shackleton	33		
OS Wheatley not out	14		
B 4, l-b 6	10		
1/12 2/109 /3/204 /4/221 5/227 6/229 7/239 8/246 9/275	323	1/0 2/73 (5 wkts, dec) 3/95 4/115 5/166	172

Bowling:

Trueman	13-6-59-2	10-6-8-1
Shackleton	38-9-101-4	19-8-38-1
Walker	28-4-64-0	9-2-21-0
Titmus	20-6-46-1	24-5-69-2
Gifford	14-4-43-0	7-0-36-0

Players

MJ Stewart c A Smith b Bailey	0	– c A Smith b Wheatley	3
JH Edrich b Bailey	19	– not out	77
PH Parfitt c Sheppard b Dexter	9	– c Dexter b Barber	63
TW Graveney c Craig b Wheatley	21	– c A Smith b Bailey	41
PJ Sharpe c and b Barber	39	– not out	12
PM Walker b Bailey	15		
FJ Titmus c Dexter b Bailey	70		
*FS Trueman c Wheatley b Barber	63		
KV Andrew c A Smith b Bailey	17		
N Gifford c A Smith b Bailey	2		
D Shackleton not out	1		
B 4	4	B 1, l-b 10	11
1/0 2/15 3/41 4/56 5/86 6/104 7/194 8/255 9/257	260	1/3 2/121 3/177 (3 wkts)	207

Bowling:

Bailey	30.3-10-58-6	13-1-45-1
Wheatley	19-6-37-1	12-1-46-1
Dexter	18-2-49-1	7-0-35-0
Barber	21-7-90-2	7-0-43-1
Pithey	8-2-22-0	4-0-27-0

Umpires: H Yarnold and AE Rhodes

Match drawn

CHAPTER 14

Championship Title Contenders

WARWICKSHIRE HAD another good season in 1963 and for a large part of it were title contenders. Their hopes of a Championship win were, however, seriously damaged by the weather in the last three games of the season. On target to win against Northants, they were deprived of an almost certain victory by the loss of two and a half hours' play on the final day; the abandonment of the match against Hampshire without a ball being bowled; and the loss of two days against Surrey. Conversely, Yorkshire, who finished up champions, had better luck with the weather, winning their last two matches against Leicestershire home and away. Warwickshire's cause was not helped when they were beaten by Yorkshire at Scarborough at the beginning of August, in a match where they had first sight of Geoff Boycott in his first full season. He scored 62 in Yorkshire's first innings, prompting Tom Cartwright to remark prophetically to Jim Stewart, 'We're going to have some trouble with this bugger for a few years to come.'[70] How right he was. Earlier in the season, in the match at Edgbaston in which Mike suffered a broken wrist fielding at short leg, they had suffered the ignominy of being bowled out by Yorkshire for totals of 35 and 55, Trueman having match figures of 10-36.

70 Conversation with Jim Stewart.

Warwickshire had been strengthened by the arrival of Bob Barber from Lancashire, who had had a pretty miserable time there. Warwickshire's wicketkeeper and vice-captain Alan Smith, who had got to know Bob on an MCC tour of Canada in 1960 and with Jim Swanton's team in the West Indies in March 1961, played a key part in Bob's move. Mike had been alerted to the fact that Bob was leaving Lancashire and considering his future and he rang Alan who was on tour in Australia with MCC and asked him for his opinion. Alan was in no doubt that Bob would be an excellent addition to the squad, primarily in the role of principal spinner, an area in which Warwickshire were deficient. On that basis, Mike contacted Bob and invited him to come down for a discussion with the chairman. Bob agreed to play several games for Warwickshire to see how it went. In the event, he was to stay with Warwickshire until 1971 when he retired from the game. Lancashire did not oppose the move, which was to revitalise his career.

Mike again topped the Warwickshire batting averages with 1,288 runs at 46.00 as well as the national averages, despite missing six games with his broken wrist. Horner, Hitchcock and Barber all made over 1,000 runs. Jim Stewart, who had made over 2,000 runs the previous season, failed to make 1,000, missing several matches after having the big toe on his left foot amputated during the winter. According to Jim, he had a bunion on his big toe, and he got hit on it while batting. It became inflamed and an operation to remove it was necessary. Unfortunately, the operation was botched and the toe had to be amputated. As Warwickshire were unwilling to support Jim in a lawsuit for compensation, he took out a private action, which was settled out of court. However, the loss of the point of balance affected his ability to drive through the 'V', his most prolific scoring shot and, even with a specially made boot, he was never able to completely readjust as it forced him to play around his front pad rather than alongside it. 'He could never quite recapture that first fine careless rapture,' wrote Leslie Duckworth, aptly quoting, with a slight modification, from Robert Browning's *Home-Thoughts from Abroad*.[71]

The fast-bowling department was strengthened by the arrival of Rudi Webster, a West Indian medical student at a Birmingham hospital who was studying at Edinburgh University. Previously, only foreign students at either Oxford or Cambridge had been allowed to play in the Championship but Warwickshire's chairman Alec Hastilow, dubbed by John Arlott 'the Squire of Edgbaston', had successfully lobbied for this change. It was just as well, as Bannister and Brown were injured for most of the season and hardly played at all. Cartwright again took the most wickets (92 at 18.35), closely followed by Webster (77 at 17.44) and Barber (64 at 21.65). Barber also performed the hat-trick against Glamorgan – three tailenders, Don Shepherd, Ossie Wheatley and Jeff Jones. For once, there were no Test calls for Warwickshire players, although Cartwright was 12th man for the first Test against West Indies. It was probably a good one for him to miss, as West Indies hammered the bowling and racked up 501/6. He had to wait another year before making his debut against Australia.

The year 1963 saw the introduction for the first time of a limited-overs competition, sponsored by Gillette, which the following year became known as the Gillette Cup. This proved enormously popular, although Warwickshire did not benefit greatly from it in its inaugural year as, with Mike out of action, they were knocked out by Northamptonshire in the first round. The final at Lord's, which drew a crowd of 25,000, was won by Sussex, who beat Worcestershire by 14 runs. This competition was clearly here to stay but not many people at the time would have appreciated the impact that this form of cricket would ultimately have on the longer game.

---

71 *The Story of Warwickshire Cricket*, Leslie Duckworth.

CHAPTER 15

Captaining Tours to East Africa and India, 1963/64

IN THE autumn of 1963 Mike was asked to captain a five-week tour to East Africa, a part of the world he was very fond of, having been there six years earlier with Freddie Brown's team. The squad, with the popular Willie Watson as the player/manager, was composed of mainly younger players, a couple of whom, Peter Parfitt and Micky Stewart, had already had a taste of Test cricket, and others like Colin Milburn, John Mortimore, Robin Hobbs, Tom Cartwright, David Larter and Jeff Jones, who would later receive Test recognition. There were to be 11 two- or three-day matches in Kenya, Uganda and Tanganyika. Mike took his wife Diana away with him for the first time, their recently born daughter Barbara left in the care of Mike's mother. The tour was a great success: of the 11 matches played, seven were won and the other four drawn. They only came close to defeat once against Kenya Kongonis in Nairobi, who, chasing 301 in the final innings, finished only 11 runs short. The matches were all played on matting, which the bowlers took some time to adjust to, but all the players made useful contributions. The leg-spinner Hobbs, who had never been abroad before, found these harder matting wickets much to his liking and was the leading wicket-taker with 46 scalps. Hobbs reckons his success on this tour probably rescued his career, as during his season with Essex he had taken only 21 Championship wickets at an average of over 50 and was seriously worried his contract might not be renewed.'[72] 'In terms of the cricket, the whole tour was a fantastic experience,' Robin says. 'Mike Smith was a terrific captain and Willie Watson was a magic manager.'[73] Mike recalls spending one night under canvas on a safari during this trip and the warden calmly telling them in the morning that lions had visited the camp during the night and 'there was us, with just the flimsy protection of tents!'

Mike was then asked to captain a side to India for an eight-week tour in January and February 1964. Dexter, England's reigning captain, could not commit on account of his parliamentary aspirations and Cowdrey, who had initially accepted the role, had not recovered sufficiently from his broken wrist in the second Test match against the West Indies. These two circumstances conspired not only to re-ignite Mike's Test match career but also to give him a run as captain. The tour programme was an excessively crowded one with five Tests and five other matches, sometimes with only a day in between to travel to the different, often distant locations. Based on MCC's previous experience of gastric problems, it was decided to take a quantity of tinned food for consumption in the more remote locations where, as EM (Lyn) Wellings rather xenophobically wrote in his summary of the tour for *Wisden*: 'European cooking is not understood.' This apparently produced some criticism from what Wellings went on to describe as 'touchy folk in India'.[74] The tinned food was corned beef and baked beans and, according to John Price, the highlight of the week was egg, chips and beans on a Wednesday night as an alternative to the endless curries. A quantity of beer was also shipped out but John

72 Conversation with Robin Hobbs.

73 *Hobbsy: A Life in Cricket,* Rob Kelly.

74 *Wisden Cricketers' Almanack 1965 edition.*

doubts whether it all reached its intended destination.[75] The team, under the benign, efficient management of David Clark, consisted of Brian Bolus, John Edrich, Phil Sharpe, Ken Barrington and Micky Stewart as batsmen, John Price, Jeff Jones and David Larter as pace bowlers, Don Wilson, John Mortimore and Fred Titmus as spinners, Jim Parks and Jimmy Binks as wicketkeepers and Barry Knight as an all-rounder.

The first match at Bangalore against the President's XI on an easy-paced pitch ended in a draw in spite of Mike's enterprising approach by declaring after only four and a quarter hours on the first day. Stewart made a century in the first innings and a half-century in the second and Bolus half-centuries in each. This augured well for the opening partnership in the Tests, or so it would seem.

The second match against South Zone at Hyderabad which started the following day was won by MCC by an innings and 27 runs, South Zone being dismissed for 140 and 313. Centuries from Barrington and Wilson, and half-centuries from Sharpe and Parks helped MCC to a total of 480.

England then travelled to Madras (now Chennai) for the first Test. The Nawab of Pataudi, captaining India for the first time in India, on winning the toss, elected to bat. India scored at a lively rate on the first day, making 277/2 by the close. They chose not to press home their advantage, however, and took most of the second day to add 180 runs, Vijay Manjrekar taking over four and a half hours for his century. The star of India's show though was Budhi Kunderan, brought in at short notice as a replacement wicketkeeper for Farokh Engineer, who was injured. His 192, together with Manjrekar's 108, Dilip Sardesai's 65 and Jaisimha's 51 put India in a virtually unassailable position

75 Conversation with John Price.

at 457/7 declared. Titmus had stuck resolutely to his task and took 5-116 in 50 overs.

Stewart and Parks had become ill during the first two days with stomach trouble and, when it was England's turn to bat, Mike went in first with Bolus but was soon out for 3, caught by Kunderan off Ranjane. Bolus then began England's rearguard action, taking almost seven hours to make 88. He received good support from the nightwatchman Wilson (42) and Barrington (80). It was during this partnership that Nadkarni bowled 131 consecutive balls without conceding a run to finish with the scarcely believable figures of 32 overs, 27 maidens, 0-5. Nadkarni was not a great spinner of the ball and relied on nagging accuracy. Manjrekar once joked that whenever Nadkarni turned the ball it was declared a national holiday. Stewart gamely came in at number ten to join Titmus. The first thing Titmus said to him was, 'Remember you're not fully fit, so no quick singles.' Soon afterwards Titmus called him for a sharp single, then changed his mind, leaving Stewart having to dive back into his crease. He and Titmus managed to put on 27 for the ninth wicket to save the follow-on. Borde put in a marathon spell of 67.4 overs to take 5-88. Titmus took another four wickets in India's second innings, which closed at 152/9. On a placid pitch India, through their slow play on the second day and England's stubborn resistance, did not have time to get England out for a second time despite using ten bowlers in an attempt to buy wickets. Mike made a determined 57 and Mortimore (73 not out) and Sharpe (31 not out) put on an unbroken 86 for England's sixth wicket to save the game.

Before the second Test MCC had one more match to play against West Zone at Ahmedabad 800 miles away. To give Mike a break, Stewart offered to captain the side, which was with hindsight very unwise, as he had not fully recovered. West Zone, batting first, were all out for 208, Ashok Mankad making a stylish

58 not out after an earlier collapse. Ashok was the 17-year-old son of Vinoo Mankad, India's former captain, who had added a new word to cricket's vocabulary when he ran out Bill Brown at the bowler's end in a Test match against Australia in 1947. MCC replied with 400/5 declared, Edrich (150) and Bolus (113) putting on 237 for the second wicket. West Zone had made 282/3 in their second innings when the match ended in a rather pointless draw. Of greater significance though was the injury to Barrington who, when attempting a catch at slip, broke a finger in his left hand and was obliged to return home. He had been averaging over 100 and, as one of the linchpins of England's batting, was a serious loss to the team.

As a result of Barrington's departure and a wave of sickness, which hospitalised Edrich, Sharpe and Mortimore, England went into the second Test at Bombay with only three specialist batsmen, Mike, Bolus and Stewart. Stewart was also suffering from the same ailment, but not quite as badly. He really should not have played at all, but when told that Henry Blofeld, who was covering the tour as a freelance journalist, was being considered, he decided that, even in his debilitated state, 25% of him would be better than 100% of Henry.[76] Blofeld had been a fine schoolboy cricketer until a serious bicycle accident put an end to any thoughts of a cricketing career. According to Fred Titmus, some of the players were disappointed that Henry was not brought in, perhaps for the novelty value.[77] And so Stewart persuaded Mike that he was well enough to play. Binks, Jones and Price all made their Test debuts. India, again winning the toss, were in some difficulty early on a livelier pitch against some good seam bowling from Knight and Price. At one stage they were 99/6 with England well on top. They were saved by a seventh-

76 Conversation with Micky Stewart.

77 *My Life in Cricket*, Fred Titmus.

wicket stand of 153 between Borde (84) and Durani (90), which would not have happened had Binks stumped Borde off Titmus at the start of his innings when he was on 2. Stewart's condition had worsened and, after diving to take a catch and bringing up his lunch, he was unable to take any further part in the game and he joined the other invalids in Bombay's Breach Candy Hospital. With no fit men left, a substitute fielder had to be borrowed from India. Stewart was too ill to remain on the tour and once he was strong enough to travel, he flew home.[78] This, sadly, was to be an unfortunate end to this fine player's brief Test career.

In Stewart's absence Mike opened with Bolus and they took the score to 42 before Bolus was out, magnificently caught one-handed at mid-off by Bhagwath Chandrasekhar off Desai. This was Chandrasekhar's debut and, after Parks was run out for 1, he swiftly accounted for Mike (46) and Knight with his wrist-spin. Titmus, coming in at number five in England's makeshift line-up, proceeded to play a fine innings and together with Price put on a vital 68 for the seventh wicket. Titmus's 84 not out took him five hours and without it England would have been staring defeat in the face. Mike later described it as 'Fred's magnificent knock'. Chandrasekhar finished with figures of 4-67. It had been a fine debut and the start of an impressive career. England's innings closed at 233 and by the end of the third day India were 91/1, 158 runs ahead. If ever there was a time to force the pace, it was on the morning of the fourth day. However, for whatever reason, India were only able to score 150 runs in the next five hours. Pataudi declared at 249/8, leaving England just over a day to score 317 to win. At the close Bolus and Binks, who had been sent in as nightwatchman, were together with 17 runs on the board. They were still there at lunchtime on the final day with

78 *Micky Stewart and the Changing Face of Cricket,* Stephen Chalke.

229 still needed. When they both went in quick succession, soon to be followed by Wilson, England decided to call off the chase and Parks (40 not out) and Mike (31 not out) batted out time in a 72-run partnership. England's illness-ridden team had escaped with a draw when a more attacking approach by India should have given them victory.

Colin Cowdrey and Peter Parfitt had been flown out to replace Barrington and Stewart. Parfitt, very popular on the county circuit, was a cheerful addition to the squad and, according to Edrich, the most successful operator in negotiating a favourable exchange rate for rupees![79] Both immediately went into the team for the third Test. India won the toss and batted first again and although the first four batsmen all got starts, they were never able to get on top of Price, who bowled magnificently to take 5-73. Wilson was also hard to get away and took 2-17. At one point India were 169/8 and, had it not been for Nadkarni (43 not out) shepherding the tail, they would not have reached their modest total of 241. England took a first-innings lead of 26 mainly thanks to a careful century from Cowdrey, which took him over six hours. With the loss of two and a half hours through rain on the third day, England's innings did not end until the morning of the fourth.

India's second innings was dominated by Jaisimha who, opening with Kunderan, raced to 49 in the first 12 overs but then took another 12 overs to reach his fifty. He was finally out for 129 after five hours. The other batsmen chipped in with useful, if not spectacular, contributions and India were able to declare at 300/7. Both sides' lack of urgency had left insufficient time for a result and England batted out the day for 145/2, Mike playing with the freedom the situation allowed for an attractive 75 not out. It was becoming difficult to see how a result could be obtained on such

79 *Runs in the Family*, John Edrich.

placid pitches without either side showing the will to be more adventurous.

A match against East and Central Zones at Nagpur was sandwiched between the third and fourth Tests and England brought in Edrich, Sharpe and Mortimore, who had all now recovered sufficiently. Mike sat this one out. East and Central Zones scored 246 but they made heavy weather of it, their innings not being completed until halfway through the second day. MCC declared 73 behind on first innings in the hope of some reciprocation, but it was not forthcoming and East and Central Zones' second innings continued at the same pedestrian pace, condemning the match to another boring draw. 'Another match best forgotten,' wrote *Wisden*.[80] On the plus side, Parfitt played two good innings for not-out half-centuries and Mortimore's 5-75 in East and Central Zones' first innings earned him a place in the Test team as a third spinner.

England lost the toss for the fourth time in the series in the fourth Test at Delhi and again spent the first day and a half in the field. The wicket was just as easy-paced as its forerunners and like the previous Tests was predestined to end in a draw. Hanumant Singh on his debut as a replacement for the injured Manjrekar really impressed, making an attractive century out of India's total of 344. Titmus and Mortimore were rewarded with three wickets each for their skilful, controlled bowling. The England openers, Bolus and Edrich, now fit and playing in his first Test on the tour, put on 101 for the first wicket and by the end of the second day England were 124/2, with Mike and Wilson, as nightwatchman, at the crease. Wilson went cheaply the following morning and Mike departed soon after for 37. A fifth-wicket partnership of 115 between Parfitt (67) and Cowdrey put England in a safe position,

80 *Wisden Cricketers' Almanack 1965 edition.*

but the rate of scoring was so slow that by the time England were all out for 451, there were only four and a half sessions of play left. Cowdrey's 151 took over six hours. Nadkarni's nagging accuracy was partly responsible for the slow scoring rate and his 58 overs cost him 97 runs for three wickets. Kripal Singh and Chandrasekhar also each took three wickets.

It was evident from the outset of India's innings that they were not inclined to go for a win and, after Kunderan was out for his second century of the series, Pataudi duly completed a double century, the first for an Indian player in Tests against England. Although he batted well and played some fine drives, it would be untrue to say it was hard-earned, as his second century was made against some tired and indifferent bowling. Mike even gave himself 13 overs, which went for 52. India finished up with 463/4 in a match whose only interest was to statisticians.

The fifth Test was at Kanpur and, although Mike lost the toss for the fifth time, Pataudi decided, to general astonishment, to put England in, perhaps thinking that the rain which had fallen a few days previously would assist his bowlers. If that was his belief, he was much mistaken, as England racked up their biggest total of the series, 559/8 declared. Bolus made 67, Parks 51 not out, but the bulk of the runs came from a fourth-wicket stand of 191 between Knight (127) and Parfitt (121). Against a total of this magnitude, India knew they had no chance of winning and their determination not to lose was reflected in their batting the next day when they scored a mere 136 runs for the loss of four wickets. Sardesai (79) and Pataudi started more brightly on the fourth day but, after they were out, the innings slumped to 188/7 and it was only a defiant 52 not out from Nadkarni which helped the score to a more respectable 266. Titmus had bowled 60 overs, including 37 maidens, for 73 runs and six wickets and Mortimore 49 overs, including 31 maidens, for 39 runs. The total was not enough to avoid the follow-on which Mike unhesitatingly enforced. By the end of the fourth day India's score stood at 86/1. On the final day, after Kunderan went for 55, Nadkarni put on 144 for the third wicket with Sardesai, who made 87 before falling to Parks for his only Test wicket. By this time it had become evident that the game was no longer being taken seriously. Nadkarni finished up with 122 not out, his only Test century, and Durani 61 not out. In addition to Parks, Mike also gave Bolus, Edrich and Cowdrey a bowl. Mike remarked after the match that even a World XI would have found it difficult to dismiss either of the teams on the Kanpur pitch within the allotted five days. In an attempt to break the deadlock of draws, at the end of the first day, with England comfortably placed on 271/2, Mike had offered Pataudi the chance to produce a result by agreeing to a mutual first-innings declaration, not unlike what often happened in county cricket. Pataudi, who had got the captaincy job on the casting vote of the chairman, was not at that stage confident enough to accept the challenge and said he would have to consult with the Indian board. They were apparently shocked at this heretical suggestion and another match was condemned to be a draw.

It was a disappointing end to a disappointing series. Perhaps Mike should have declared earlier on the second day, say at tea, when England were 490/5 with surely enough runs, and had two hours' bowling at tired players when they may have got two or three wickets. India were left with no incentive other than to play for a draw on wickets where it was difficult to remove defensive players. In truth though, neither side pushed hard enough for a win in any of the Tests, so a drawn series was probably a fair result.

Before heading back to England there was one more game to play against North Zone in Amritsar, where the players had the opportunity to visit its fabled Golden Temple. This again was inevitably drawn. MCC batted first against a side containing Test players Pataudi, Kunderan and Vijay Mehra and a 17-year-old left-arm spin bowler who was to become an Indian legend – Bishen Bedi. He only took one wicket in MCC's first innings, that of Bolus for 52. Sharpe, Knight and Parfitt all made half-centuries in MCC's total of 299/3 declared. North Zone declared 92 runs behind in an attempt to produce a result and Mike declared again at 136/5, leaving North Zone three hours to score 229. Sharpe made 80 in MCC's second innings before being bowled by Bedi. With North Zone 48/4 in the first hour, MCC looked favourites but 63 from Pataudi stopped the rot and North Zone ended up 14 runs short with seven wickets down.

The tour was a success inasmuch as it gave several players the chance to experience Test cricket in difficult conditions. Nearly all the players fell ill at some stage because of poor food hygiene standards, only Mike and Parfitt not succumbing to gastric ailments. Parfitt attributes his immunity to advice given to him by a Norfolk medical practitioner, Dr Corran, the father of Andrew Corran, captain of Nottinghamshire in the early 1960s, who recommended a glass of whisky every night before bedtime, with which remedy he was happy to comply whenever he could obtain it.[81] As a spectacle, the Test matches could not have been very exciting, although, such is the interest in cricket in India, it did not deter large crowds from watching. The two late arrivals, Cowdrey and Parfitt, headed the Test batting averages, Cowdrey with 309 runs at 103.00 and Parfitt 192 at 64.00. Mike was third with 306 runs at 51.00, Bolus fourth with 391 at 48.87 and Parks fifth with 211 at 42.20. Titmus was the pick of the bowlers with 27 wickets at 27.66, although Price had a slightly better average with 14 wickets at 27.35. Both these performances were remarkable given the easy-paced pitches. 'It was almost impossible to get the ball to bounce

81 Conversation with Peter Parfitt.

higher than stump-height,' says Price.[82] It was a series that India should have won, had they been more adventurous when they had the whip hand in the first two Tests. For India Nadkarni topped the batting averages with 294 runs at 98.00, Kunderan scored 525 runs at 52.50, and Hanumant Singh 152 at 50.66.

Overall, there were no major controversial incidents, the matches were played in a good spirit and full credit should be given, as *Wisden* said, 'to Smith's leadership, Clark's management and the admirable co-operation of all their players'.[83] Clark later paid tribute to Mike in a letter to the Warwickshire club: 'It is difficult to imagine a better person to captain a side in India. Under conditions where leadership is a first essential, he could not be faulted. When conditions were difficult he was completely unflappable. On the field he set a fine example, being a great fielder and always tried to score runs fast when the situation demanded it. Although at times he must have been very tired, he never showed it. He was the greatest help to an inexperienced manager and any success that the tour achieved must largely be due to his efforts.'[84]

'Tours to India and Pakistan were a challenge,' says Mike. 'The main problem was having 11 fit players for each match. You could guarantee that at least one person would be ill with some stomach complaint or other on account of the poor hygiene. Things are probably quite a bit better today but 60 years ago the standard of food preparation wasn't very high, to put it mildly. On top of that you had injuries, particularly among the fast bowlers because of the hard pitches, which take a toll on the body, as well as injuries sustained batting and fielding.

---

82 Conversation with John Price.

83 *Wisden Cricketers' Almanack 1965 edition.*

84 *The Story of Warwickshire Cricket,* Leslie Duckworth.

'There was the additional problem of dehydration because of the heat, which was energy-sapping. Also the distance between matches was considerable and the means of transport uncomfortable and occasionally precarious. On one of the journeys I seem to remember a door falling off the plane just as we were about to take off. The concentrated programme left little time for rest and recovery. I was fortunate to never get sick or injured in India or Pakistan, but I was probably the only one. Our hosts always tried to look after us as best they could, however, and you ate what they gave you and kept your fingers crossed.

'Their players suffered rarely from illness because their bodies had built up better resistance to infection over time. Because it had a reputation for being a difficult tour for these reasons, a lot of our top players opted out of touring India and Pakistan, which meant we rarely went with our strongest Test team. In spite of all this, though, morale was good, we made the best of things and the crowds were knowledgeable and appreciative of good cricket. Because of the generally lifeless wickets, it was difficult to get sides out and consequently there were a lot of drawn games.'

For the visit of the Australians in the coming season many believed Mike should be given the captaincy on the strength of his leadership abilities. 'If there is any justice in cricket, Mike Smith must be the man,' wrote Clive Taylor in the *Daily Herald*.[85] The selectors, however, decided to revert to Dexter, also ignoring Mike for selection as a player.

85 *MJK Smith: No Ordinary Man,* Douglas Miller.

CHAPTER 16

Championship Runners-up

WARWICKSHIRE HAD their best season to date in 1964 under Mike's captaincy, finishing second in the Championship to Worcestershire, having led for most of the season. They won 14 of their 28 matches, lost five and drew nine. Mike headed the Warwickshire batting averages again with 1,586 runs at 39.65. Jim Stewart, who missed part of the season through injury, was second with 786 runs at 30.23 and three batsmen, Bob Barber, Billy Ibadulla and Norman Horner, all made over 1,000 runs. Barber's elevation in the batting order to open with Horner proved a great success and he scored centuries against Nottinghamshire and the touring Australians as well as one against Northants in the second round of the Gillette Cup. He was then recalled for the final Test against Australia to open the innings for England with Geoff Boycott and chosen for the party to tour South Africa in the winter. Of the younger players, John Jameson made the most improvement, scoring his maiden first-class century against Oxford in a partnership of 255 with fellow centurion Dennis Amiss.

Tom Cartwright headed the bowling averages with 128 wickets at 13.78 and was fourth in the national averages. He made his Test debut for England in the fourth Test at Old Trafford where, on a perfect batting wicket, Bill Lawry and Bobby Simpson put on

201 for the first wicket and Australia made a massive total of 656/8 declared, Simpson making 311 of them. Apart from the run-out of Lawry, Cartwright got the only other wicket to fall on the first day, that of Ian Redpath, and finished with 2-118 off 77 overs, receiving great praise from Sir Learie Constantine, John Woodcock in *The Times* and Charles Bray in the *Daily Herald.* His former coaches, Tiger Smith and Derief Taylor, greeted the news with great pride, Tiger saying in his autobiography that Cartwright's selection pleased him more than anything he'd done in his own career.[86] Tom also played in the final Test at the Oval, taking 3-110 in 62 overs. This match fizzled out into a draw because of the weather, but not before Boycott had scored the first of his many Test centuries and Fred Trueman had taken his 300th Test wicket.

Jack Fingleton's prediction that Cartwright would be in the England side for years to come sadly did not come to pass, the selectors continuing to ignore the merits of medium-paced seamers. Cartwright was, however, selected to tour South Africa along with team-mates Bob Barber, Mike and David Brown, who took 76 wickets at 19.72 for Warwickshire during the season. Brown had made his debut for Warwickshire three years earlier but was not able to command a first-team place until the following year. David feels he owes a great debt to Warwickshire's coach, Tiger Smith, who he says made him into a bowler. 'A big lad like you should be bowling,' he said. 'We were all terrified of Tiger, but he was a fantastic judge of a player and a great coach. He'd come into the dressing room, shut the door and say "Right, you can all stop talking about me now."' He is also grateful to Jack Bannister for taking him under his wing at the start of his career. A lot of opening bowlers might have felt threatened by

86 *Tom Cartwright: The Flame Still Burns,* Stephen Chalke.

a newcomer, but Brown says Bannister was kind to him.[87] The pair were to become the mainstay of Warwickshire's opening fast bowling attack and Brown went on to have a successful Test career, his greatest contribution being his 5-63 in the first innings of England's victory at Sydney in the 1965/66 series. Brown was a big-hearted bowler and a great competitor. Jamie McDowall, who played several matches for Warwickshire as wicketkeeper in the early 1970s when Alan Smith was absent, recounts an incident when Brown was bowling at Boycott. 'Geoffrey had lost a contact lens and I was helping him look for it,' says Jamie. 'Brown came running up to me and asked me what I was doing.' "I'm helping Geoffrey find his contact lens." "Why?" said David.'[88]

Rudi Webster with 43 wickets at 19.11 also played when he could get time off from his medical studies. Against Yorkshire at Edgbaston in his first match of the season he was virtually unplayable and had the remarkable analysis of 7-6 from 13.4 overs when the visitors were bowled out for 54 in their first innings. Brown took 76 wickets at 19.72 and Bannister 51 at 19.74, including match figures of 8-42 against Nottinghamshire. He also took 6-16 in Sussex's second innings when they were bowled out for 23 in 12.2 overs on a minefield of a pitch at Worthing. Brown took 2-7 from his six overs and Cartwright, pleading for the ball, got the last two wickets with the first two balls of his only over. Les Lenham, after being hit on the chest by a lifter from Bannister, was lbw next ball to a shooter. On his way out he said to Bannister, 'I don't think that was out – it would probably have gone under the stumps.'[89] The match honours, though, must go to Sussex's Ian Thomson, who took all ten for 41 in Warwickshire's first innings but still finished on the losing side. The pace

87 Conversation with David Brown.

88 Conversation with Jamie McDowall.

89 *The History Of Warwickshire County Cricket Club*, Jack Bannister.

bowling department was one of Warwickshire's strengths, but it was spinners they were lacking. Basil Bridge, who had been first in the country to 100 wickets in 1961, apparently got the 'yips' and lost form completely even, according to Cartwright, embarrassingly bowling balls which went over the wicketkeeper's head. Warwickshire tried to help him by arranging hypnosis, but there appeared to be no cure and he sadly disappeared from the scene,[90] leaving Barber as the only spinner Warwickshire could count on with 41 wickets at 21.63. 'It's hard to understand', observes Ossie Wheatley, 'as Basil had such a smooth action.'

One of the highlights of the season was an exciting victory against the touring Australians by nine runs with only two balls to spare. Batting first, Warwickshire made 384, Barber scoring a century before lunch and Horner, Jameson and Mike all making forties. Brian Booth sportingly declared 131 runs behind and Mike closed Warwickshire's second innings at 63/1 in an attempt to produce a result. Set to make 195 in two and a half hours, Australia were bowled out for 185 in the last over. Bannister claimed the prized wickets of Bill Lawry, Peter Burge and Brian Booth. Roger Edmonds, a PE teacher at King Edward's School, Birmingham, took 5-63 with his fast off-breaks.

Warwickshire also enjoyed a good run in the second year of the Gillette Cup, eventually losing to Sussex in the final. Given a bye in the first round, they defeated Hampshire by 172 runs, Jameson making 100 not out and Mike 88. In the third round against Northants they made 300, Barber scoring 114 in cavalier fashion. Some, including team-mates Alan Smith and David Brown, have claimed that this innings was the watershed when Barber decided to play with more abandon, but Bob dismisses the notion that there was ever a Damascene moment when he consciously decided

90 *Tom Cartwright: The Flame Still Burns,* Stephen Chalke.

to change his style of play. He had previously on occasion scored freely at Lancashire in partnership with Alan Wharton, but it was apparent that, rid of the burden of captaincy responsibilities and with a stronger batting line-up at Warwickshire to follow him, he was playing with much more freedom and was now thoroughly enjoying his cricket in a more convivial team atmosphere. Bob also attributes the transition to the adoption of the front-foot no-ball rule as giving him a fraction more time to decide on an attacking shot, and the absence of bowlers' footmarks on a half-volley length making driving less risky.[91] In Northants' innings Ibadulla with 5-34 was principally responsible for dismissing them for 153.

The semi-final against Lancashire a month later was not without drama. Warwickshire, having been put in, made another big score, 294/7 off their 60 overs, Barber making 76, Mike 58 and Ray Hitchcock 47 not out against an attack which included Brian Statham, Ken Higgs, Peter Lever and Sonny Ramadhin. Lancashire started well with David Green and Duncan Worsley taking 67 off the first 12 overs before Worsley was out. Mike then tightened up the game by putting six of his fielders on the boundary and the scoring rate inevitably slowed. When the fifth Lancashire wicket fell at 161, it was evident that victory was highly unlikely and in protest the Lancashire wicketkeeper, Geoff 'Chimp' Clayton played negatively on purpose for 19 not out, even refusing to run easy singles. With a scoring rate of only two an over against Barber and Hitchcock, Lancashire finished on 209/7.

Warwickshire's tactics and Clayton's response to them did not please the crowd, to put it mildly, and after the match the supporters were calling for Clayton's head. Cyril Washbrook, Lancashire's former captain and newly appointed team manager, intercepted Clayton on his return to the dressing room and gave

91 Email correspondence with Bob Barber.

him a furious dressing-down. The Lancashire team refused to socialise with Warwickshire after the match and the celebrations had to take place at a pub on the way home. John Kay, writing in *Playfair Cricket Monthly*, described the match as 'a disgraceful display of cricketing bad manners'. Clayton, Peter Marner, Jack Dyson and the captain Ken Grieves, who was party to the go-slow, were all released at the end of the season and the members voted out the unpopular committee. Bob Barber must have been happy that he had made the move to Warwickshire.

Mike won the man of the match award partly for his batting but also for three excellent leg-side catches. Certain members of the press, EW Swanton in particular, were not enamoured of the more defensive tactics of limited-overs cricket. 'I trust the award was not for his captaincy,' was Swanton's caustic comment,[92] which Mike says was the source of a lot of future dressing-room laughter and leg-pulling.

And so, Warwickshire were now, in the second year of the competition, in the final at Lord's against Sussex, which took place at the beginning of September. Mike won the toss and decided to bat, having previously visited the ground for a pitch inspection with several of his players two days earlier. This policy, in which Mike was a general believer on the basis that it is easier to get runs at your own pace than against the clock, had worked well in the previous rounds. It did not work well this time, however, as by lunchtime Warwickshire were 61/6, having fallen prey to some outstanding swing and seam bowling from Ian Thomson, who took 4-23 in 13 overs. 'The ball was swinging round corners in the overcast atmosphere,' says John Jameson, one of Thomson's victims. John Snow accounted for Mike, whose 28 took 100 minutes, and Ted Dexter polished off the tail with 3-6. Alan Smith with 35

92 *MJK Smith: No Ordinary Man,* Douglas Miller.

not out was the only other batsman to offer any resistance. Set to score 128 to win, the task was easily accomplished in 41 overs, the opening pair of Les Lenham and Ken Suttle paving the way with a partnership of 92.

CHAPTER 17

Victorious in South Africa, 1964/65

MIKE WAS appointed to captain MCC in South Africa after some speculation as to whether it would go to him or Colin Cowdrey. Ted Dexter, who had captained against Australia, had ruled himself out as he was contesting the Cardiff South-East constituency as the Conservative candidate in the general election. Mike read the news in the paper and apparently put the paper down without saying anything to Diana, who only found out when she picked it up herself![93] This was presumably unintentional on Mike's part, and just typical of his absent-mindedness.

The England team contained several surprises. There was no place for Cowdrey or John Edrich, both of whom had finished near the top of the 1964 Championship and Test match averages, nor for Brian Statham or Fred Trueman, who had both taken over 100 first-class wickets in 1964. Trueman had topped the Test match averages against Australia with 17 wickets at 23.47 in a series which Australia had won two games to nil, with three matches drawn. The selectors were, however, apparently of the opinion that, at the age of 33, Fred was not as fast as he had been and was not likely to be successful on South African wickets. Also, if not selected for the Tests, he might prove to be a disruptive force on

93 *MJK Smith: No Ordinary Man*, Douglas Miller.

the tour party. They had some reason to be wary on this issue, as the following tale demonstrates.

Dennis Amiss and John Jameson recount an incident in a Warwickshire match against Yorkshire at Middlesbrough when Fred, as was his wont, came into the visitors' dressing room before the game uttering his boasts about how he was going to skittle the Warwickshire batsmen. Alan Smith was out in the middle tossing up with Brian Close. When Alan asked Brian for his team, Brian said Fred was going to be 12th man. On Alan's return to the changing room, Fred was still there 'telling us how he was going to knock our heads off'. When Alan said, 'Guess what, chaps, Fred's 12th man,' to much hilarity, Fred dashed out into the bar area and confronted his captain. According to Amiss, the air turned blue for several minutes as Fred exploited the richness of the English language to its full potential and a furious row between him and Close erupted.[94] With anyone other than Close, it may have led to fisticuffs, but Fred was actually quite scared of Brian, who was as hard as nails and had once or twice pinned him against the dressing room wall to get him to behave. Fred once said of Brian, 'If you punched him on the nose, he'd feel f… all.'

Irrespective of this, it was probably a mistake not to take him. Fred was naturally hurt and disappointed, as he had never before toured South Africa, apart from with the Cavaliers. On hearing of David Brown's selection ahead of him, he reportedly said with slow emphasis in his broad Yorkshire accent, 'David f…ing Brown.' As only a certain type of Yorkshireman can, he bore a grudge about it for the rest of his life. When many years later he was invited to a gathering of former Test players in honour of Mike Smith, he is said to have replied, 'No, I won't be going. I'll be staying at

94 Conversations with Dennis Amiss and John Jameson.

home, as I was in 1964.'[95] Trevor Goddard, the South African captain, was pleasantly surprised at the omission of Cowdrey and Trueman, and suspected that in Cowdrey's case there may have been a difference of opinion with the selectors, possibly over the captaincy issue. According to tour manager Donald Carr, however, Cowdrey had only made his availability known on the day when the final additions to the touring party were made, and the need was for an additional opening batsman. As Cowdrey had in the past been reluctant to fulfil this function, the selectors instead opted for the 22-year-old Mike Brearley who, still at Cambridge University, had scored over 2,000 runs during the summer. Ted Dexter eventually lost the Cardiff South-East seat by some 8,000 votes to James Callaghan and joined the tour party as vice-captain after the first Test.

According to Boycott on the plane out, Mike Smith had observed, 'Ted will be with us shortly.' 'Why's that?' asked Boycott. 'He's just told some dockers in Wales that some people are more fit to rule than others.'[96]

According to Mike, Ted was in no way put out by having to play under him and was a cheerful, constructive team member. Crawford White's prediction in the *Daily Express* that the presence of England's dynamic former captain would be a constant embarrassment to 'professor-like' Mike proved to be completely unfounded. Nothing could have been further from the truth. Peter Parfitt regards Edward Dexter, as he calls him, as a terrific team man and a really unselfish batsman, unlike some of the others he played with.[97] Some considered him aloof, but Tom Cartwright recalls Ted humbly asking him and Ian Thomson if he could join them for dinner soon after his arrival in Salisbury.

95 *Bob Barber: The Professional Amateur,* Colin Schindler.

96 *Being Geoffrey Boycott,* Geoffrey Boycott and Jon Hotten.

97 Conversation with Peter Parfitt.

'This bloke is not as flamboyant or as pushy as people think,' thought Tom.[98]

England took Boycott, Barber and Brearley as openers as well as Barrington and Parfitt as batsmen. The wicketkeepers were Jim Parks and John Murray, the pace bowlers John Price and David Brown, and medium-pacers Tom Cartwright and Ian Thomson. England also took three spinners in David Allen, Fred Titmus and the 22-year-old Robin Hobbs. Thomson, who was now 35 and had been playing for Sussex for over ten years, was not originally selected and was brought in at the last moment to replace Tony Nicholson, Fred Trueman's Yorkshire opening bowling partner, who had had to withdraw because of a back injury sustained during the Scarborough Festival. Nicholson unfortunately never got another chance to represent England.

Based on the form South Africa had shown in Australia and England's home defeat by Australia, South Africa were considered strong favourites. The emergence of players like 20-year-old Graeme Pollock, Colin Bland and Eddie Barlow, who had scored over 600 runs in the Test series in Australia the previous year, together with the shrewd captaincy of Trevor Goddard, the pace and aggression of Peter Pollock and the efficiency of John Waite, made South Africa a team to be reckoned with. England were, said Gordon Ross, editor of *Playfair*, 'a useful side, but no more'. Jackie McGlew, the former South African captain, was not so sure and in his first column for *The Sunday Times* wrote: 'The side without a star might well become a star side.'

The players were under strict instructions not to discuss politics which, with Rhodesia pushing for independence in a long-running dispute with the British government, was not so easy as it was a constant topic of conversation for South Africans and

98 *Tom Cartwright: The Flame Still Burns*, Stephen Chalke.

Rhodesians. The issue of apartheid was also starting to smoulder in the background, and John Arlott and even EW Swanton decided not to make the trip on a matter of principle. Returning from his coverage of the 1948/49 tour of South Africa, Arlott had refused to fill in the 'race' column on the departure form and when asked by an irritated immigration officer what race he was, he had defiantly said that he was a member of the human race.

Most of the players, either through ignorance, disinterest, or the belief that politics should not interfere with sport, had no qualms, but Mike Brearley and Bob Barber, who both had reservations, were keen to go so that they could see things for themselves. Whilst there, the pair made a couple of clandestine visits to the townships to see what life was like. They made sure Mike and Donald Carr were unaware of this as it could have been seen as an embarrassing breach of the 'no politics' mandate.[99] Brearley was in fact invited by a hotel worker to his home and despite the warmth of his welcome he was left with a sense of the bleakness of the townships. He stayed on for several weeks after the tour to get a fuller impression and even got to meet Alan Paton, author of *Cry The Beloved Country* and a strong anti-apartheid campaigner. Cartwright, who had strong left-wing leanings from his background as a car worker in Coventry, also had reservations. However, as a professional whose livelihood was cricket, it was more difficult for him to get directly involved, although he was disgusted by what he saw.[100] He had previously coached in South Africa and had witnessed at first hand the injustices of the system. Ironically, it was Cartwright's withdrawal from the proposed 1968/69 tour of South Africa which led to Basil D'Oliveira's belated inclusion and the ultimate cancellation of the

99 *Bob Barber: The Professional Amateur*, Colin Schindler.

100 *Tom Cartwright: The Flame Still Burns*, Stephen Chalke.

tour. Hobbs also maintains that he was shocked by some of the things he observed under this abhorrent policy, but his view was that there was nothing they as cricketers could do about it and they were there to play cricket.[101]

Mike himself has said that he had no regrets about playing against South Africa in the apartheid era and even fair-minded cricket writers like John Woodcock felt the tour should proceed. 'Personally, I decided I would disregard the politics in South Africa,' says Mike. 'We were out there to win a Test series. The political shit hadn't quite hit the fan. I knew Brearley had gone into the townships but I didn't know Bob had. The feeling was that if you wished to get involved in politics you shouldn't go on a cricket tour.'[102] The issue is a complex one, summed up so succinctly by the doyen of cricket writers, John Arlott, at the time of the D'Oliveira affair: 'Few of those within world-class cricket are political animals. That, however, is no excuse for being politically unconscious.'

After travelling out by air for the first time on two separate planes, MCC's first fixture was a two-day game in Bulawayo against a Matabeleland XI, which the visitors won by ten wickets, Mike top-scoring with 60, Parfitt making 55 and Titmus taking 7-58 in Matabeleland's second innings. From there it was on to Salisbury for the match against Rhodesia, where the team was joined by Dexter, although he did not play. Rhodesia made 281 in their first innings with half-centuries from Test players Colin Bland and the captain Tony Pithey. MCC bettered this by 17 runs, with Parfitt making 82 and Barrington 74. Joe Partridge, an experienced campaigner who had taken 25 wickets in the Tests in Australia, was Rhodesia's most successful bowler with 4-66.

---

101 *Hobbsy: A Life in Cricket,* Rob Kelly .

102 *MJK Smith: No Ordinary Man,* Douglas Miller.

Godfrey Lawrence, 6ft 7in tall and the only Rhodesian survivor from MCC's 1956 tour, took the wickets of the Warwickshire trio, Mike, Brown and Cartwright. Rhodesia were all out for 225 in their second innings, Brown bowling well for his 4-42, ably supported by Cartwright with 3-21. Barber's second-innings 108 clinched victory for MCC by five wickets shortly before the heavens opened. With Mike Brearley having recovered from the shock of his spectacular run-out by Bland in the first innings from what he had assumed was a comfortable single, he provided Barber with unselfish support in a second-wicket stand of 115. Bland was arguably one of the most brilliant fielders cricket has ever known. His presence in the field during the series not only produced run-outs but saved innumerable runs through exceptional stops and by preventing batmen from taking singles for fear of being run out if the ball went anywhere near him. David Brown, who got to know him well in South Africa and became a good friend, witnessed him practising and says: 'Colin took fielding to a new level and set new standards.'[103]

After a day spent sightseeing at Victoria Falls, the team travelled to Benoni, a town 20 miles west of Johannesburg for a match against a South African Colts XI. Mike decided to sit this one out, Dexter taking over the captaincy. After Price had reduced the Colts to 35/2, nobody expected the final total of 398. Two 19-year-olds, Barry Richards (63) and Neil Rosendorff (83), and 18-year-old Norman Crookes (60) took the score to 286/9, before an unlikely last-wicket partnership between Jackie Botten (57) and Mike Macaulay (55), aided by several dropped catches, added 112 runs in less than an hour. MCC replied with 267, Brearley top-scoring with 68. The Colts were dismissed for 161 in their second innings, Titmus taking five wickets. Set to make 293 to

103 Conversation with David Brown.

win in four hours, MCC reached 241/8 at the close. Had the Colts not been handicapped on the last day by illness and injury, with only two fit bowlers, things might have been different. The off-spinner Crookes kept up one end tirelessly, finishing with 5-108 off 38 overs. At one point the Colts had an unprecedented six substitutes on the field, one of whom was Ken Barrington and another Jim Pressdee, the Glamorgan left-arm spinner who was coaching in South Africa and had only come along to watch. A partnership of 94 between Boycott (53) and Dexter (50), which had temporarily put MCC in control, was ended by Crookes when he took stunning catches to dismiss both batsmen.

MCC then travelled 40 miles each day for a two-day match against a Transvaal Country Districts XI at Vereeniging, the town where the treaty ending the Second Boer War was signed. MCC, batting first, made 337/5 declared, Mike scoring 102, Brearley the same score and Parks 50 not out. The former Test fast bowler Peter Heine was included in the home side but at the age of 36 he bowled at a lot less than his former fiery pace and did not trouble the tourists unduly. When it was the Country Districts' turn to bat, they collapsed to a miserable 107 all out and were asked to follow on. They were saved from defeat by an unlikely century in 65 minutes from the aforesaid Heine which contained five sixes and 11 fours. When he was finally out for 108, with the total standing at 271, there was no time for MCC to bat again.

Before the next match against Transvaal at the Wanderers ground Mike had his team out for fielding practice to try and remedy the lapses that had been made in earlier matches. This was to prove beneficial. Ali Bacher, the 22-year-old who had taken over the Transvaal captaincy from John Waite the previous year, had taken his oral examination at Witwatersrand University on the morning of the match. He unwisely opted to bat on a softish wicket, possibly because one of his key players, Tony

Vorster, also had exams that morning. With the ball swinging and cutting, Price and Thomson were almost unplayable and at the end of the first hour only 17 runs had been scored in 17 overs. When the innings came to an end just before tea, 73 overs had been bowled for just 125 runs. Price, Thomson, Cartwright and Titmus had shared the wickets. Although MCC were 99/4 at the close, with Barber run out for 59, the pitch became much more benign on the second day and a partnership of 232 between Mike (124) and Barrington (169) put MCC in an unassailable position. *The Times* reported that Mike 'showed the full range of his leg-side repertoire, much of which is highly irregular and distinctive. He was chipping the ball away to square-leg from outside the off-stump as if there was nothing to it.'[104] Heine finished up the main wicket-taker for Transvaal with 5-110 off 41 well-controlled overs. His taking of the second new ball was not without some mild controversy, however, as Mike sent out a message of protest because he had been off the field for an hour immediately prior to this. In spite of MCC's commanding position, Mike was always a stickler for protocol with regard to the Laws of the game, but on this occasion the umpires allowed Heine to continue, probably incorrectly, as he had almost certainly been resting. After MCC declared at 464/9, they proceeded to bowl out Transvaal for 257 (Barber 4-78) to win by an innings and 82 runs with a day to spare.

The next stop was Durban, where Mike lost the toss for the fifth time in succession. Natal, captained by Jackie McGlew, the former South African captain who had retired from Test cricket in 1962, opted to bat, with a strong side that contained nine present and future Test cricketers. These included Trevor Goddard, who many thought, as South Africa's captain, should have been

104 *MJK Smith: No Ordinary Man,* Douglas Miller.

given the captaincy for that match as a rehearsal for the Tests. Natal scored 360/9, Derek Varnals making a century, Richard Dumbrill 68 and McGlew, demoting himself to number nine to give wicketkeeper Dennis Gamsy a chance to impress, 49 not out. Thomson with 5-58 was MCC's most successful bowler. MCC started slowly in reply and had lost three wickets by the close. Brown then came in as nightwatchman but the umpires took the players off for bad light before he reached the crease.

The next day was a Sunday and Barber, who at the beginning of the tour had taken a rather introverted Boycott under his wing in an attempt to get him to socialise more, rather than stay in his room thinking about his batting, arranged for them both to visit a game reserve at Hluhluwe, some 150 miles up the coast from Durban. They left at 4am armed with Polaroid cameras (Boycott's was apparently loaned to him by Harry Secombe) and met the head warden, Ian Player,[105] the older brother of the golfer Gary Player. Ian suggested that he get a black rhino to charge him so they could film it. 'They are practically blind', said Ian, 'and if you stand still they can't see you properly, so I won't be in any danger.' So, a rhino having been located and Barber and Boycott positioned at extra cover with their cameras at the ready, the rhino started

105 Ian Player (1927–2014) was born in Johannesburg and was educated at St John's College. During the Second World War he served in the 6th Armoured Division of the American 5th Army in Italy in 1944–46. His career as a conservationist started in 1952 as warden of Hluhluwe Umfolozi Game Reserve. He is credited with bringing the white rhinoceros back from the brink of extinction and was awarded the Decoration for Meritorious Service and honorary doctorates from the University of Natal and Rhodes University. For many years he faced widespread hostility in his homeland from farmers, hunters and businessmen. He was the older brother by eight years of Gary Player, who says his brother fashioned his first golf club from a tree branch and taught him the rudiments of the game. He was the founder of the World Wilderness Congress, an international forum which brings together scientists, financiers and environmental activists. He stood out for his outspoken support of black culture in South Africa and one of his closest friends was a Zulu park ranger named Magqubu Ntombela who taught him how to track animals in the bush. 'The wilderness has no perception of race,' he told *The Washington Post* in 1984.

to charge Ian. Suddenly, however, halfway through the charge, it stopped and started to head towards Bob and Geoff. Neither batsman questioned whose call it was and both took to their heels. This is where their accounts diverge. According to Bob, Geoff was up the nearest tree like a shot. According to Geoff, Bob was first up the tree. Boycott maintains he was at the foot of the tree and about to climb it when the rhino lost interest and wandered off. Maybe it had heard about Boycott's impregnable defence. 'They tell you you're supposed to stand still when a rhino charges you', says Boycott, 'but just try it. It's like if you're in Alaska and a grizzly bear comes after you, you're supposed to curl up into a ball and pretend to be dead, but who the f...'s going to do that?'[106]

When play resumed on Monday, as Brown had not faced a ball on the Saturday, Mike made to go in himself instead of Brown but the umpires ruled that, as Brown had crossed with Dexter on the way to the wicket, Brown had to continue. This in fact turned out rather well as Brown made 69. After Parfitt was out for 74, Mike joined Brown and the partnership between the Warwickshire pair raised 68. Parks (80 not out) and Cartwright (35) helped MCC to a total of 445. The games against state sides were four-day matches and, with only two innings having been completed by the end of the third day, a draw looked inevitable but Natal were shot out for 102 on the final day. Overnight rain had dramatically changed the character of the pitch and it was the bowling of Thomson (3-16 off 23 overs) that precipitated Natal's downfall. In 13 overs before lunch he took 2-6, Gamsy being brilliantly caught at short leg by Mike and Varnals by an equally fine catch by Parks. Brown accounted for Goddard, well caught by Parks off an inside edge and McGlew, who had gone in first, was run out after being sent back by his old buddy Roy McLean. Natal were in a perilous

106 Telephone conversation with Sir Geoffrey Boycott.

position at 25/4. Only Richards with 29 offered any resistance and Allen cleaned up the tail with 4-12. MCC needed only four overs to knock off the 18 runs required.

A jubilant MCC flew out of Durban for Port Elizabeth for the next match against Eastern Province, a side containing Eddie Barlow and both Pollock brothers. After winning the toss Mike chose to bat, but things did not go well at first, with Brearley, Dexter and Barrington all going cheaply. However, a stand of 278 between Boycott (193 not out in eight hours) and Mike (153 in half that time) created a winning platform and MCC were able to declare at lunch on the second day at 447/9. Mike had sent a message out saying that he was going to declare but in the last over Boycott was prevented from reaching his double-century by the tactics of Peter Pollock, who deliberately bowled him a succession of wide leg-side deliveries, bouncers and beamers, which were in those days not penalised as no-balls. That evening in the bar when Pollock was boasting and laughing about it, Barber went up to him and said, 'Let me tell you, you'd better f...ing hit me with one of those, because otherwise I'm coming after you with the bat. And if you ever bowl another one at him again, when I'm at the other end, you're for it.'[107] 'Bob was like an older brother to me on that tour,' says Boycott. 'He was a very strong man who knew how to look after himself.'[108]

Eastern Province were bowled out twice for 133 and 164 to give MCC victory by an innings and 150 runs within three days. Titmus took ten wickets in the match for 70 runs, five in each innings, Barlow falling both times to him and Graeme Pollock once to him and once to Allen. The premature finish gave the players and journalists time to visit the beach, where in a game

---

107 *Bob Barber: The Professional Amateur,* Colin Schindler.

108 *Being Geoffrey Boycott,* Geoffrey Boycott and Jon Hotten.

of barefoot football Bob Barber managed to break two toes in a tackle with the commentator Brian Johnston. He had to miss the next match against Western Province and was doubtful for the first Test. Johnston's own toes were apparently painful but only bruised. As fellow South African commentator Charles Fortune wryly observed, 'Perhaps a commentator has to fracture his jaw before he is considered to be professionally unserviceable.'[109]

Mike missed the next match against Western Province in Cape Town, which Dexter captained. He obviously felt that three centuries in his last four innings had given him enough batting practice and others could benefit from time at the crease. Instead he undertook the 12th man duties to the surprise of many reporters and commentators who had never before seen an England captain bringing out the drinks. Brearley opened with Boycott but was out cheaply in the first innings. Another century from Boycott, bowled eventually, to his disgust, by a slow full toss, and an unhurried 169 not out from Barrington helped MCC to 441, to which Western Province replied with 357. Len Weinstein, who as a 16-year-old, had played against Peter May's 1956 team, made 53 and their captain Peter van der Merwe a chanceless century. He had been South Africa's vice-captain in their recent drawn series in Australia but had not done well in the Tests and had been dropped for the last two. In England's second innings Brearley made 64 and Barrington 82. MCC declared at lunch on the last day, leaving Western Province four hours to make 313. They were never in the hunt and with eight wickets down and 20 minutes left, defeat looked a possibility but the ninth-wicket pair managed to hold on for a draw. Dexter's declaration was overly defensive and, had it come an hour earlier, MCC would surely have been able to extend their winning sequence.

---

109 *MCC in South Africa 1964–65*, Charles Fortune.

The England team selected for the first Test at Durban was pretty much as predicted. Barber's toes had recovered sufficiently and the bowlers, Thomson, Price and Titmus, were automatic choices. The only issue up for debate was whether to play two or three seam bowlers. The answer to this was decided when Cartwright was declared unfit to play and England opted for Allen as a second spinner. South Africa did not pick Van der Merwe, in spite of his century against the tourists, and went in with only one spin bowler, Richard Seymour, who had not pulled up any trees with his off-breaks in MCC's previous game against Western Province. Denis Lindsay was chosen as wicketkeeper, Waite having made himself unavailable. Thomson was making his debut for England and Varnals for South Africa. The Kingsmead pitch looked bare and hard in contrast to the much greener surface in the earlier game against Natal. Mike won the toss and had no hesitation in deciding to bat, conveying his decision to the dressing room with an imaginary swish of the bat. Also there, at the invitation of Donald Carr and Mike, was one of England's all-time greats, Wally Hammond, who had some years earlier moved to South Africa for business reasons. Boycott maintains he was too much in awe of him to ask his advice on batting.

Barber and Boycott opened the innings, Barber having already made it clear to Boycott that he wanted half the strike and if he tried to pinch a single off the last ball of the over, he wouldn't run. Sure enough, Boycott tried to do this at the end of the first over of the Test and, although there was an easy single, Barber stayed put and Boycott was forced to run a two for nothing.[110] 'He was a bugger like that, was Bob,' says Boycott.[111] At the start of the England innings the pair made fairly slow progress against tight

110 Conversation with Bob Barber.

111 *Bob Barber: The Professional Amateur*, Colin Schindler.

bowling from Peter Pollock and Joe Partridge, but when the off-spinner Seymour came into the attack Barber immediately went after him. At lunch England were 79 without loss with Barber having reached fifty. The opening partnership had progressed to 120 when Barber was out for 74. Dexter was next out, neatly caught and bowled by Seymour for 28. Boycott was dismissed shortly after tea, lbw to Partridge after apparently getting an inside edge which the umpire missed; his 73 had taken four and a quarter hours. Parfitt followed soon afterwards, caught at slip by Goddard without opening his account. Mike and Barrington put on 73 for the fifth wicket until Mike was out for 35 the next day. The partnership that then ensued between Barrington and Parks put England in a position from which it would be difficult to lose. They put on 206, Parks batting aggressively for 108 not out in four hours and Barrington passively for 148 not out in over seven. It was hardly entertaining cricket, but Barrington never saw that as his mission. 'Kenny was an outstanding player,' says former Surrey captain Micky Stewart. 'He had all the shots but he didn't always use them, preferring to err on the side of caution and only punish the really bad ball. He had been dropped from the England team early in his career after a run of low scores and was determined it was never going to happen again.'[112] In the mood, though, he could be a very powerful, attacking player, and Pat Pocock remembers him once taking 27 off an over from Harold Rhodes.[113] 'If Barrington had a fault, it was that, at times, he was guilty of playing for himself rather than the team. He was a really good bloke, though,' says Peter Parfitt.[114]

With less than an hour left to play, Mike declared at 485/5. South Africa made a disastrous start, and by the close they had

112 Conversation with Micky Stewart

113 Conversation with Pat Pocock

114 Conversation with Peter Parfitt

lost Goddard, Barlow and Graeme Pollock for 20 runs. They very nearly lost Tony Pithey as well when he was dropped by Dexter at silly point. Things didn't get much better for them on the third day, which belonged to Allen. In 20 overs he took 5-41, no batsman making more than 30 as the South African innings crumbled to 155 all out. Three smart catches at short leg, two by Mike and one by Barber, played their part, but it was clear South Africa had a problem against quality spin bowling. Following on, South Africa had an equally disastrous start to their second innings, the score soon standing at 28/3. Barlow was caught at slip by Barrington off Price for nought, brazenly refusing to go until the umpire had raised his finger, and Graeme Pollock went for the same score, well caught by Mike at gully off Titmus. Only a fourth-wicket partnership of 95 between Pithey (43) and a defiant Bland (68) gave the score some respectability before Pithey fell again to Allen and Bland to Titmus. A ninth-wicket stand between Seymour (36) and Peter Pollock (18 not out) took the score to over 200, but by then every South African knew it was a lost cause. In South Africa's second innings nine batsmen were out caught, and this time it was Titmus's turn to bag the honours with 5-66. So, England completed a convincing win by an innings and 104 runs on the fourth day. They had clearly benefitted by winning the toss, but had ground South Africa down with a solid batting performance, skilful captaincy and a pair of spinners who the conditions had suited perfectly. 'The difference between the two sides in South Africa was very simple,' says Mike. 'We had a high-class spin attack and they didn't. We were brought up on wet wickets and we could play spin.'[115]

115 *Bob Barber: The Professional Amateur,* Colin Schindler.

ENGLAND v SOUTH AFRICA
First Test Match

England

G Boycott lbw b Partridge	73
RW Barber b Goddard	74
ER Dexter c and b Seymour	28
KF Barrington not out	148
PH Parfitt c Goddard b Partridge	0
*MJK Smith c Lindsay b Partridge	35
JM Parks not out	108
B 2, lb 1, nb 16	19
1/120 2/169 (5 wkts, dec) 3/205 4/206 5/279	485

FJ Titmus, DA Allen, NI Thomson and JSE Price did not bat

PM Pollock	33-1-80-0
Partridge	45-14-85-3
Barlow	20-5-36-0
Seymour	46-4-144-1
Goddard	32-8-79-1
RG Pollock	10-1-32-0
Bland	4-1-10-0

South Africa

*TL Goddard c Smith b Price	8	– c Thomson b Titmus	15
EJ Barlow b Thomson	2	– c Barrington b Price	0
AJ Pithey b Allen	15	– c Dexter b Allen	43
RG Pollock b Titmus	5	– c Smith b Titmus	0
KC Bland c Barber b Allen	26	– c Barber b Titmus	68
JD Lindsay c Price b Barber	38	– c Dexter b Titmus	10
RA.McLean c Smith b Allen	30	– c Smith b Allen	9
D Varnals b Allen	3	– c Parks b Thomson	11
MA Seymour not out	15	– b Titmus	36
PM Pollock c Dexter b Barber	3	– not out	18
JT Partridge b Allen	6	– run out	1
B 4	4	B 9 lb 6	15
1/10 2/10 3/19 4/54 5/67 6/120	155	1/4, 2/28 3/28 4/123 5/142 6/145	226
7/130 8/131 9/142		7/157 8/178 9/225	

Price	6-2-19-1	9-7-7-1
Thomson	15-5-23-1	13-6-25-1
Titmus	20-9-20-1	45.5-19-66-5
Allen	19.5-4-41-5	47-15-99-2
Barber	14-1-48-2	6-2-8-0
Parfitt		2-0-6-0

Umpires: HC Kidson and JG Draper

England won by an innings and 104 runs

There were two more matches to be played before the start of the second Test at Johannesburg, the first against South African Universities at Pietermaritzburg and the second against North Eastern Transvaal at Pretoria. The South African Universities put up a poor show, being dismissed for 114 in their first innings and 130 in the second. Barrington with his leg-breaks was the destroyer with 5-29 and 4-25. MCC put together a total of 356 thanks to century partnerships between Boycott and Parfitt, and Murray and Mike. The students blamed their performance on the match being part of the Universities Cricket Week when too much revelry and too little sleep had taken their toll – a poor excuse for serious cricketers and rather disrespectful to a touring side.

MCC then travelled to Pretoria by rail to play North-Eastern Transvaal. Put into bat by Mike, the home side progressed slowly to a total of 204 on a dampish pitch against a tight bowling attack and a network of close fielders. Several batsmen got starts, but no one made a significant score. Titmus was the most effective bowler with 4-29 from 23 overs. MCC put together a total of 350. The best batting of the second day came from the Middlesex pair Titmus (65) and Murray (142), who put on 137 together for the seventh wicket at a run a minute under the approving eye of Denis Compton, who was present as a reporter for the *Sunday Express*. Compton had scored 300 in just over three hours on the same ground in MCC's tour of South Africa in 1948/49. North Eastern Transvaal's second innings never promised much, and they were all out for 135 to give MCC victory by an innings and 11 runs. Price took 4-42, bowling faster than at any time on the trip. MCC had recorded their seventh win of the tour and the fifth by an innings.

Both teams were unchanged for the second Test at the Wanderers ground in Johannesburg, South Africa somewhat surprisingly after their hammering in the first. Mike was again lucky with the toss and England batted first on an excellent surface. After losing Boycott early on, England took complete control as Barber, partnered by an initially restrained Dexter, went on the offensive immediately. He was lucky to escape when McLean dropped a difficult low chance at slip with only ten runs on the board, but thereafter he never looked back. He responded to a barrage of bouncers from a frustrated Peter Pollock by turning his cap around and going down on one knee and pretending to play a sweep shot. When Pollock pitched one up, he would drive him superbly through the covers.[116] At lunch England were 121/1, Barber having made a dashing 75 and Dexter, who was now starting to open up, 42. Barber perished three runs short of his first Test century after telling Dexter he was going to reach it in spectacular style with a six. 'Don't be daft,' said Ted, but his words fell on deaf ears as Barber took an almighty heave at the next ball from Seymour and dragged it from well outside his off stump on to the wicket.[117] Barber is not one for milestones and averages and feels strongly that often they do not reflect the true ability of a player, believing that each innings or bowling performance has to be viewed in the context of the game.[118] He would approve of Robertson-Glasgow's view of averages, expressed in his *46 Not Out*, 'How I loathed them. What a mess mathematics make of man, damning his generous currents, frowning on joyous fallibility, pursing the dry lip at admirable error.' When asked recently what he thought of Barber, Boycott replied, 'In all my life I've never met anybody like Bob Barber. He played cricket like it was just a bit of fun. I think he was serious underneath, but it didn't look like it. That's not how I was taught to play in Yorkshire. It was a matter of life and death there. If we ever lost a match, there were

116 *Being Geoffrey Boycott*, Geoffrey Boycott and Jon Hotten.

117 *Bob Barber: The Professional Amateur*, Colin Schindler.

118 Conversation with Bob Barber.

repercussions. When I was batting in the nets, if ever I hit the ball in the air, the coach would say, "Don't do that, yer daft bugger, yer'll get caught." Bob was a great guy to bat with though, because by scoring so fast, it took the pressure off me.'[119] Barber's approach to batting was without doubt in complete contrast to Boycott's. Essentially Bob came to see cricket as a game to be enjoyed and one which had to be made attractive for spectators. For him it was a form of entertainment with the emphasis on positive attacking cricket, although he doesn't like the phrase 'brighter cricket'.

After Barber was out, Dexter was joined by Barrington and he continued on his majestic way, dispatching the ball to all corners of the ground with an array of powerful shots. When he eventually fell for 172 with the total at 337/3, he had hit 108 of his runs in boundaries. Joined by Parfitt, who made 52, Barrington continued in his usual measured way, progressing to his second consecutive century with a straight six, gesturing to the players' balcony to show Barber how it was done. England batted almost to the close on the second day for 531 all out, thus guaranteeing, barring miracles, they could not lose. Peter Pollock had bowled tirelessly, taking 5-129. In reply, South Africa compiled 317, with substantial contributions from Goddard (40), Barlow (71) and Pithey (83), but it was not enough to avoid the follow-on, which Mike enforced. At the end of the fourth day South Africa's score stood at 146/4 and England must have had high hopes of going two up. Goddard and Barlow had put on 50 for the first wicket, but two fine catches by Mike at short leg brought about their downfall. Allen took the first three wickets to fall and Titmus accounted for McLean, who was bowled off his pads after an uncharacteristic and irresponsible wild swipe. At the age of 34, his race was run as a Test player. At one of the drinks breaks Mike received a note from Gubby

---

119 Conversation with Sir Geoffrey Boycott .

Allen, who had come out from England to watch. 'Why don't you change the bowling?' According to Bob Barber, Mike borrowed a pen from the waiter and wrote as his reply, 'Why don't you get stuffed?' Mike has no recollection of this and it does seem a bit out of character, but Barber swears to having witnessed it.[120] On the final day play started three-quarters of an hour late after heavy overnight rain. Pollock and Bland were still there at lunch with the deficit down to 27. When Pollock was out soon after lunch for an attractive 55, England must have fancied their chances. But they had not reckoned with the mastery of Bland, who played the innings of his life, scoring 144 not out by the time play was abandoned for bad light three-quarters of an hour before the close. Varnals, who stayed with him for close on two hours, scored 23 out of a partnership of 124, which saved the game for South Africa. Varnals had been lucky to survive an appeal for a catch in the leg trap by Barber, which most of the England team thought should have been given out.

The third Test at Cape Town started on New Year's Day, three days after the end of the second. It was a huge disappointment from the spectators' point of view as, after each side had completed their first innings, there was never any possibility of a result. The match was also marred by a couple of controversial incidents relating to whether a batsman should walk. Goddard won the toss for the first time and, opting to bat, made the most of it by putting on 80 for the first wicket with Barlow before being bowled by Titmus. When Barlow, on 40, was given not out, caught by Parfitt at slip off Titmus after playing the ball on to his boot, an unpleasant exchange between him and Titmus ensued, which soured relationships to the point that none of the England players applauded his subsequent half-century and century. According

120 *MJK Smith: No Ordinary Man,* Douglas Miller.

to Parfitt, who has a vivid recollection of the incident, Barlow definitely edged the ball on to his boot and it never touched the ground. 'Eddie, I've caught it,' said Parfitt. 'Eddie, Peter's caught it,' added Parks. When it became obvious Barlow was not going to walk, Titmus called Barlow a 'cheating bastard', in reply to which Barlow walked down the wicket with his bat raised, saying, 'Don't you call me a f...ing cheat or I'll hit you with this.'[121] At this point Bob Barber intervened with 'Calm down, Eddie, you're not big enough to start hitting anybody.'[122] To add insult to injury, Barlow and Pithey proceeded to put on 172 for the second wicket, Barlow finally departing for 138 at the beginning of day two. Pithey batted on slowly for most of the second day, sharing partnerships of 61 with Graeme Pollock and 99 with Bland. On reaching his fifty, he received excessively warm congratulations from several of the England team, clearly as a means of showing contempt for, in their eyes, Barlow's ill-merited century. After Bland was run out by Dexter for a fine 78, the batting lost momentum and Goddard declared at 501/7 an hour before the close.

Boycott and Barber played out the remaining time with their wickets intact. Boycott did not last long on the morrow but substantial scores from Barber (58), Dexter (61), Barrington (49), Parfitt (44), Parks (59) and 121 from Mike enabled England to reach a total of 442 on a pitch that continued to behave benignly. The runs were made slowly, however, Dexter's innings uncharacteristically taking four hours. Barrington's dismissal sparked off another controversial incident when he edged a ball from Pollock to the wicketkeeper and was not given out. He appeared to start to walk, then stopped for several seconds before deciding to go. This delay was regarded by several members of the press as theatrical and his

121 Conversation with Peter Parfitt.

122 *My Life in Cricket,* Fred Titmus.

decision to walk a snub to Barlow's decision to do the opposite. The *Daily Mail* thought his action too ostentatious, but Barrington himself maintained afterwards that he was having a conversation with his conscience and what he did was not for effect.

When South Africa went to the crease again there were only seven hours left to play and they basically used it as batting practice with no intention of declaring. They were finally out for 346, Barlow, Graeme Pollock, Bland and Lindsay all making half-centuries. As an indication of the futility of the final day, England used all ten outfield players as bowlers; Parfitt bowled 19 overs and Mike even gave himself 11. Boycott sent down 20 overs, bowling Bland and Graeme Pollock and finishing with 3-47. But by then it was too late. When asked why he had not declared, Goddard said that he did not think it would have been possible to bowl out England in about two hours. He was probably right, but perhaps an attempt should have been made if only out of consideration for the spectators. Rather pointlessly, England were required to bat eight overs, which Boycott and Barrington played out. Overall, the match was adversely affected by poor umpiring and was a dreary, ill-tempered affair which did no credit to cricket. Former captain McGlew described it as 'a farce and a circus'.

At one of the intervals during the match, Titmus was taken to one side by the manager Donald Carr and ordered to apologise to Barlow for his outburst. 'I'm not apologising,' said Titmus. 'Well, if you don't, there's a plane leaving for England at nine o'clock tomorrow morning and you'll be on it,' said Carr. Parfitt says that the following morning he accompanied his Middlesex team-mate downstairs to the South African dressing room, where, after opening the door, Titmus offered a less than contrite apology, saying 'I've come to apologise, so I've f…ing done it.' According to Parfitt, they then both left without waiting for a response.[123] Another version has Barlow asking Titmus if he was asked to apologise and Barlow saying that he wouldn't have done so and a further one having Barlow say, 'I'm sorry it all blew up.' Parfitt has no recollection of these latter two possible exchanges, but they could have happened after the match ended. This incident rather overshadowed the cricket and was much commented on in both the British and South African press, with journalists and administrators taking different sides, some fervently believing that a batsman should 'walk' if they know they are out, others taking the view that 'walking' undermines the umpires. It is, and has always been, one of cricket's most controversial areas of debate. Goddard, who was not watching at the time of the Barlow incident, and was clearly saddened by it, maintains that Barlow gave him his word that he did not hit it.[124] For the record, Mike says that he always 'walked', as one would have expected.

After the match Goddard was called before the selectors and asked to resign the captaincy. He refused, on the basis he had been appointed for the whole series, but during the fourth Test said he would resign at the end of the series. This he did, to the dismay of many of his team-mates and his supporters. Goddard had been an inspirational captain. Don Bradman said of him, 'He enriched the game of cricket and set a fine example by his sincerity and integrity.'

MCC were in action again three days later against Border at East London. Batting first, Border made 215, their captain 'Buster' Farrer, who had played tennis at Wimbledon, top-scoring with 66. Barber took 6-67. MCC declared at 407/5, Dexter making 110, Parfitt 79 and Cartwright 111 not out. Border's second-innings total

---

123 Conversation with Peter Parfitt

124 *The Trevor Goddard Story,* Graham Short.

of 244 was largely due to 65 from 20-year-old Chris Wilkins who later played for Derbyshire and a sparkling century from 17-year-old Hylton Ackerman, who hit 17 fours and one six. He later had four seasons with Northamptonshire. Cartwright and Brown each claimed three wickets. Left with only 53 to make, MCC completed the win easily, losing only the luckless Brearley for 5.

The penultimate game before the fourth Test was against Orange Free State at Bloemfontein. Inserted by Barrington, skipper for this match, Bloemfontein made 170, wicketkeeper Raymond van der Poll top-scoring with 47. MCC started badly against the medium-paced outswing of Mike Macaulay, who accounted for Barber, Brearley and Barrington for one run in his first 13 deliveries. Boycott (73) and Parks (89) came to the rescue, however, with a 154-run partnership, which enabled MCC to declare 29 runs ahead for the loss of seven wickets, all of which were picked up by Macaulay for 58 runs. On the final day the Orange Free State captain Des Schonegevel sportingly declared the innings closed at 171/9, Van der Poll again top-scoring with 64. This left MCC 90 minutes to make 143 which they accomplished in the last over of the day, Boycott, Barber, Parks and Barrington all going for the runs aggressively to give MCC a win by seven wickets.

South Africa made four changes to their side for the fourth Test in Johannesburg. Waite was recalled to replace Lindsay, Partridge came in for Sydney Burke, and Athol McKinnon and Peter van der Merwe started for the first time in the series. To many people's surprise, Mike opted to field on winning the toss. To be fair, the decision was not Mike's alone and was made after Mike, Donald Carr, Dexter and Barrington had taken a long hard look at the pitch for almost 30 minutes. Anyway, it proved, on Mike's own later admission, to be a very bad decision with South Africa's score standing at 118/0 at lunch. The partnership was finally broken when Goddard, dawdling, was run out at the bowler's end by a powerful throw from Barrington and quick thinking by Boycott, who had raced to the wicket at the bowler's end to gather the ball and take off the bails. He had made 60 and Barlow carried on to make 96, caught and bowled by Cartwright for his only wicket in the innings. Not all the players had been happy with the decision to play Cartwright ahead of Allen, one of the bowlers responsible for the victory in the first Test, and when Mike announced the team there were rumblings of dissent, not least from Titmus. According to Parfitt, Titmus, who was no shrinking violet, proffered his opinion aloud in no uncertain terms with 'You must be f...ing joking.' Mike did not reprimand Titmus for this insubordinate outburst, but he was clearly irritated by it and proceeded to forcefully repeat the announcement of the team.[125] Tom admitted to Allen later that he thought it was a bad choice. Bland was out for 55 on the second day, well caught by Parks off Price after Mike had taken the new ball. Graeme Pollock fell in the same way to an even better catch low down off a bottom edge. Pithey, who had been playing in his usual patient manner, then put on 157 with Waite for the fifth wicket, which ended only when Waite was run out. It was in fact Bland who was run out at the bowler's end by a strong throw from Barrington while acting as a runner for Waite, who had succumbed to cramp. Soon afterwards Goddard called a halt at 390/6.

England replied with 384 all out, Barber making 61, Barrington 93, Mike 42 and Parfitt 122 not out. England had more than their fair share of luck in arriving at this total. Barber, Parfitt and Barrington were all missed off the left-arm spinner McKinnon, who should have had a much better return than his 4-128. Waite was particularly culpable, missing several catches and the chance to stump Barber. A potentially controversial incident

125 Conversation with Peter Parfitt.

arose during England's innings. Mike, on 5, missed a ball down the leg side from Partridge, which Waite took and tossed to Van der Merwe, the vice-captain, at leg slip. Seeing that Mike had wandered out of his crease to do a bit of 'gardening', he threw the wicket down and appealed. The umpire gave Mike out and Mike departed, bemused. Parfitt, who was the non-striker, said to the umpire, 'That can't be right, the ball was dead, for God's sake.' He then turned to Goddard and said, 'Trevor, this is not good, the ball was dead.'[126] Goddard, after consultation with the umpire, sprinted after Mike, who by then was close to the gate and sportingly recalled him. Mike remembers the umpire apologising to him when he returned to the crease.

Going in for the second time after lunch on the fourth day, South Africa needed to score quickly to stand a chance of winning. This they did, Goddard batting superbly for a well-deserved century, his first in 62 Test innings. When he achieved it, almost the entire England team moved over to congratulate him. He nearly didn't make it, though, as he was almost run out by Cartwright on 99 when short of his ground. Tom, showing his softer side, said afterwards, 'I picked up the ball and threw it side on at the wicket – and I missed by a whisker. I almost ran him out for 99 – and forever I've been glad that I didn't. He was such a nice man. I'm glad he got a hundred.'[127] Goddard's dismissal, though, had serious consequences for England, for in the process of taking what was a fairly comfortable catch off a skier at long leg, Barber broke a bone in his right hand. He was not only unable to open in England's second innings, but his tour was over. He had to miss the final Test and made the sad journey back to England alone. After Goddard's dismissal South Africa cracked on, Bland

---

126 Conversation with Peter Parfitt.

127 *Tom Cartwright: The Flame Still Burns,* Stephen Chalke.

and Graeme Pollock putting on 96 in the remaining 71 minutes before lunch, at which point Goddard declared.

England were left with two sessions to score 314. Titmus came in to open in place of Barber and it became pretty clear early on that they were not going for the runs. Pollock, bowling like a demon, removed Titmus and then Dexter for nought, brilliantly caught by his brother Graeme at short leg. When Barrington was out caught in the gully, England's score stood at 33/3 and the prospect of defeat loomed. A doughty Yorkshireman had other ideas, though, and it is in situations like this that one can appreciate Boycott's true worth. He batted for four hours for 76 not out and his innings saved the match. Parfitt provided solid support for an hour, and Mike and Parks for half an hour each. Cartwright was there with him at the end and a relieved England finished on 153/6. Barber was also padded up and prepared to bat if needed. There was no doubt South Africa had had the better of the match. Missed chances in England's first innings had cost them dearly and an earlier declaration would have given them more time to bowl England out. But in Test matches safety first almost always overrides the risk of losing. Donald Carr admitted afterwards that they had misread the pitch and should have batted. 'It was a bit too close for comfort,' Mike said.

There were two matches to play before the final Test, one against Griqualand West in Kimberley and the other against an Invitation XI at Cape Town. The match against Griqualand West was a three-day affair, played at the De Beers stadium and won easily by MCC. The 21-year-old Weston Symcox was the only player to put up much of a fight, making 62 stubborn runs out of a total of 140 in 92 overs. The MCC bowlers were always on top with Brown taking three wickets in an over near the end. Allen took 2-15 in 19 overs and Cartwright, miserly as ever, had figures of 0-6 in 14 overs. With Barber now out of the picture,

Brearley and Murray opened in what was effectively a contest for the opening slot. Brearley batted doggedly for 43 runs, but with wickets falling regularly around him England found themselves still behind with seven wickets down. The tail wagged, however, and useful contributions from Cartwright, Thomson and Brown helped them to 226, their lowest total of the tour for a completed innings. Griqualand's meagre second-innings total of 107 left MCC needing only 24 to win, which Murray and Brearley knocked off quickly. Barrington once again showed his skill against weaker opposition, taking 7-40.

The last match before the final Test was against a strong Invitation XI, captained by Van der Merwe. After losing the toss on a perfect batting strip, Mike remarked, 'I'm going to be anything but popular when I get back to the dressing room.' He was right. After the loss of an early wicket, a magnificent partnership of 186 between Gamsy (88) and Bland (116) in a little over two hours put the Invitation XI in a strong position. Van der Merwe made an unconvincing 50 but it was an eighth-wicket partnership of 105 between bowlers Robbie Muzzell (70) and Jackie Botten (53) which brought the total to 437. Cartwright, an ever-willing workhorse, bowled 38 overs to take 5-107. Mike again had Brearley and Murray open to decide which of the two would play in the final Test, with Boycott shunted down to number three. In the event, the experiment was inconclusive, as both batsmen were out cheaply with only 14 runs on the board. Boycott, apparently playing with much more freedom than usual, then proceeded to make an excellent century, without which MCC would have been in dire straits. At 113/5 things had looked bleak, but later contributions from the bowlers, particularly Cartwright (53 not out) and number 11 Hobbs (36) helped MCC to reach 326. In Invitation's second innings they went for it from the start, Gamsy (55) and Bland (67) putting on 97 for the second wicket, followed by a stylish 91 from Graeme Pollock and another half-century from Muzzell. They declared at 316/7 at close of play, setting MCC the unlikely target of 428. Boycott was MCC's most successful bowler, taking 3-69 from 21 accurate overs, including the wickets of Graeme Pollock, Van der Merwe and Richards. On the final day the openers failed again. Boycott was given out caught at the wicket from one he swears he never touched, and he made little attempt to hide his dissatisfaction. Wickets fell steadily to Pat Trimborn, Clive Halse and Botten and at 100/7 with almost three hours left, MCC looked to be in serious danger of losing their unbeaten record. However, an imperturbable 78 not out from Mike and 42 not out from his reliable Warwickshire team-mate Cartwright saved the day. As John Woodcock wrote in *The Times*, 'The Invitation XI played unquestionably the better cricket in this match – but Warwickshire held them at bay.'

There was criticism in some quarters of Van der Merwe's failure to declare on the previous evening, but equally some who found justification in it by having reduced MCC to 100/7. In the face of uncertainty there will never be agreement on the appropriate degree of risk, but in this case Van der Merwe may have missed an opportunity to give South Africa a morale-booster going into the final Test. This overly defensive approach did not, however, deter the South African selectors from choosing Van der Merwe as captain for the forthcoming tour of England.

South Africa made only one change for the final Test at Port Elizabeth, bringing in Macaulay for Partridge. England opted for Murray, England's reserve wicketkeeper to open with Boycott, leaving Brearley to wait another 11 years for his first Test cap. England could also have called on John Edrich, who was coaching in South Africa to open with Boycott, but, for some unexplained reason, chose not to. Cartwright, who in his early career with Warwickshire was an opening batsman, would probably have been preferred to Murray but he was injured, as were Price and Brown. England were forced to call on Ken Palmer, the Somerset fast-medium bowler, who was coaching in South Africa, as a replacement bowler. Allen was also recalled. It was something of a surprise that Parks held on to the wicketkeeping position, as Murray was generally regarded as his superior as a gloveman.

South Africa won the toss and chose to bat on a docile pitch. An opening partnership of 114 between Goddard (61) and Barlow (69) set them well on their way to a big score. Bland, not at his best, made 48 and at close of play South Africa were 262/3 with Graeme Pollock 56 not out. England's bowlers had stuck to the task tirelessly for scant reward. The following day, after Pithey and Waite, playing his last Test, departed, Pollock was joined by Van der Merwe and the pair made hay, putting on 113 for the sixth wicket. Pollock was finally out caught and bowled by Allen off a very hard-hit drive for 137. 'If Allan hadn't caught it', said Goddard, 'it would have drilled a hole right through him.'[128] Van der Merwe later went for 66, giving Palmer his first and only Test wicket. The South African innings finally closed on 502, an hour before the end of play on the second day. England had bowled 189 overs, Boycott 26 of them, Palmer 35 and Thomson 47. At one point Thomson bowled 21 overs in succession for 27 runs and two wickets, a remarkable feat of accuracy. In the remaining period England lost Murray lbw to Macaulay. The following morning, after Titmus the nightwatchman was yorked by Pollock, Dexter entered and played in fine style until a mix-up with Boycott led to him being run out, both batsmen finishing up at the same end. Boycott had called for a quick single, then changed his mind. In came Barrington and both batsmen played defensively until tea. Barrington finally departed for 72 and Boycott for 117. All the

128 *The Trevor Goddard Story*, Graham Short.

later batsmen chipped in with useful contributions and England finished up with 435. The innings had lasted 208 overs, and only two hours and one day remained to produce a result. South Africa scored 62 runs in the last session, putting them 129 ahead with one day left. When play resumed Mike set an ultra-defensive field to ensure South Africa did not build up a substantial lead. It did not endear him to the spectators or the South African press, but he was determined not to let the series slip from his grasp at the eleventh hour. The last day was noteworthy for little other than Graeme Pollock's 77 not out against a tired attack. When Goddard declared at lunch, England needed 246 to win in four hours. Boycott was out early on, but the weather settled the outcome, persistent rain bringing the match and the series to a premature end. Mike was unrepentant about his defensive tactics in the final two Tests. 'You obviously try your hardest to win, but if you can't, you make damn well sure you don't lose.'

England's tour of South Africa was indisputably a great success in terms of results, with one win in the Tests, four drawn games and victories in nearly all the other matches. Charles Fortune in his book *MCC in South Africa 1964/65* gives great credit to Mike for this. He writes:

> 'On the field his captaincy always had plan and purpose. The purpose may not always have made much for popular appeal but always it made matters more difficult for his opponents. Never once throughout the tour did we ever see or hear Mike Smith specifically asserting authority, but authority he always had and a great deal of warm respect as well. It was his fixed belief that his task was to lead England to victory in the series: if this could best be achieved by defensive field placings, slow over rates and other manoeuvres that were within the laws, then use such tactics when they served.

> Smith can with some justification claim that he achieved victory slightly against the odds and the overall run of play. But I think there will be some shaking of heads at Lord's and I would not give Mike Smith more than an even chance of the captaincy for the MCC Australian tour of 1965/66.'

Charles was wrong about that!

Trevor Goddard had this to say about Mike, 'I cannot say that I enjoyed playing against Mike Smith on the field, but I have not met a nicer chap than he is and it is a long time since England have had such a genuine and well-meaning fellow as skipper. He and Donald Carr were tact and dignity itself.'[129]

In his summary of the tour for *Wisden*, Basil Easterbrook wrote: 'MCC have sent more powerful teams from Lord's than this one, but never one superior in corporate effort on the playing pitch and harmony in the pavilion. Manager and captain set the tone by behaving naturally and unchangingly to all with whom they had to deal. On any occasion which offered for fun they identified themselves as members of the team.'[130]

Barrington topped the England Test match batting averages with 508 runs at 101.60, followed by Barber with 290 at 72.50, Dexter 344 at 57.33 and Boycott 298 at 49.66. Three other batsmen, Parfitt, Parks and Mike, averaged over 40. Allen was the most successful bowler with 17 wickets at 26.94. Titmus took 18 at 38.55, Thomson nine, Price eight and Boycott five. Mike took the most catches, ten, and Parks eight. It is most unusual for the wicketkeeper not to collect the most victims in a series – clearly a testimony to Mike's exceptional ability and athleticism at short leg. Brearley, Hobbs and Brown did not play in any Test matches

---

129 *The Trevor Goddard Story,* Graham Short.

130 *Wisden Cricketers' Almanack 1965 edition.*

but made useful contributions in the provincial matches. Brearley started well but faded as the tour progressed, making fewer than 200 runs in his last 14 innings. Such was his deterioration that John Murray was preferred to him as a makeshift opener in the final Test after Barber had returned home. He earned the nickname of 'the refugee' for his less than sartorial appearance. Hobbs picked up 27 wickets and fielded so well that he was frequently used as 12th man in the Test matches, which earned him the sobriquet 'the waiter'. Brown, an eternal trier, took 23 wickets, but was never properly able to adapt his bowling to less helpful South African pitches. 'David and I did make another useful contribution at the end of the tour,' says Robin with a chuckle. 'We were entrusted with bringing the cricket bags back from South Africa.'[131]

For South Africa, Bland scored 572 runs at 71.50, Graeme Pollock 459 at 57.37, Barlow 558 at 55.80, Pithey 462 at 51.33 and Goddard 405 at 40.50. Peter Pollock was the only bowler to take more than ten wickets with 12 at 37.08. McKinnon got eight, Harry Bromfield seven and Partridge and Goddard six each. From the above it is clear that batsmen dominated the series, but England were vastly superior in the spin department.

131 Conversation with Robin Hobbs.

CHAPTER 18

Defeat by the South African Tourists

WARWICKSHIRE HAD a very disappointing season in 1965, dropping to 11th position in the County Championship, winning only five matches, losing five and drawing 18, several on account of the weather. They lost the services of Ray Hitchcock and Norman Horner, who only played in two matches. Both had given sterling service to the club, Hitchcock both on and off the field, and both were model professionals and excellent team players. The side was also weakened by Test match calls on Mike and Bob Barber who both played in all six Tests that summer, three against New Zealand and three against South Africa. Of the ten Championship matches without this pair, Warwickshire lost two, drew seven and won only one. Had it not been for these call-ups, both would have undoubtedly scored 1,000 Championship runs. Jim Stewart had another good season, topping the Warwickshire averages with 1,175 runs at 39.16 and scoring the only Warwickshire century that season.

It was pleasing to see the development of Dennis Amiss and John Jameson, who were the only other two to score 1,000 runs. At the start of the season Amiss, who had only played four first-team matches in 1964, had been experiencing doubts over whether he would command a regular place in the side. After the first winter net session he found himself in the showers with

Mike and, seeking reassurance, told him that Gloucestershire had shown some interest in signing him. 'Should I stay or go?' he asked Mike, only to receive the rather dispiriting response of 'Suit yourself.'[132] There is no doubt Amiss would have preferred a more encouraging reply, but, whether or not this non-committal response was a deliberate ploy, it had the effect of producing in Amiss a strong desire to prove himself. He was awarded his county cap later that season and never looked back, at least not as far as Warwickshire were concerned, although his England career was to have a few stutters.

In the bowling department, Tom Cartwright was arguably by now the best medium-pace seam bowler in England and he headed the Warwickshire bowling averages with 94 wickets at 13.45 and finished fourth in the national averages. In the only match Warwickshire won without Mike and Barber against Middlesex, Cartwright took 12 wickets in the match for 100 runs. Jack Bannister took 75 wickets at 18.93 and David Brown 56 at 26.19. Rudi Webster was a useful addition to the pace attack when he was available. Spin bowling was still Warwickshire's Achilles heel and Basil Bridge, who played hardly any matches, was not re-engaged at the end of the season. Barber was used infrequently and John Jameson even less, although he performed the unlikely feat of a hat-trick against Gloucestershire when he polished off their innings with his off-breaks. After he had taken the first two wickets, Tom Cartwright said he would eat his hat if he got the hat-trick but, according to John, he never fulfilled his promise. In the Gillette Cup, Warwickshire reached the semi-final stage, beating Cambridgeshire, Lancashire and Hampshire easily. They then lost to Yorkshire, the eventual winners, by 20 runs in the semi-final. Having bowled Yorkshire out for 177, they contributed

132 *Not Out at Close of Play*, Dennis Amiss.

to their own downfall with five run-outs (Billy Ibadulla, Amiss, Stewart, Cartwright and Webster). Mike still has nightmares about hitting a gentle Don Wilson full toss to Fred Trueman at mid-on when well set.

Mike retained the England captaincy for the three-match series against New Zealand and the three-match series against South Africa which followed immediately afterwards. Both Ted Dexter and Colin Cowdrey, previous England captains, were happy to play under him and Mike felt there was never any problem with the arrangement. Cowdrey in fact played in all six Tests.

England went into the first Test at Edgbaston against New Zealand with the nucleus of the successful team in South Africa, but also including Cowdrey, with Trueman and Fred Rumsey as the opening bowlers. Rumsey had made his debut the previous summer against the Australians at Old Trafford and this was his second Test match. The batting line-up proved too strong for the New Zealand bowlers who, with the exception of Mike, lbw to the 19-year-old left-arm fast bowler Richard Collinge for a duck, all made runs. Boycott and Barber put on 54 for the first wicket, Dexter made 57, Barrington 137 in over six hours and Cowdrey 85 in England's total of 435.

As recounted by Fred Rumsey, at the start of the New Zealand innings, Mike asked him which end he wanted. Rumsey, somewhat taken aback, being junior to Trueman, said, 'Shouldn't you be asking Fred first which end he wants?' Mike retorted, 'Are you the England captain?' 'No skipper,' replied Fred meekly. 'So, which end do you want?' repeated Mike.[133] In the end it made little difference, as New Zealand succumbed to the spinners, being all out for 116 with Fred Titmus taking 4-18 and Barber 2-7. They were not helped by the loss of the 41-year-old Bert Sutcliffe, who

133 Conversation with Fred Rumsey

was forced to retire hurt on 4 after being struck behind the ear after ducking into a Trueman delivery which did not get up as much as expected. He had been the mainstay of New Zealand's batting for the last two decades but was clearly past his best and had been backing away. At one point Trueman had ribbed him with the comment, 'If you back away any further, you'll be in the bus queue for Birmingham.' At the lunch interval, according to Rumsey, he and Fred were summoned to the committee room where both captains, the New Zealand team manager and the England selectors were gathered. Both Freds were asked to stop bowling bouncers at Sutcliffe on the understanding that this was to be his final Test match. This request was greeted by an astonished expletive from Yorkshire's Fred and this weapon in the fast bowler's armoury was reluctantly laid aside.[134] Following on, New Zealand made a much better effort in their second innings, scoring 413. Sutcliffe, under the agreed protection, made 53 and the 19-year-old Vic Pollard[135] 81 not out. Barber took 4-132, Titmus 2-85 and Trueman 3-79. They had managed to avoid an innings defeat, but it did not prevent England from knocking off the runs required to win by nine wickets, Barber departing with only three required for victory in trying to finish the match with a six after an entertaining half-century.

The second Test followed a similar pattern, the only difference being that New Zealand batted first after winning the toss. They must have regretted the decision as they struggled against the England pace bowling attack of Trueman, Rumsey and John Snow

134 Conversation with Fred Rumsey.

135 Vic Pollard (1945–) was born in Lancashire and moved with his family in 1952 to New Zealand. He was fast-tracked into the New Zealand side after only six first-class matches for their 1964/65 tour of India and Pakistan where he played in all four Tests against India and three against Pakistan. He was a devout Christian whose refusal to play on Sundays probably cost him the captaincy of New Zealand. He became a lay preacher after retirement from first-class cricket in 1975 and later entered politics.

who had been bought in for his Test debut to replace Cartwright. At one point New Zealand were 28/4, Rumsey having taken all four wickets for seven runs, and at lunch they were not much better off at 62/6. A seventh-wicket stand between Pollard (55) and Bruce Taylor (51), brought in to replace Sutcliffe, realised 92, but after they were out, the innings fizzled out for 175. Rumsey finished with 4-25, Trueman 2-40, Snow 2-27 and Titmus 2-25.

Barrington had been omitted as a disciplinary measure for slow scoring in the previous Test in favour of Peter Parfitt, but it was Cowdrey with 119, Dexter with 62 and Mike with 44 who were principally responsible for England's total of 307. As before, New Zealand did a lot better in their second innings, with Graham Dowling, Barry Sinclair and Pollard making half-centuries in a total of 347. Snow took two wickets, Titmus two and Barber three. Trueman finished wicketless in what was to be his final Test. He had given England great service over the past 13 years and had created a record with 307 Test wickets.

Needing 216 to win, England again made a good start with 64 for the first wicket but because of time lost for rain on the final day, they needed to make 152 to win in three hours. A partnership of 126 between Boycott (76) and Dexter (80 not out) brought England to within 22 and Dexter and Cowdrey finished off the job to bring England victory by seven wickets with a quarter of an hour to spare.

Boycott and Dexter were unavailable for the third Test at Headingley; Boycott was injured and Dexter more seriously, having broken a leg when it became trapped between his car and a warehouse door, which effectively curtailed his career at the age of 30. This Test was made memorable by a marathon innings of 310 not out by a reinstated John Edrich in just under nine hours. Together with a forgiven Barrington, they put on 369 for England's second wicket, Barrington making 165 in five and a half hours. Mike declared at 546/4 on the afternoon of the second day.

David Larter had replaced Snow and England played a second spinner, Ray Illingworth. New Zealand were soon in trouble at 53/3 and the later batsmen succumbed to Illingworth, who took 4-42. Larter finished with 4-66 and New Zealand were all out for 193, the captain John Reid making 53 and Bryan Yuile 46. Made to follow on, they could only manage 166 second time round to lose by an innings and 187 runs. Pollard made a good half-century in the second innings, bringing his aggregate for the three matches to 281 at an average of 56.20. Rumsey took 3-49, Larter 2-54 and Titmus 5-19.

It was a disappointing tour from New Zealand's point of view. Of the 19 matches played they won three, lost six and drew ten. They were outclassed by England in the Test series, neither being able to put a decent first-innings score on the board nor to restrict England when bowling. Edrich scored 310 not out in his only innings, Barrington 300 at an average of 150.00, Dexter 199 at 99.50, Cowdrey 221 at 73.66 and Boycott 157 at 52.33. Mike only scored 46 runs in the series but was hardly required to bat. Titmus was England's most successful bowler with 15 wickets at 15.60 and Rumsey and Barber both took nine wickets. No New Zealand batsman, apart from Pollard, made many runs. Dick Motz took 11 wickets and Richard Collinge eight.

South Africa were likely to be a different proposition, however. Smarting from their recent home defeat, they came to England under a new captain, Peter van der Merwe. They had an indifferent start to the tour against the counties, going down to Derbyshire and drawing the next four but by the first Test Eddie Barlow, Ali Bacher and Denis Lindsay had all made centuries and Dennis Gamsy, Tiger Lance, Colin Bland and Graeme Pollock half-centuries. Bacher, Jackie Botten and Richard Dumbrill were all making their debut for South Africa and David Brown was given his first outing after having toured South Africa in the winter without having played a Test. He joined Rumsey and Larter as the fast bowling attack, England leaving out Illingworth. Boycott was fit again and resumed the opener's slot with Edrich dropping down to number three and Parfitt losing out as a consequence.

South Africa won the toss and batted in front of a capacity Lord's crowd who had expectations of an exciting match. They were not to be disappointed. After Rumsey claimed the early wicket of Barlow, neatly caught at leg slip by Barber, Lance and Lindsay put on 59 for the second wicket before Brown removed Lance for his first Test wicket and Rumsey accounted for Lindsay. Graeme Pollock (56) and Bland (39) then put on 80 for the fourth wicket. A mini-collapse then ensued and with the score at 212/8 an inadequate total looked on the cards. Resolute batting by the last three South African batsmen, Botten, Peter Pollock and Harry Bromfield, took the score to 280. Brown took 3-44, Rumsey 3-84, Titmus 2-59 and Barber 2-30.

England replied with 82 for the first wicket, Boycott making 31 and Barber 56. An innings of 91 from the ever-prolific Barrington and 59 from Titmus enabled England to reach 338, giving them a handy first-innings lead of 58. The most memorable feature of the innings was the wonderful fielding of Bland, who ran out both Barrington and Parks with direct hits on the stumps. South Africa made 248 in their second innings with Barlow 52 and Bland 70 being the main contributors. At 120/4 South Africa had been in some danger but Bland saved the day with good support from Bacher and Van der Merwe. Brown and Rumsey again each took three wickets.

England were left to score 191 to win in just under four hours, a task which should have been well within their capabilities, but the innings never really got going, Cowdrey top-scoring with 37.

Matters were not helped by Edrich being struck a sickening blow on the forehead from a Peter Pollock bouncer which forced him to retire hurt and which put him out of action for the rest of the match and the series. Dumbrill was South Africa's most successful bowler with 4-30 in 18 overs. After falling well behind the clock and losing seven wickets for 140, England were content to bat out for a draw.

For the second Test at Trent Bridge England made three changes. Edrich was replaced by Parfitt, and Snow and Cartwright came in for Brown and Rumsey. Rumsey, who was in the original 12, but suffering from a minor thigh strain, was walked round the ground by the chairman of selectors, Doug Insole, before the game and was effectively talked out of playing lest he break down. He maintains that there was an implicit promise that it would not affect his England career and still regrets volunteering to stand down as he was never invited to play for England again.[136] Asked to field first, England started well and had South Africa in serious trouble at 43/4 early on, Cartwright accounting for Barlow, Lance and Lindsay and, according to one newspaper report, 'threatening total destruction'. With much depending on him, Graeme Pollock, fresh from an unbeaten double century against Kent, played cautiously at first, but after lunch his innings blossomed with an array of glorious drives in one of the finest innings ever seen at Trent Bridge. He made 91 of the next 102 runs before he was finally out to Cartwright for a magnificent 125 which set South Africa well on the way to victory. Van der Merwe's 38 and Dumbrill's 30 helped the total to a respectable 269. Cartwright was the pick of the bowlers with 6-94 but unfortunately he dislocated his right thumb going for a caught and bowled off Dumbrill. He pulled it back into place himself and carried on bowling, getting two further wickets but, after being driven to hospital by Doug

136 Conversation with Fred Rumsey.

Insole, it was discovered to be broken and he was unable to bowl in South Africa's second innings. This sadly proved to be Tom's last appearance for England, although he was to continue to trouble batsmen on the county circuit for many years to come.

England were not able to match this total despite 105 from Cowdrey, 41 from Barber and 32 from Mike. England, required to bat for half an hour at the end of the first day, had made a disastrous start, losing Boycott and Barrington to Peter Pollock with only eight runs on the board. Titmus had come in as nightwatchman to successfully prevent the fall of any more wickets but on the following day, after hopes had been raised by a partnership of 92 between Cowdrey and Mike, Pollock and Botten wrapped up the innings. England were all out for 240 and Pollock had taken 5-53 in 24 hostile overs.

Graeme Pollock made a half-century in South Africa's second innings in a third-wicket stand of 99 with Barlow (76) and, with 67 from Bacher at number six, South Africa were able to reach a total of 289, giving them a lead of 318. Larter took 5-68, Snow 3-83 and Titmus 2-46. Boycott also bowled 26 overs as a stand-in for Cartwright but took no wickets.

England had to bat for half an hour on Saturday evening and after Barber was out caught at the wicket off Pollock for 1, Titmus was sent in as nightwatchman. This time he was not able to see the day out, also being snapped up by Lindsay off McKinnon for 4. A second nightwatchman was then employed as Snow joined Boycott at the crease. When play resumed on Monday Snow did not last long, being bowled by Botten for nought. Worse was to follow, Barrington edging one off a Peter Pollock bouncer to Lindsay for 1. With England's score now at 13/4, South Africa had their tails up and when Cowdrey was out for 20, stumped off McKinnon, the writing was on the wall with England at 41/5. Boycott was next to go, bowled by an arm-ball from the left-arm spinner McKinnon which he maintains to this day he spotted but did not react fast enough to keep out. He had been at the crease for two hours and 20 minutes for 16 runs. Mike and Parfitt then knuckled down in an attempt to rebuild England's innings, but Mike fell lbw to Graeme Pollock with the score at 114/7. Parfitt and Parks then cast caution to the wind and went on the attack in a stand that produced 93 runs at more than a run a minute. It could not last, however, and Parfitt finally fell for 86 to the hero of the hour Pollock, who quickly finished off the tail by dismissing Larter and Cartwright, who had gamely gone out to bat. England were all out for 224 and South Africa were one up in the series, having won by 94 runs on the fourth day. Pollock finished with another five-wicket haul, giving him the excellent match figures of 10-87. McKinnon took 3-50 but it was really the Pollock brothers' show, Graeme making 184 runs in the match and Peter taking ten wickets. The match raised the issue of the wisdom of employing nightwatchmen which, by using two in this case, pushed Parks down from number seven to number nine and left him stranded on 44 not out.

And so to the final Test at the Oval, with the series at stake. England brought in the Lancashire pair of Brian Statham, now 35, and Ken Higgs, for whom it was his first game for England. One wonders why Statham had not been considered for the first two Tests, although he hadn't played for England since 1963. Brown, now fit again, came back in as the third pace bowler. Boycott was dropped and Eric Russell brought in to open. South Africa kept the same XI with Lindsay moving up to open and Lance dropping down the order.

Mike won the toss and put South Africa in. The move paid off as England dismissed them for 208, Lance benefitting from his reshuffled position to number six by top-scoring with 69. Statham more than justified his recall with 5-40 and Higgs his inclusion with 4-47.

England now needed a good total to seize the initiative but it was not forthcoming. Barber uncharacteristically took two and a quarter hours to make 40, Cowdrey almost four hours to make 58 and Barrington an hour and a half for 18. Mike failed again, falling lbw to Peter Pollock for 7, and only Parks with a lively 42 demonstrated that the pitch, slow though it was, was not a minefield. Peter Pollock again took the bowling honours with 5-43. England finished a disappointing six runs behind on first innings.

South Africa were well placed at the end of the third day on 160/3 with Bacher not out on 70 but he went early the following day, bringing Lance in to join Bland. The pair then proceeded to put on 96 for the fifth wicket before Lance was out for 53. Van der Merwe departed without scoring, bowled by Higgs, but Bland and Dumbrill then put on 83 for the seventh wicket. Bland was in magnificent form and drove powerfully for his 127 to put South Africa in a commanding position. They were all out eventually for 392, leaving England 399 to win in seven hours – a pretty tall order. England batted with much more purpose in their second innings with Russell, Barrington and Cowdrey all making scores in the 70s. At tea, England needed 109 in 85 minutes with Cowdrey and Mike at the crease and six wickets standing. Unfortunately, after about half an hour rain stopped play for the day, killing off the chance of an exciting finish, with England on 308/4.

And so South Africa avenged their home defeat by England by the same 1-0 margin. It had been a good series, played in a friendly spirit with a lot of attractive cricket and exciting matches, even the two that had finished as draws. South Africa were worthy winners, largely thanks to the Pollock brothers and Colin Bland. Graeme Pollock scored 291 runs at an average of 48.50 and Bland 286 at 47.66. Peter Pollock took 20 wickets at 18.30, Dumbrill, McKinnon and Botten eight each. For England, Cowdrey scored

327 runs at 65.40 and Parfitt 174 at 43.50. Mike did not prosper with the bat, scoring 112 runs at 22.40 but his captaincy could not be faulted. England used ten bowlers in the series – Higgs, Brown and Titmus took eight wickets each, Statham and Larter seven each and Rumsey and Cartwright six each.

CHAPTER 19

Captaining England in Australia and New Zealand, 1965/66

THE TEAM that left England for the 1965/66 tour of Australia was considered by the majority of sportswriters and commentators in both hemispheres to be one of the weakest to visit Australia since the Second World War. There was no Trueman, Statham, Tyson, Lock or Laker, nor any Dexter, May or Graveney. Nobody gave them much of a chance. Apart from Jeff Jones and David Brown, there was little genuine pace, with Ken Higgs and David Larter the other fast-medium bowlers. In Fred Titmus and David Allen England did have two top-class off-spinners and Bob Barber and Ken Barrington, though principally batsmen, as leg-spinners. Cowdrey, Barrington, Parfitt and Mike were the key batsmen along with the four openers Barber, Boycott, Edrich and Russell. They also took two wicketkeepers, Parks and Murray. Although England had lost the second Test and subsequently the home series against South Africa in the summer of 1965, the selectors had kept faith with Mike ahead of Colin Cowdrey, Dexter's career having been effectively curtailed by his car accident. 'Retired, ran himself over,' should have been the *Wisden* entry, sportswriter John Clarke callously suggested.[137] EW Swanton, in spite of his probable

137 *With England in Australia*, John Clarke.

preference for Cowdrey, applauded the decision on the basis of Mike's 'good leadership qualities of serenity, fair-mindedness and unselfishness which have made him so popular with the players'. Mike's appointment was also welcomed by his opposite number Bobby Simpson, who had captained the Australian side in England in 1964. He stated that he was pleased that Mike had been given the job and that it would be nice to be on the same wavelength, perhaps implying that he had not been with previous captains. In his foreword to John Clarke's book covering the tour, *With England in Australia*, Simpson writes: 'Although this year a greater friendship and understanding existed between the two sides, it did not lessen the will to win by either.'[138]

For the first time ever the team flew out with the obvious advantage of being able to make the journey more quickly and avoid the perils of seasickness. What could have been lost, though, was the opportunity for bonding that a lengthy sea voyage provides, but the able leadership of team manager Billy Griffith, assistant manager Jack Ikin and the man-management skills of Mike would have soon compensated for this. Following the appointment of Billy Griffith as team manager it was announced that he would have overall control of cricket with a view to ensuring that attractive, attacking cricket would be played. This was an unusual, never to be repeated precedent, which Mike with his easy-going temperament was prepared to accept. At a meeting at Lord's when this concept was being discussed, Gubby Allen posed the question as to who would have control on the field. Mike remembers Billy Griffith immediately shouting 'Mike', which forestalled any further discussion of the issue.

The team, as was the custom, broke the journey by stopping off in Colombo, where they played two one-day matches on successive

138 *With England in Australia*, John Clarke.

days, the first against the President's XI and the second against Ceylon. Both were one-innings matches and both were drawn, with Barber making 64 not out in the first. In the second England were lucky to escape with a draw, having been bowled out for 127, only Cowdrey with 47 making a score. The off-spinner Neil Chanmugam took 5-26. Four years later he was to take eight wickets against the touring Australians, including Bill Lawry twice. He was later to marry the daughter of Ceylon's cricket captain Fredrick de Saram – a good way of keeping your place in the side! Ceylon's innings was interrupted by a monsoon-like storm at 27/1 which turned the ground into a quagmire. For the sake of the 15,000 spectators Mike agreed to play on using only slow bowlers. Ceylon finished only 50 runs short for the loss of one wicket when time ran out.

After a stop-off in Singapore, where they had left an unwell Geoff Boycott in hospital, the MCC team arrived in Perth. Billy Griffith and Mike had to go through the usual PR formalities, not something that Mike particularly relished, but he handled it laconically at the first press conference, saying, 'We have come here to get back that miserable urn, not at all costs, but by playing hard but good cricket.'[139] Generally speaking, relations with the press were convivial, somewhat in contrast to England's previous tour. Then, they were more interested in Dexter's beautiful model wife Susan than the cricket, and the Reverend David Sheppard was tricked by a rogue journalist into making a comment about Sydney's red light district, which made the headlines the following day suggesting he was enquiring about it.

MCC started their tour with a match against a Western Australia Country XI in Moora, a small farming community some 100 miles north of Perth. This they won easily by 82 runs,

139 *Quest for the Ashes*, Ken Mackay.

Edrich making 66 and Parks 48. Barber took five wickets with his leg-breaks. Two days later they took on Western Australia, whose side included Graham McKenzie, Tony Lock and three other former Test players. MCC achieved a narrow victory by nine runs, following a declaration by Mike which almost cost them the match. Apparently, Mike, in the spirit of the earlier discussions at Lord's, had consulted with his team manager on the timing of the declaration, saying 'When do you think I should declare?', to which Billy Griffith had replied 'Now!' 'That's the last time I ask for that sort of advice,' said Mike. In fairness though, the target of 301 to win in the fourth innings was not overly generous, as they could not have bargained for two Western Australians, Peter Kelly and Murray Vernon, making centuries in the run chase. For MCC, Barber and Parks both made centuries, Russell 81 and Mike 67 not out. At 244/5 Western Australia were heading for a win but Jones, Higgs and Larter wrapped up the tail almost on the point of time. A 21-year-old Terry Jenner took 4-72 in MCC's second innings against batsmen going for quick runs. The game had been halted for half an hour at around lunchtime on the final day so that players and spectators could listen to a broadcast of the Melbourne Cup – not something that would have happened at Lord's!

The next game, also in Perth against a Combined XI, ended in an evenly-matched, rain-affected draw with Bob Barber and Mike both scoring centuries, Edrich making 92 and Titmus 69. For the Combined XI Bob Cowper gave a foretaste of things to come with 89 and 122 not out and Peter Burge restated his class with half-centuries in each innings.

The MCC team then travelled to Adelaide for their match against South Australia with Geoff Boycott, now happily recovered from illness, playing his first match in Australia. To give Mike a break, Cowdrey took over the captaincy for this match, which for South Australia included a 21-year-old Ian Chappell.

Put in by Cowdrey, South Australia were dismissed for a paltry 103 in two and a half hours, the bowling honours being shared by Larter, Brown and Allen. In reply MCC made a good start with 116 for the first wicket (Boycott 94, Edrich 61) and with Barrington weighing in with his first good score of the tour (69), MCC totalled 310. Cricketers have long memories and nearly 60 years later Parfitt is still cursing his bad luck after being given out caught off his arm at backward short leg for 1 in the first innings. He departed rubbing the spot ostentatiously. Boycott was disgusted with himself for having missed out on a century, ruefully lamenting, 'What will they say in Yorkshire, caught off a full toss in the nineties?'[140] This was not to be the end of his troubles, however, as before the end of the match he went down with sciatica and finished up in hospital again, this time in Adelaide. It was suspected that the problem had been caused by a badly aimed needle intended to cure his earlier stomach complaint touching his sciatic nerve. Frustratingly for him, this was to keep him out of action for the next four matches. He was visited in his sick bed by the other openers, where he complained about them making his runs, vowing to get his place back when he had recovered. Bob Barber replied that he would be quite happy to spend his tour on the beach if he were to be the one displaced.[141] EW Swanton also visited Boycott in hospital, becoming acutely aware for the first time of Boycott's intensity and passion for the game.[142]

South Australia fared much better in their second innings, with Les Favell, their experienced captain and former Australian Test player, making 96 and Lynn Marks 67 in a first-wicket partnership of 150. An innings of 61 from wicketkeeper Barry Jarman, for many years Wally Grout's understudy and strongly fancied to

140 *Quest for the Ashes*, Ken Mackay.

141 Conversation with Bob Barber.

142 *Swanton in Australia with MCC 1946-1975*, EW Swanton.

replace him during this Test series, and 83 from 22-year-old Alan Shiell helped Australia to a total of 364. Brown and Higgs with four wickets apiece were MCC's most successful bowlers. It had been hard work on a hot day. MCC duly knocked off the 158 required for the loss of four wickets, Barrington completing his second fifty of the match.

Following a light-hearted one-day match against Victoria Country Districts in Hamilton which the tourists won by six wickets, MCC took on Victoria at Melbourne in what was to be their first defeat of the tour, the first by a Victoria side against MCC for 41 years. The home side posted a total of 384/7 declared, thanks mainly to 153 from opposing captain Bill Lawry, 60 not out from wicketkeeper Dave Cowper, Bob Cowper's elder brother, 59 not out from Graeme Watson and 53 from 23-year-old Ian Redpath. David Brown maintained his good form with 4-74 but, to quote one English journalist, the bowling overall had about as much penetration as a cardboard dagger. MCC's 211 left a substantial deficit and although they restricted Victoria to 165 in their second innings (Lawry 61), they finished up losing by 32 runs despite a valiant 158 from Barrington and 52 from Cowdrey. Two run-outs at the end of the innings did not help the cause. Mike's contribution was 46 not out in the first innings and 22 in the second. Keith Stackpole took four first-innings wickets for Victoria, Alan Connolly four in the second and Graeme Watson three.

A controversial incident occurred in Victoria's first innings shortly after Lawry had reached his century when he trod on his wicket after stepping back to pull a ball from Titmus. The umpire, who was watching the flight of the ball, missed this and in spite of protests from the MCC fielders, Lawry was given not out. Lawry was a self-professed non-walker but, in fairness, on this occasion he maintained that he neither saw nor heard anything but later agreed he must have touched the stumps with his foot. Mike's 'forget-it' gesture quickly defused the situation.

After this defeat a one-day game was scheduled against a Victoria Country Districts XI at Euroa, a small town some 100 miles north of Melbourne, whose only prior claim to fame was that its National Bank branch there was robbed by Ned Kelly and his gang in 1878. On this occasion the locals were robbed of the opportunity to see the MCC team as no play was possible because of rain, which was quite bizarre, as this area had not seen a cloud for several months. Following what had proved to be an unnecessary detour, MCC travelled to Sydney for their encounter with the New South Wales side captained by Brian Booth, Australia's vice-captain. The team included Doug Walters, who was to have a major impact on the Test series. Born and raised in the small agricultural town of Dungog, where he worked on his father's farm, Walters hit a sparkling 129 out of a total of 288, his third-wicket partnership with Booth (80) yielding 142. This was in reply to a massive 527/6 declared in which seven MCC batsmen scored 50s but none centuries. A superb opening stand of 151 between Barber and Eric Russell in just over 100 minutes set them on their way. Titmus, who was now coming into his own as a batsman, scored 80 not out.

Asked to follow on, New South Wales could muster only 240 in their second innings in which Mike took five catches, including three exceptional ones at short leg. Titmus took 5-45 in New South Wales' second innings to go with his 3-54 in the first. With MCC needing only two runs for victory, Booth asked Barry Rothwell, a batsman, to open the bowling, whereupon Barber thumped Rosswell's first ball, a full-toss, straight to mid-off to be caught for a duck. Rothwell took only one other wicket in his entire career. Parfitt took two off Rothwell's next ball to win the match. Worryingly, though, Jeff Jones was banned from bowling during the second innings for running on the pitch. The English press generally agreed with the umpire's decision, but Peter Smith of the *Daily Sketch* called it 'hasty and ill-advised' and Crawford White of the *Daily Express* 'a brutal punishment that never fitted the crime'. Some work would need to be done to iron out Jones's follow-through to get England's main strike bowler ready for the first Test. An Australian evening newspaper carried the headline 'English Bowler Banned', a double insult to Jones, who was born in Wales.[143]

MCC then moved on to Brisbane to play Queensland. Boycott, now recovered, opened with Barber, whose turn it was to fall ill. He was forced to retire on 21 not out and took no further part in the game. Batting first, centuries by Eric Russell and John Edrich, 80 not out from Barrington and 51 not out from the reinvented all-rounder Titmus took MCC to a formidable total of 452/5 declared. Queensland replied with 222 all out, largely thanks to Peter Burge's 114 not out. This time, for whatever reason, Mike did not enforce the follow-on. If he had wanted to give Boycott some more batting practice after his disappointing first-innings dismissal for 30, it did not work, as Boycott was out without scoring after touching an outswinger from Peter Allan. A brisk century stand between Edrich and Russell enabled MCC to declare at 123/2, before Russell was forced to retire with a hairline fracture of his right thumb. Queensland made a brave effort to score the 354 runs required to win and had reached 315/8 when bad light brought play to a close. Ken Higgs took 3-35 in Queensland's first innings and Titmus 3-56 in the second.

A one-day match against Queensland Country Districts XI followed the next day at Beaudesert, a town some 40 miles to the south of Brisbane in the Gold Coast hinterland. MCC won

143 *With England in Australia*, John Clarke.

by seven wickets with Barber, now recovered from his gastritis, scoring 56 not out in 35 minutes and Boycott 48 not out. One of Barber's sixes dented the bonnet of an Australian Broadcasting Corporation car, causing a flurry of anxious drivers to shift their vehicles to safer ground.

Two days later the first Test started in Brisbane. England were without Cowdrey, the latest victim to fall ill. Russell was declared fit to play but, after he split the webbing of his right hand while fielding, he was relegated from opening batsman to number 11. Boycott, who had originally been pencilled in at number six, took his place. Australia were without their captain Bobby Simpson, who had a broken wrist, and their leading fast bowler Graham McKenzie, who had back trouble. Ian Redpath, on debut, replaced Simpson and Peter Allan replaced McKenzie for what turned out to be his only Test. Brian Booth, standing in for Simpson as captain, on winning the toss, elected to bat after due consideration. Because of numerous interruptions for rain, there was never any likelihood of the match reaching a conclusion, particularly after play was completely washed out on the second day. Very early on in his innings, Lawry was once more the centre of controversy when he, according to some, turned a ball off his hip from Brown to be brilliantly caught down the leg side by Parks. Parks and Mike at short leg appealed but Lawry was given not out. He was later dropped by Barrington at slip on 32. He gave no further chances, going on doggedly to make 166 over seven hours. At the fall of the fourth wicket, Lawry was joined by the 19-year-old Doug Walters, fresh from his hundred at Sydney. Mike brought the field in to crowd the debutant but Walters, with attractive attacking shots, soon dispersed it. In the words of *The Australian*, 'Nothing seemed to worry him. He was powerful off the back foot, everything he did was positive and confident and he quickly gave the impression that hitting the ball was what he was there for and that was what he would do.' The contrast in styles between him and Lawry, playing with measured caution, was striking but the partnership flourished and had yielded 187 runs before Lawry finally departed, caught Parks (some would say for the second time), bowled Higgs. Walters, then on 87, a supposedly unlucky number for Australians, was joined by Tom Veivers. Walters progressed to 90 but became becalmed on this number for almost an hour. Four runs later a dog wandered on to the field and halted proceedings. While it was being pursued by an army of small boys trying to catch it, Walters merely sat on the pitch and waited for the drama to play out. On the resumption he took a two and then completed his century by on-driving Allen to the boundary. As Robert Gray wittily, if slightly inaccurately, put it in *The Australian*, 'At 98 [sic] in one's first Test, is no time to tangle with dogs and Englishmen in the afternoon sun.'

The 2,000 eager listeners in Walters' home town of Dungog must have roared their delight for their 'Dougie' along with the 9,000 spectators at the Gabba. The following day after Walters and Veivers had put on 100, and with Brown absent with a stomach strain, Boycott offered to take the new ball in tandem with Higgs. 'A new ball in a Test, Geoff, better make the most of it,' joked Veivers. Boycott's reply is unrecorded. Booth declared when Australia's total had reached 443/6 but the match was already into the fourth morning with only a miracle likely to produce a result. England's modest reply of 280 (Titmus 60, Barrington 53 and Parks 52) meant they did not avoid the follow-on, but insufficient time remained for Australia to bowl out England twice and the match petered out into a draw with England finishing on 183/3. Boycott contributed a stubborn 63 not out, although he was lucky to survive a 'handled the ball' incident when in ignorance of the law he diverted a ball from Peter Philpott with his hand when it was rolling back on to his stumps. Had anyone appealed, he would have been given out. 'I wouldn't do that again if I were you, matey, you might find yourself out,' said the keeper Wally Grout sternly.[144] Boycott, surprisingly, was unaware of the law. Earlier Barber had thumped it about a bit with gay abandon for 34 in spite of the necessity of saving the match; it was the only way he liked to play. As Ken Mackay, not known for his flamboyant batting as a player (hence his sarcastic nickname, 'Slasher') wrote, 'I don't quite go along with Bob's attitude. I know if I were Mike Smith I would have been having the tremors [sic] watching him waving his wand when the order must have been to consolidate. But one thing is certain. Whatever county Bob plays for at home, be it Warwickshire, as at present, or any other, that county will never go broke.'[145] 'Bob was a one-off,' says Mike with a grin. The highlight of the match was clearly Walters' 155 on debut, which produced almost 100 congratulatory telegrams, one of his team-mates even taking the opportunity to run a book on how many would be received. The papers the next day were full of unwanted comparisons to Don Bradman and Neil Harvey.

The next fixture two days later against the Prime Minister's XI, captained by Richie Benaud at Canberra's Manuka Oval, offered some light relief, with a young Paul Sheahan making a dazzling 79, Jim Burke 60 and Benaud, now retired from Test cricket, 45. The side also included Neil Harvey, Bob Cowper, Wally Grout and Wes Hall, who was playing club cricket in Sydney. England won by two wickets, scoring the last 90 runs in half an hour, Mike (51 not out) making the winning hit off the last ball of the day bowled by Burke, who, on a more serious occasion would probably have been no-balled for his suspect action. It was a pleasant interlude, with the cricket-loving Prime Minister, Sir Robert Menzies, who

144 *Quest for the Ashes*, Ken Mackay.

145 *Quest for the Ashes*, Ken Mackay.

was to leave office a few months later, speaking wittily at the post-match dinner. The team were all presented with a signed copy of the memorial address he gave at Winston Churchill's funeral earlier that year, while Jim Burke entertained everyone with his impersonations of Test cricketers.

Two further one-day matches against New South Wales Country Districts at Bathurst and Albury produced wins for MCC by five and six wickets respectively with Edrich scoring 70s in both, Barrington 61 in the first and Mike 81 in 69 minutes in the second. Barrington also took ten wickets in the two matches with his leg-breaks. England possibly missed a trick by not using him more in the Tests. A one-day game two days later at Mount Gambia against a South Australian Country XI was won by MCC by eight wickets, Boycott making 99, which, even given the lesser importance of the fixture, must have irked him, and Parfitt 52 not out.

The final first-class match before the second Test was against South Australia at Adelaide which MCC won by six wickets in spite of South Australia's first-innings total of 459/7, which Alan Shiell illuminated with a not-out double-century. After 23 matches for South Australia, at the age of 22 and with a glittering cricket career beckoning, he left the state side to become a cricket reporter for the *Adelaide Advertiser*, having based his decision on journalism providing a longer and more secure career than cricket. In that regard he was correct, as he was still writing 40 years later, but he could still perhaps have deferred his decision for a few years and added a few Test caps to his CV. In the match he was ably supported by Ian Chappell who made 59 and Barry Jarman with 70. MCC replied with 444 all out with Mike making 108, Murray 110, Barry Knight in his first match 79 and Ken Barrington 63. Les Favell sportingly declared South Australia's second innings at 253/4 with Chappell 113 not out but MCC knocked off the

270 needed for the loss of four wickets. Boycott and Barber put on 138 in 18 overs for the first wicket and with Cowdrey 63 not out and Knight 46 in 41 minutes, MCC cruised home with more than half an hour to spare.

Higgs, Brown and Larter were all unfit to play in the second Test at Melbourne, Higgs through illness, Brown with an elbow problem and Larter with a damaged heel. Knight, after his showing in the South Australia game was an obvious replacement, not least because he was the only other fast-medium bowler available. He had been flown over from England to cover for injured players and had quickly established himself as a valuable member of the squad. For Australia, Simpson replaced Booth as captain and Lawry's opening partner, and Redpath was dropped. McKenzie, now fit, was recalled in place of Allan. The latter, who had left the field in England's second innings in the first Test feeling unwell, was in the 12 but was omitted in favour of local boy Alan Connolly for whom it was his first Test match against England. Australia, batting first, compiled a useful total of 358, Simpson and Lawry putting on 93 for the first wicket. Bob Cowper, coming in at number four, just missed out on a century, falling to a catch at slip by Titmus when trying to cut Jones. Knight with 4-84 fully justified his summons from his Essex fireside. Jones, having overcome his follow-through problems, finished with 3-92.

England started well with Boycott and Barber putting on 98 for the first wicket and Edrich and Cowdrey following up with centuries. Parks with 71, Barrington with 63, Titmus with 56 not out and Mike with 41 gave England a very healthy 200-run lead. McKenzie's five wickets cost him 135 runs. When Australia batted again, the openers prospered with a partnership of 120 and centuries from Peter Burge and Walters ensured the draw. This was Walters' third successive century against the tourists and he was beginning to be hailed as a prodigy. His innings was witnessed by the only other Australian player to score centuries in his first two Test matches, Bill Ponsford. Things might have been different had Parks not missed Burge from a clear stumping chance off Barber from a ball which spun and jumped when he was on 34, or if Barber's shy at the stumps had not missed with Burge well out of his ground. Walters was also lucky to be given not out from a run-out before he had scored, a photo in a Melbourne newspaper clearly showing that he had not made the line. In most games of cricket there are at some stage critical potential turning points which are usually the result of either fielding lapses, rash strokes or umpiring errors. There is little doubt that if any of these things had gone England's way, they would have gone one-up in the series.

The third Test at Sydney started three days later with Booth again taking over the captaincy on account of Simpson having mysteriously contracted chickenpox; no one seemed to know from whom. According to Booth, Sir Donald Bradman, the chairman of selectors, had approached him at practice the previous day and said, 'Bob has chickenpox, Brian. You're captaining tomorrow.' Sincock was brought in for Tom Veivers and Neil Hawke replaced Alan Connolly. Grahame Thomas was given the opening slot in preference to Ian Redpath and with a half-century on debut did enough to hold his place for the rest of the series, but at number three. England went in unchanged except for Brown, who was now fit, replacing the unlucky Knight who had been England's most successful bowler in the previous Test.

Mike won the toss for the first time in the series and batted. What followed was the greatest opening partnership since the Second World War. In front of a full house Bob Barber played the innings of his life, flaying the Australian attack with an array of majestic drives and cuts. When his partner Boycott finally departed for 84 after four hours, caught and bowled Philpott off a checked drive, with the total at 234, England had put themselves in a match-winning position. Barber's innings of controlled aggression delighted even the Sydney Hill spectators, who gave him a standing ovation when he was finally out for 185. EW Swanton, covering the tour in Australia for the *Daily Telegraph*, in a piece of glorious prose, described the innings thus:

> 'Often in bleak moments do I cast back to Bob Barber's 185 in front of 40,000 on that sunny Friday in January '66. He batted without chance for five hours, starting decorously enough and then hitting the ball progressively harder and with superb disdain to every corner of the field. One recalls the exceptional vigour of his driving and how he brought his wrists into the cut, making room for the stroke. It made blissful watching to English eyes – to one pair in particular, for by a wonderful chance father Barber had flown in from home that very day.'

That magnificent innings will stay forever in the memory of those who were privileged to see it. It was a perfect example of what can be achieved when skill, adventure and judgement are applied in the right proportions. Walter Robins described it as the greatest innings he had ever seen by an Englishman on the Sydney Cricket Ground. The cricket that followed was always going to be a side-show but, after losing four quick wickets to Hawke (Barrington, Cowdrey, Mike and Brown), Edrich steadied the ship with a patient century the following day. After Titmus was out for 14, having passed the milestone of 1,000 runs and 100 wickets in Test cricket, a partnership of 55 for the last wicket between Allen and Jones enabled England to reach a total of 488. Allen had just gone to 50 when Jones was bowled by Hawke, who finished with 7-105. EW Swanton recalls passing the nets just after tea on the first day when England were 234/1, where he witnessed, to his surprise, Mike Smith bowling alone to Jeff Jones. To what extent this would have prepared Jones to take on Hawke and McKenzie is debatable, as Mike's bowling has been described rather unkindly as 'right arm indifferent', but it must have helped, as Jones contributed 16 valuable runs to the partnership.[146] It is indicative of Mike's team-mindedness and dedication to the cause, as it would have probably been more enjoyable watching the progress of England's innings with the prospect of a double-century from Barber. As EW Swanton wrote in *Swanton in Australia with MCC 1946–1975*:

> 'Smith, though outwardly unconventional and in manner casual to a degree, succeeds as a captain for the conventional reasons. He is thoughtful for his players, unselfish, does not "fuss" them or panic, shows a grasp of the situation which they deem is generally sensible and not least gives an inspiring example in the field.'

Mike's former England and Warwickshire team-mates would wholeheartedly endorse those sentiments.

England's total of 488 put them in a commanding position and, ironically, word had come through at lunch on the second day that the Queenslander Peter Allan, not selected for this Test, had taken all ten wickets for 61 runs in a Sheffield Shield match against Victoria. Australia started their innings badly. When Lawry was caught by Parks off Jones for nought, the normally impassive Mike was quite unable to contain his joy at this unexpected bonus, as Lawry had made over 300 runs in his previous three innings. Thereafter Australia struggled on a wearing pitch, and after a second-wicket partnership of 81, to which Thomas contributed

146 *Swanton in Australia with MCC 1946–1975,* EW Swanton.

51 stylish runs, they collapsed to 221 all out. Brown (5-63) and Jones (2-51) bowled with hostility and were backed up by some excellent catching, all their victims being caught. After Thomas had departed, Cowper batted stubbornly, taking four hours to make 60 before being stumped by Parks off Allen, as was Walters. At the end of the innings, the hero of the hour, David Brown, was sought out by England's most feared fast bowler of the 1930s, Harold Larwood, for congratulations.

THREE WICKETS IN OVER

In one devastating over with the new ball immediately after lunch yesterday, lanky David Brown gathered up three wickets without a run being taken.

His victims were David Sincock (29), Neil Hawke (0) and Wally Grout (0).

What with Lawry's dismissal in the first innings and Bob Cowper's in the second, Australian batsmen have recorded four "ducks" in the match so far.

Red-haired Sincock earned great credit by hanging on throughout the pre-lunch two hours.

Australia at that adjournment were 5-174. But Brown's swift clean-up made the score 8-174.

Some joyous consolation —brief though it was—came for the third-day crowd of 37,000 from beautiful sixes hit by Graham McKenzie and Doug Walters.

Wickets crash

After an opening partnership of 46 runs by Lawry and Thomas in the second innings, three wickets fell with the addition of only five runs.

Were those Englishmen jubilant?

They knew then they had this Test "in the bag."

The wickets went this way:

4-48pm: Graeme Thomas caught at slip by Cowdrey off Titmus when he mistimed a sweep shot. 1-46.

4-56pm: Bob Cowper (0), who had faced five balls, splendidly caught, knee-high, by Geoff Boycott, at short mid-wicket, from a hard pull off Titmus. 2-50.

Tragic loss

5pm: Peter Burge run out when Lawry did not respond to his call for a single. 3-51.

The loss in such a fashion of Burge, one of Australia's most experienced players — and experience was most important in this desperate situation — was tragic.

Burge had taken a single from the last ball of Titmus' over.

This brought him up against fast bowler Brown.

Burge pushed the first ball he received from Brown fairly straight, and just wide of Lawry, and called for a single.

Lawry shouted: "Stop." Lawry then looked around at the ball moving beyond him. He did not budge from his position at the bowler's end.

Burge came through, well down the pitch. When he realised that Lawry was stuck fast Burge doubled back.

But Boycott, stationed at mid-on in line with the bowling crease, had moved back for the ball, and skipper Mike Smith had dashed in front of the stumps, at the striker's end.

Boycott's return to Smith clearly beat Burge and Smith removed the bails.

Burge walked off slowly, scowling, as well he might. The stolid Lawry made no gesture.

It was the striker's call in such a case, and there seemed no doubt that Lawry could have made his ground.

A ludicrous happening in the circumstances.

It appeared that Lawry, grimly intent on doing a job of keeping at the wickets, had decided not to run any sharp singles.

Burge, cheerful enough at the end of the day's play, when asked by a team-mate had he not heard Lawry call "Stop," said:

Lawry's hook

"All I know is that I saw a run in it, and I went."

Lawry has batted for 130 minutes. His leg-side play was especially good. He played one great hook to the fence off a nasty bouncer from left-hander Jeff Jones.

Thomas shaped nicely against the new-ball bowlers; he began with a neat glance from Brown (from the Randwick end) for four.

In Jones's third over Thomas took four, four and two from successive balls, with two brilliant cuts and a hook.

He steadied against the spinners, until he made that fatal swing at Titmus.

Thomas, when the ball flew behind him, started for a run, turned back, and then saw umpire Rowan signal him "out," on the bowler's appeal.

Dogged batting

Titmus had begun this second innings with his bowling analysis for the series 1-175 off 114 overs.

It had been dogged batting before lunch. Australia had resumed at 4-113, with left-hander Cowper 46.

The crowd, though eager for entertainment on this sunny day, appreciated that the batsmen had a struggle on their hands.

Sincock, the stubborn "nightwatchman" from Saturday, had batted for 42 minutes in all before he opened his score by driving Titmus for three.

But Sincock, who has scored 61 in Shield cricket, got well behind the ball, pace or spin, and generally put on an excellent "show."

Runs, as well as time, were important. Cowper might have tried to do more about it.

There was relief when Sincock slammed Titmus over mid-off for four; he was 20 when a half-century stand was recorded.

Cowper, severely disciplined, got to 60 after 250 minutes' batting; then he was beaten by Allen's spin and flight and stumped.

Sincock, 29, and Doug Walters, six, were together at lunch (5-174), and noting that spin had taken only one wicket in the two hours, the position was rather reassuring.

But then came Brown with that rattling good over, in which he had Sincock caught behind the wicket, and Hawke at short fine-leg, and bowled Grout middle stump, first ball.

Walters, joined by McKenzie, could not control the strike.

However, McKenzie, with an amazingly easy swing, lifted Allen for a great six on to the "Hill," just beyond the outer stand.

A big thrill for the crowd, and there came another one soon afterwards.

Walters, with a lovely drive, also cracked Allen for a six—a massive hit well on to the "Hill" to the left of the sight screen.

Walters went for his shots but he was stranded by Allen and stumped by Parks.

Parks twice dropped McKenzie off Jones and missed the chance to equal Wally Grout's 'keeper's Test record of six dismissals in an innings.

Peter Philpott, with the index finger of the left hand badly bruised (he had broken it in November), batted No. 11.

English fast bowler David Brown, who took five wickets for 63 in Australia's first innings, is toasted in the dressing-room by Harold Larwood, England's great speedster of the bodyline era.

Harold Larwood congratulating David Brown on his 5-63 in England's victory against Australia in Sydney, January 1966.

Larwood, persuaded by Jack Fingleton, had given up his sweet shop in Blackpool to emigrate to Australia in 1950, where he received a warm welcome. Coincidentally, he travelled on the same ship, the *Orontes*, which had carried him and Douglas Jardine's team there 17 years earlier for the infamous Bodyline series.

Worse was to follow for Australia in their second innings after Mike enforced the follow-on, as they tamely succumbed to 174 all out to the spin of Titmus (4-40) and Allen (4-47), leaving England victors by an innings and 93 runs. Only Walters with 35 not out offered any real resistance. Geoff Boycott played a prominent part

HE Packer running up the Stamford School flag on hearing of England's victory at Sydney.

in Australia's second-innings downfall, first by neatly catching Cowper off Allen before he had scored off a hard-hit pull to mid-wicket, chipping a bone in his finger in the process, and secondly by his calm return to Mike who had beaten Parks to the stumps to run out the dangerous Burge, who had been sent back by Lawry. In addition to this smart piece of work, Mike took three sharp short leg catches to supplement a fine captaincy performance, having used his bowlers intelligently to exploit the conditions.

The esteem in which Mike was held by his team-mates was clearly evidenced when, on leaving the field, Mike offered his most successful bowlers, David Allen and Fred Titmus, the honour of leading the team off the field, only for this gesture to be declined and Mike himself being thrust forward to the applause of his side. 'He's done a lot towards this. He's our leader. Let him take the plaudits,' said David Allen, one of the match heroes.[147]

147 *MJK Smith: No Ordinary Man*, Douglas Miller.

AUSTRALIA v ENGLAND
Third Test

England

G Boycott c and b Philpott	84
RW Barber b Hawke	185
JH Edrich c and b Philpott	103
KF Barrington c McKenzie b Hawke	1
MC Cowdrey c Grout b Hawke	0
*MJK Smith c Grout b Hawke	6
DJ Brown c Grout b Hawke	1
JM Parks c Grout b Hawke	13
FJ Titmus c Grout b Walters	14
DA Allen not out	50
IJ Jones b Hawke	16
B 3, l-b 8, w 2, n-b 2	15
1/234 2/303 3/309 4/309 5/317 6/328 7/358 8/395 9/433	488

McKenzie	25-2-113-0
Hawke	33.7-6-105-7
Walters	10-1-38-1
Philpott	28-3-86-2
Sincock	20-1-98-0
Cowper	6-1-33-0

Australia

WM Lawry c Parks b Jones	0	– c Cowdrey b Brown	33
G Thomas c Titmus b Brown	51	– c Cowdrey b Titmus	25
RM Cowper st Parks b Allen	60	– c Boycott b Titmus	0
PJ Burge c Parks b Brown	6	– run out	1
*BC Booth c Cowdrey b Jones	8	– b Allen	27
DJ Sincock c Parks b Brown	29	– c Smith b Allen	27
KD Walters st Parks b Allen	23	– not out .	35
NJN Hawke c Barber b Brown	0	– c Smith b Titmus	2
ATW Grout b Brown	0	– c Smith b Allen	3
GD McKenzie c Cowdrey b Barber	24	– c Barber b Titmus	12
PL Philpott not out	5	– lbw b Allen	5
B 7, l-b 8	15	B 3, l-b 1	4
1/0 2/81 3/91 4/105 5/155 6/174 7/174 8/174 9/203	221	1/46 2/50 3/51 4/86 5/86 6/119 7/131 8/135 9/140	174

Jones	20-6-51-2	7-0-35-0
Brown	17-1-63-5	11-2-32-1
Boycott	3-1-8-0	
Titmus	23-8-40-0	17.3-4-40-4
Barber	2.1-1-2-1	5-0-16-0
Allen	19-5-42-2	20-8-47-4

Umpires: C Egar and L Rowan

England won by an innings and 93 runs

Two days after the heady atmosphere of this comprehensive victory, MCC travelled by train to Newcastle to play a three-day game against a Northern New South Wales Country Districts XI in a match not designated as first-class. MCC won by ten wickets, Mike making 164, his highest score in Australia, and Fred Titmus 114.

MCC then flew to Tasmania for a three-day match in Launceston which ended as a tame draw with time only for three innings. In MCC's first innings of 371/9 declared Mike, opening, scored 96, Parks 91, Cowdrey 63 and Knight 45 not out. Knight followed this up with 51 not out in the second innings after Cowdrey had made a century and Parks another fifty. Tasmania's reply of 322 included a century from the amateur Brian Richardson, a horticulturalist by profession, and 67 not out from Brian Patterson. The following day MCC took on a Combined XI at Hobart, captained by former Australian wicketkeeper Len Maddocks and strengthened by the inclusion of Lawry, Cowper and Walters. The Combined XI total of 199 would have looked pretty sick without these three who contributed 146 between them. Richardson and Patterson both played again but failed to impress this time. Titmus was the principal destroyer with 6-65. With Mike rested, MCC scored 471/9 in their only innings, Boycott making an assured 156, Cowdrey 70 and Murray 83. Kerry Hooper, nicknamed the gentle giant, from Burnie, a port city on Tasmania's northern coast, took 5-106 with some high quality left-arm medium-pace bowling. The Combined XI fared much better in their second innings and after the dismissal of Kevin Brown for a duck, Lawry with 126 not out and Cowper 143 not out used the final day as batting practice for the fourth Test. During the Combined XI's second innings Boycott was induced to bowl having been told mischievously by Cowdrey that the game was not a first-class one and his century would not count. Cowdrey promised to use his influence with the

ICC to get the match upgraded and Boycott fell hook, line and sinker for this good-humoured leg pull to the amusement of his team-mates who were in on the joke. He bowled his heart out for seven eight-ball overs, only to be told afterwards that the match had always been a first-class one.

The Australian selectors, irreverently known by Aussie cricket fans as the Three Blind Mice, dropped a bombshell when the team for the fourth Test at Adelaide was announced. They had omitted McKenzie in favour of Peter Allan. Peter Philpott and David Sincock were also left out. Simpson, now recovered from chickenpox, was back as captain, replacing Booth, who was dropped, having done little in the preceding three Tests with only 84 runs in five innings. This brought an end to his five-year Test match career, during which he had averaged over 42. Booth was also a talented hockey player and had been a member of the Australian squad at the 1956 Melbourne Olympic Games. Some sections of the press were even calling heretically for Lawry to be dropped. Keith Stackpole was to make his debut. As it transpired, Allan injured himself in a Sheffield Shield match against Western Australia and, to the delight of Australian fans and groans from the English, McKenzie was reinstated. England fielded an unchanged side from the third Test. There was a further shock for Australian supporters when it was announced that Cowper was to be 12th man despite having top-scored in the first innings of the previous two Tests. Mike again won the toss and opted to bat, signalling the fact to the dressing room with a swish of an imaginary bat, departing, as one writer put it, from his usual sphinx-like inscrutability.

England started badly with Barber being bowled for a duck off an inside edge. Soon afterwards Boycott was brilliantly caught by Chappell at third slip, followed by Edrich at first slip by Simpson. England were in serious trouble at 33/3, the reinstated McKenzie having accounted for the two left-handers. However, a partnership of 72 between Barrington (60) and Cowdrey (38) restored some respectability until Cowdrey was disastrously run out after being sent back by Barrington. Apparently, Grout had called to the fielder Hawke at wide mid-on 'Watch for the one', which Cowdrey misheard as Barrington calling him for a single.[148] Mike (29), Parks (49) and Titmus (33), all batting responsibly, helped England to a total of 241 which always looked inadequate. It looked even more inadequate after Australia passed it without the loss of a wicket, finally registering a total of 516. The opening partnership of 244 between Simpson (225) and Lawry (115) should have been broken earlier had Boycott taken a relatively easy catch off Simpson at long leg when he was on 84 – a very costly miss. He had a bad day in the field and also dropped Burge. After Lawry was out, Thomas continued the onslaught, batting with great fluency until he fell on 52, made in 74 minutes. Play resumed on the second day with Australia's score standing at a formidable 333/3. Simpson's innings came to an end with the score at 480 and only Stackpole with 43 made any other significant contribution, Walters going for nought, caught by Parks attempting a hook off a Brown bouncer, and Chappell in his second Test making only 17 on his home ground before being brilliantly caught by Edrich at gully. Australia were finally all out for 516.

Near the end of Simpson's innings the spectators witnessed a rare sight – Mike Smith dropped a catch! Simpson was on 215 at the time, so it made little difference. Jones was the pick of the England bowlers with 6-118 off 29 overs. England's second-innings reply was equally disappointing and at 32/3 after the first hour with Barber, Boycott and Edrich gone, there looked little hope of saving the game. Ultimately, only Barrington (102), the

148 *With England In Australia*, John Clarke.

Warwickshire players inspecting the pitch prior to the Gillette Cup Final against Sussex in 1964. From left to right are: Norman Horner, John Jameson, Mike Smith, Alan Smith and Tom Cartwright.

Jim Stewart batting in the 1964 Gillette Cup Final.

MCC team in South Africa in 1964/65. Back row: PH Parfitt, JT Murray, JM Brearley, G Boycott, RNS Hobbs; Middle row: RJA Nichols (physiotherapist), JSE Price, NI Thomson, D Brown, RW Barber, TW Cartwright, M McLennan (baggage master); Front row: DA Allen, KF Barrington, DB Carr (manager), MJK Smith (captain), ER Dexter, FJ Titmus, JM Parks.

Mike bowling in the nets – looks like a leg-break.

Mike congratulating Trevor Goddard on his maiden Test century.

Mike catching Dennis Gamsy off Ian Thomson. MCC v. Natal, November 1964.

Mike catching Eddie Barlow off Fred Titmus. MCC v. Eastern Province.

Graeme Pollock batting in the second Test at Trent Bridge in 1965. His 125 was largely responsible for South Africa's victory.

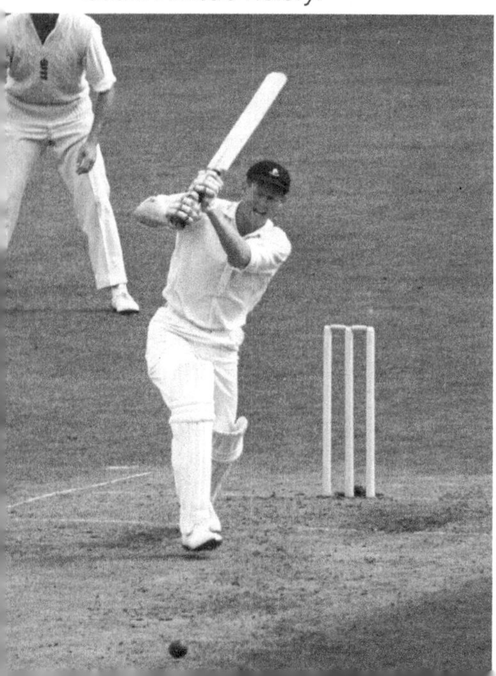

Colin Bland batting in the third Test at the Oval in 1965. His second-innings 127 saved the match for South Africa.

John Edrich pole-axed by Peter Pollock in the first Test against South Africa at Lord's in 1965. He retired hurt and took took no further part in the game or the series.

England team v South Africa at Trent Bridge 1965. Standing: Jeff Jones (12th man), Peter Parfitt, Bob Barber, John Snow, David Larter, Tom Cartwright, Geoff Boycott, Dennis Amiss. Seated: Jim Parks, Colin Cowdrey, Mike Smith, Ken Barrington.

Jim Parks' bat autographed by the MCC team in Australia, 1965/66.

MCC team in Australia, 1965/66.

Bob Barber batting in the third Test at Sydney, January 1966.

Mike flicking one off his legs in the Gillette Cup Final against Worcestershire in September 1966 at Lord's.

Warwickshire, Gillette Cup winners in 1966 – Mike holding the trophy aloft.

ever-reliable Titmus (53) and Cowdrey (35) offered any resistance. McKenzie had done the damage in England's first innings with 6-48 but this time it was Hawke with 5-54. Australia had won by an innings and nine runs with over a day to spare on a wicket that had been good for batting throughout. They had outplayed England and their victory was thoroughly deserved. Although Mike was gracious in defeat, according to EW Swanton, he described the England effort as 'appalling' and it still rankles with him to this day. Of the several theories advanced for this comprehensive defeat, one was that the preceding three less important matches had softened England up; another that they had gone into the match determined to continue to play attacking cricket rather than defend their series lead. There is no doubt that England got off to a bad start by playing too rashly at the outset but full credit has to be given to the efforts of McKenzie and Hawke with the ball and the excellent batting by Australia's openers.

The series was now all square and whether Mike could bring back 'that miserable urn' depended on England winning the final Test as Australia were already in possession of the Ashes. In the one final match against New South Wales to be played before the series decider Simpson opened with Norman O'Neill, whose best years were now behind him. O'Neill made 36, with glimpses of his former prowess, in an opening stand of 77 before falling dubiously lbw to Knight. When Thomas joined Simpson, they carried on where they had left off in the fourth Test, putting on 146 for the second wicket. Simpson finally fell to Barber for 123 and Thomas to Boycott for 129. An innings of 57 from Walters helped New South Wales to a total of 488. Only Knight with 3-87 and Allen with 4-97 produced creditable bowling figures. England's reply of 329 was not enough to avoid the follow-on which Simpson duly enforced. Several batsmen got starts but Parfitt's 87 was the only half-century, Barber making 49 and Mike 40. England's second innings turned into a run-fest, however, with Barber (77) and Boycott (75) putting on 120 for the first wicket. Edrich weighed in with 47 and Russell showed his true class with 101 not out. Mike made 64 and Knight 94 in only 71 minutes. The game ended in a draw but England had gained some useful batting practice.

Australia made just one change for the final Test, bringing back Cowper to replace Burge. England brought in Knight for Allen, believing the conditions would suit pace better than spin. There was some doubt as to whether Mike would be able to play as he was suffering from a viral infection. In the event he declared himself fit and on winning the toss elected to bat. Wally Grout, playing his 51st and final Test, was given the honour of leading the fielding side out. After a steady start, disaster struck when Barber was run out with the total on 36, nobly sacrificing himself when he could have easily returned to his crease at the non-striker's end. Walters had run from leg slip ahead of Grout to neatly pick up McKenzie's throw on the half-volley to remove the bails after a slight fumble. It was a poor call from Boycott, which may have unsettled him, as he did not survive much longer, being held at slip by Stackpole after a tantalising juggling act. A third-wicket stand of 178 ensued between Edrich (85) and Barrington (115), who played with unaccustomed abandon, scoring the fastest century of the series. Cowdrey (79) and Parks (89) put on 138 for the sixth wicket after Mike had gone for a duck, caught Grout, bowled Walters off too fine a leg glance, capping a miserable series for him with the bat. Walters also accounted for Barrington, Cowdrey and Edrich to give him four prime scalps for 53 runs, an impressive return considering England's total of 485/9 declared.

When Australia batted, a hostile spell from Brown accounted for Simpson, a fast outswinger uprooting his off stump. Thomas followed soon afterwards, caught at slip by Titmus off Jones. This was to be England's last success for some time as Lawry and

Cowper proceeded to put on 212 for the third wicket. After Lawry was out for 108, nicely caught by Edrich in the gully, Cowper was joined by Walters and they were still together at the end of the third day. A result was now looking improbable and, after almost an inch and a half of overnight rain completely washed out play on the fourth day, an improbability became a virtual impossibility as Cowper and Walters took their partnership to 152 and the total to 420/4. When Cowper was finally out for 307, Simpson declared at 543/8, having withheld the closure to allow Cowper his chance at the world record. As Robert Gray wrote at the time in *The Australian*:

> 'Cowper's marathon innings took over 12 hours and lifted an otherwise pointless final day to memorable heights. Cowper, maintaining unflappable concentration throughout the longest innings ever played in Australia in first-class cricket, smashed seven records. Only a gem of a leg-cutter from Barry Knight after tea thwarted his aim of hitting the highest Test innings of all time. The game wasn't England against Australia – it became a battle between Cowper and the dusty bones of history.'

In the remaining 75 minutes left for play, England lost Barber, Boycott and Edrich, all to McKenzie for 17 runs, and finished on 69/3. Thus the series was squared and the Ashes retained by Australia. Not everyone was happy about the events of the last day, however, and Keith Miller in a newspaper article even proposed that the Ashes be scrapped if a series result was to become more important than the proper conduct of individual games.

By any objective measure the tour was a great success. Of the 15 first-class matches played, five were won, two lost and eight drawn. On balance England were probably the better side, at least at the beginning of the series and, had a couple of catches been taken and a crucial stumping not missed, they would almost certainly have won the second Test. There are some, like EM Wellings, in his summary of the tour in *Wisden*, who believed a side should always play its best keeper – in this case, Murray. But to prefer him to Parks would have deprived England of many valuable runs. There were no recriminations as far as Mike was concerned. His view was that, by dint of their position, wicketkeepers get the most chances and are therefore likely to make the most mistakes and no fielder is infallible.

Clearly, the batting on both sides was stronger than the bowling and with hindsight, in spite of the Herculean efforts of David Brown and Jeff Jones, Mike wishes they had taken John Snow. Also, perhaps Mike could have used Bob Barber and Ken Barrington more as wrist-spinners. A myth exists that Barber was a reluctant bowler which he is keen to dispel. 'I was always happy to bowl my leg-spin,' says Bob, 'but at the right time, although I never asked to be put on.'[149] Certainly, England were unlucky with illness and injuries but so too were Australia – though obviously the home side have more options in overcoming such problems. Although we do not know what went on behind the scenes, the dubious co-captaincy arrangement never really materialised as an issue. As EM Wellings shrewdly wrote, 'In fact, Griffith did not use his powers. Griffith is not the sort of which dictators are made.' This was probably just as well, for a ship cannot sail easily with two captains. Wellings was also critical of wives being allowed on tour, as Mike's and Barber's were, believing them to be a distraction 'however well they behave and aim to keep themselves in the background'.[150] These sentiments would not go down too well today.

149 Conversation with Bob Barber.

150 *Wisden Cricketers' Almanack 1967 edition.*

One thing stands out above all though and that is that it was a very happy tour with a lot of entertaining, attractive cricket with even normally cautious players like Boycott and Barrington at times playing with attacking flair. Although Mike had a poor tour with the bat, his captaincy both tactically and motivationally was excellent and in his own inimitable way he developed a team spirit second to none. As Ken Mackay said in his book on the tour, *Quest for the Ashes*, his team would follow him into outer space if necessary. Mike also set an outstanding example in the field for both athleticism and courage.

'Mike's team did not win back the Ashes,' Mackay wrote, 'but they had a pretty good go, and after the third Test match looked an odds-on chance of pulling it off. In fact, he out-performed many previous Ashes-winning England skippers by leaving behind happy memories of an enterprising series played, for the most part, in a good spirit.'[151] There was no doubt about that and from a public relations point of view, it was one of the most successful.

As far as the Test averages were concerned, Barrington was top of the batting with 464 runs at 66.28, Titmus second with 258 at 64.50 and Cowdrey third with 267 at 53.40. Parks, Boycott, Edrich and Barber all averaged over 40. Knight took eight wickets at 31.25, Jones 15 at 35.53 and Brown 11 at 37.18. Allen and Titmus took nine wickets apiece, both at a high cost.

Simpson headed Australia's batting averages with 355 runs at 88.75, followed by Lawry with 592 at 84.57, Cowper 493 at 82.16 and Walters 410 at 68.33. Hawke was Australia's most successful bowler with 16 wickets at 26.18, closely followed by McKenzie with 16 at 29.18 and Walters nine at 31.44. Ironically, two of the players who had thwarted England's chances of an Ashes victory,

151 *Quest for the Ashes*, Ken Mackay.

McKenzie and Cowper, had both been dropped by the selectors during the series.

MCC then travelled to New Zealand for three Test matches without Barber, Barrington, Titmus and Larter, who had opted out of this leg of the tour. Prior to the first Test they played the President's XI, the match ending in a draw as a result of slow scoring and interruptions for rain and bad light. Parfitt, with a century, Mike and Boycott with half-centuries and Cowdrey and Edrich with forties had all gained some useful batting practice.

This was not reflected in England's start in the first Test at Christchurch, as they lost their first four wickets for 47 on a difficult pitch, three to the bowling of Dick Motz and one to Bob Cunis. It was left to Mike and Parfitt to retrieve the situation, which they did with a stand of 113, both making 54. Allen (88) and Brown (44) then put on 107 for the eighth wicket under easier conditions to give England a total of 342. Motz and Gary Bartlett each took three wickets. New Zealand replied with 347, Bev Congdon making a century at number three and Eric Petrie, on his return to Test cricket after a five-year absence, and Motz putting on 89 for the eighth wicket to give New Zealand a slender first-innings lead. The wickets were shared by the pace bowlers, Jones taking 4-71, Higgs 3-51 and Brown 3-80.

The Tests in New Zealand were only of four days' duration and the first innings of both teams had taken up the best part of three days, rendering a result improbable. England lost Boycott and Edrich before the close on the third day but the following morning Mike (87) and Parfitt (46 not out) again revived England's fortunes with a partnership of 125. Mike declared at 201/5, leaving New Zealand two hours and 20 minutes to score 197 – hardly a generous declaration. New Zealand's 'run chase' started disastrously, Brown striking first and then Higgs taking four wickets for five runs in nine overs. At one point New Zealand were 22/7 and in danger of recording their lowest total ever. Vic Pollard, New Zealand's best batsman in the previous series in England, and Cunis managed to save the match by holding out for the last half an hour with eight wickets down. As a last throw of the dice, Mike had put on Parfitt and Parks to try and take the last few wickets. Parfitt got 2-5 with his off-breaks and, with Edrich quickly donning the pads, Parks bowled three overs but neither could break the partnership, New Zealand finishing on 48/8. Parks took five catches in New Zealand's first innings and eight in the match. In catching Murray Chapple in New Zealand's first innings, Cowdrey took his hundredth catch in Test cricket.

For the second Test at Dunedin, Parks and Brown were left out in favour of Murray and Knight. New Zealand's captain Chapple was injured and Ross Morgan, who had scored 72 not out in the first innings for the President's XI, came in to replace him, with the captaincy passing to Barry Sinclair. The match was played in miserable weather conditions and there was never much chance of a result. Less than four hours' play was possible on the first day on which New Zealand struggled to 83/5. On the second day an eighth-wicket partnership between Petrie (28) and Motz (57), who hit 22 off one over from Allen, gave the score some respectability and the innings closed at 192. Jones and Higgs took three wickets apiece and Knight and Allen two each but it had been a laborious process, taking 90 overs.

England's scoring rate was not much better and when they declared at 254/8, 104 overs had been bowled at them. Cowdrey was England's top scorer with 89 not out, made in just under six hours, and Murray made 50. Just two hours' play had been possible on the third day and when England declared on the final day, only two sessions remained. Although England managed to take nine New Zealand wickets in their second innings, the Kiwis finished 85 runs ahead when time ran out. Allen took 4-46 and Higgs and

Jones two wickets each. Once again, bad weather and slow play by both teams had killed the match as a contest.

England made two changes for the final Test at Auckland. Boycott was left out and Parfitt moved up to open. Brown was brought in as an extra bowler and Parks took over from Murray. England were reduced to ten men after the first day, however, when Edrich went down with appendicitis. For New Zealand, Chapple was still injured and Bruce Taylor was brought in to replace Gary Bartlett after some doubts about the legitimacy of his action. Taylor had made history the previous winter in India, becoming the first Test player to score a century and take five wickets on debut.

New Zealand batted first in favourable weather conditions and put together a total of 296, largely thanks to 114 from Sinclair, his first century against England, and 64 from Congdon. Once again, the scoring rate was pedestrian. Allen took 5-123 and Jones and Higgs two wickets each. In reply England were all out for 222, Cowdrey making 59 and Russell 56 in a second-wicket partnership of 118. England had equally shown no sense of urgency to push the score along and their innings took 88 overs. Taylor took 3-46 and Pollard 3-3 to bring England's innings to a speedy end.

New Zealand's second innings got off to a terrible start when they lost both openers without a run on the board, one to Brown and one to Jones. The later batsmen had no answer to Higgs, who took 3-27 in 28 overs and Jones who took 3-28 in 25. New Zealand were finally all out for 129 in 103 overs, a scoring rate of little over 1.25 per over. England were left with the task of making 204 to win in four and a half hours. Determined to stave off defeat, Sinclair set an ultra-defensive field with no slips or close leg-side catchers but, in spite of this, England should have made a better effort to get the runs. In the event, they finished up with 159/4 off 75 overs. Parks, with 45 not out, was the only batsman to score at a reasonable rate in yet another undecided, boring contest.

For the record, Parks topped the England batting averages in New Zealand with 117 runs at 58.50, Allen was second with 104 runs at 52.00, Cowdrey third with 196 at 49.00 and Mike fourth with 209 at 41.80. Higgs topped the bowling averages with 17 wickets at 9.34 and Jones was second with 14 at 17.29. Brown got six at 21.00 and Allen 13 at 27.62.

CHAPTER 20

Mixed Fortunes

WARWICKSHIRE MADE a good start to the 1966 season and, apart from being bowled out for 38 by Derbyshire in August at Coventry, finished well. A mid-season slump, however, dented their Championship chances and they ended up in sixth position, Yorkshire winning the title, with Worcestershire, the previous year's champions, runners-up. Out of 28 Championship matches played, Warwickshire won eight, lost eight and drew 12. The batting was boosted by the emergence of Neil Abberley as an opening batsman and the continued development of John Jameson and Dennis Amiss, all three of whom scored 1,000 Championship runs. In what was Warwickshire's best win of the season, Abberley played a patient innings of 54 not out against Yorkshire at Hull to get them over the line by three wickets, defying for two and a half hours everything Yorkshire could throw at him on a drying pitch. He had a remarkable start to the season, with almost 400 runs in his first seven innings at an average of 77. Mike was the only other batsman to make over 1,000 and his 1,824 runs at 44.48 put him fourth in the national averages behind Tom Graveney, Colin Milburn and Jim Stewart. Jim, however, was absent for most of the season following an operation on the knuckle joint of his right index finger and he only played seven matches for Warwickshire. Bob Barber was less frequently available because of business commitments but generally did well when he played, especially in the Gillette Cup competition which Warwickshire won for the first time. He was also honoured in *Wisden* by being named one of their five Cricketers of the Year.

In the bowling department, Tom Cartwright was the mainstay, taking exactly 100 wickets at 16.97. The pace bowlers Jack Bannister, Rudi Webster and David Brown also performed well, Bannister taking 42 wickets at 19.09, Webster 57 at 20.47, and Brown 71 at 22.14. The best bowling performance of the season was Rudi Webster's 8-19 against Cambridge University, who were bowled out for 38 in their first innings. The middle order was boosted by Jimmy Allan, Mike's former university opening partner, whom Mike persuaded to turn out for the county. His left-arm spin also helped to fill a gap in that area of weakness and he took 31 wickets at 25.22.

1966 also saw the advent of Sunday cricket in some counties but not at Edgbaston, in spite of a referendum of members which showed a large number in favour of it. Clubs would not be allowed to take gate money, although they could charge for car parking, seating, scorecards and refreshments. Because of the extra manning costs on a Sunday, the committee decided it was not financially viable.

Mike retained his captaincy of the England team despite his mediocre batting performance in Australia, no doubt helped in part by a splendid innings of 140 for MCC against the touring West Indians at Lord's. This was to be short-lived, however, as Cowdrey was given the captaincy after England lost the first Test by an innings. In the event, Cowdrey kept the job for only the next three Tests, losing two and drawing one, before being replaced by Brian Close. Warwickshire did not suffer as much as in the previous season from Test match calls as Mike and David Brown played in only the first and Barber in the last two. Amiss made his Test match debut in the fifth, after scoring 69 and 47 for the President's XI against West Indies and 160 not out when Warwickshire played them.

Batting first at Old Trafford, West Indies posted a score of 484, Conrad Hunte making 135, after having been dropped by Ken Higgs on 7. Garry Sobers gave a masterclass performance, making 161, his highest score in England. Lance Gibbs was virtually unplayable in England's first innings and at one point he had 3-3 from nine overs and finished with 5-37. England were dismissed for 167, having been 85/6 at one stage. Jim Parks attacked belatedly for a top score of 43 and Allen made 37. England were forced to follow on and did somewhat better, making 277, Gibbs again taking five wickets. Colin Milburn, who had been run out without scoring by Gibbs in a one-sided race to the wicket in the first innings, made 94 with some lusty blows and Cowdrey 69. Mike had a poor match, dismissed by Gibbs in both innings for 5 and 6, the second time a little unluckily as the spinning ball went back off his boot on to the stumps. To keep a place in the team, a batsman has to score runs and it was Mike's failure to do this at Test level, rather than his captaincy, which ended his career at the helm.

Mike took the news from the chairman of selectors Doug Insole philosophically and with good grace, as could be expected of someone with such a fair-minded and phlegmatic temperament. 'I was, of course, disappointed,' says Mike, 'but I was in no position to complain as I hadn't got enough runs.' Some commentators and players thought he had been hard done by, though, losing the job after one defeat considering his previous record. Richie Benaud described it as 'the most drastic chop in post-war cricket'.[152] There was much speculation as to who should replace him, many

152 *The Story of Warwickshire Cricket*, Leslie Duckworth.

advocating Brian Close, but in the end the selectors took the safe option and appointed Cowdrey. Doug Insole, chairman of selectors, provoked some hostile reaction by saying England would probably have won if they had batted first, but most impartial observers believed that England had been outplayed and outspun by the 'human cobra' Gibbs.

One player who was more upset than most about Mike's sacking was John Edrich. In his eyes it was a harsh decision and he could see no justification for it. In his autobiography *Runs in the Family* he writes:

> 'Mike had been considered good enough to skipper a team that very nearly brought back the Ashes. He had been widely acclaimed for the enterprising cricket his team had produced. Yet just this one Test and a few months later he was thrown out. Surely he should have been given the captaincy for all five Tests against the West Indies? That is the way to breed confidence. How can a skipper feel completely in command when everyone knows he has only been appointed for part of a series?'

He continues:

> 'The paradox of it all was that Mike was liked and respected by his players. That is why the tour to Australia under him was such a happy one. He knew the game inside out and he set a great example by his close catching. If there was any fun off the field, he was in the middle of it. He possessed this casual, unflappable way. He didn't mope if he made a low score. He would just flop down on the dressing room bench seat, remove his boots, put on his sandals and exclaim with a grin, "That wasn't very good, was it?" (and then forget all

> about it). He accepted that his players knew something of the game. If you didn't get runs, he knew you felt bad enough about it without any strictures from him. Some skippers will order extra practice and lay down the law if the game goes wrong, but not Mike. He treated every day as a new day, every match as a fresh challenge. He had no time for recriminations, but he would certainly speak his mind if he thought anyone wasn't pulling his weight.'[153]

Mike himself has gone on record saying that one of the worst faults a captain can deploy is destructive criticism, which is bound to affect team morale. Likewise, he believes that nothing is more calculated to destroy a team's confidence than a pig-headed captain who does not listen to suggestions from other members of his side.

Edrich's Surrey captain Micky Stewart shares his opinion of Mike. 'Our careers ran side by side,' says Micky. 'I first encountered him in the Public Schools' matches in 1950. He was a fine batsman and a competitive, intelligent captain. We had a similar sense of humour. As a person he was a top bloke and a great people person.'[154]

Heads other than Mike's had to roll and for the second Test England dropped Eric Russell, David Brown and David Allen and brought in Geoff Boycott, Tom Graveney, Barry Knight and Basil D'Oliveira. D'Oliveira had been in the 12 for the Manchester Test at a time when the policy was to not decide on the 12th man until the morning of the match. When Mike wandered up to him and said 'You do 12th, Bas', he must have been acutely disappointed after such an heroic struggle to get to that stage.[155] It probably worked out well for him in the end though, as the pitch may not

153 *Runs in the Family,* John Edrich.

154 Conversation with Micky Stewart.

155 *Basil D'Oliveira,* Peter Oborne.

have been a good one on which to make his debut. He was given an assurance by the selectors that he would play in the second Test and was in the side for the rest of the series, making three half-centuries. Graveney was astonished at his recall as, although he had been consistently in the runs at county level, he had assumed his Test career was over. He thoroughly justified his inclusion though by scoring 96 in the second Test, 109 in the third and 165 in the fifth.

Although he had lost the England captaincy, Mike must have been cheered by Warwickshire's winning of the Gillette Cup, their first trophy in his reign. Having received a bye in the first round, they beat Glamorgan in the second. Batting first, they amassed 266/8 in their 60 overs, Dennis Amiss making 113 and Mike 48 in a partnership of 126 for the third wicket. They then saw off Glamorgan for 101 all out. David Brown dismissed Alan Jones and Tony Lewis for nought in his first over and finished with figures of 5-18. In the third round they defeated Gloucestershire by six wickets, dismissing them for 193 and passing their total for the loss of four wickets in 40 overs. Bob Barber made 113 and Amiss 62. In the semi-final they beat Somerset by five wickets, bowling them out for 189 in the 60th over. They passed Somerset's score in the 52nd over, Barber making 45, Mike 47 and Amiss 80 not out.

Their opponents in the final were Worcestershire who had progressed by beating Essex, Nottinghamshire and Hampshire. They were captained by 43-year-old Don Kenyon, for whom Mike had great respect as a player and captain. 'I got on well with him and enjoyed his company,' says Mike. 'He was a smashing chap.' Kenyon won the toss and opted to bat, a decision Mike was not unhappy with as, having learnt from the experience against Sussex two years earlier, bowling first at Lord's in September could be an advantage. Worcestershire were unfortunate to lose their captain early on when he trod on his wicket, having been forced back by

GILLETTE CUP FINAL
WARWICKSHIRE v WORCESTERSHIRE

Worcestershire		Warwickshire	
D Kenyon hit wkt b Webster	13	RW Barber c Horton b d'Oliveira	66
MJ Horton b Cartwright	20	K Ibadulla c Horton b Cartwright	10
JA Ormrodc AC Smith b Cartwright	9	DL Amiss c Booth b Coldwell	44
TW Graveney c Ibadulla b Cartwright	18	MJK Smith b Brain	12
B D'Oliveira c Ibadulla b Brown	12	JA Jameson c Booth b Flavell	0
DW Richardson b Ibadulla	23	RN Abberley not out	3
B Booth c AC Smith b Bannister	0	AC Smith not out	21
N Gifford b Ibadulla	38	TW Cartwright did not bat	
BM Brain not out	14	RV Webster did not bat	
L Coldwell not out	1	DJ Brown did not bat	
JA Flavell did not bat		JD Bannister did not bat	
B 1, l-b 6	7	L-b 2, n-b 1	3
1/33 2/33 3/48 (8 wkts, after 60 overs)	155	1/44 2/95 3/130 4/133 (5 wkts)	159
4/65 5/86 6/88 7/104 8/154			

Bowling:

Brown 12-2-27-1	Flavell 12-2-31-1
Webster 12-2-28-1	Coldwell 12-1-34 -1
Cartwright 12-4-16-3	D'Oliveira 10-3-26-1
Bannister 12-3-27-1	Gifford 11-3-32-1
Ibadulla 9-3-33-2	Brain 11.4-2-33-1
Barber 3-1-17-0	

Umpires: JS Buller and CS Elliott
Warwickshire won by 5 wickets

the pace of Rudi Webster. Thereafter Warwickshire restricted Worcestershire to 155, Tom Cartwright taking 3-16 in his 12 overs, including the prized wicket of Tom Graveney, brilliantly caught one-handed in the leg trap by Billy Ibadulla. At 104/7 after 49 overs, Warwickshire looked odds-on to win, but Norman Gifford at number nine hit two sixes and three fours in his 38 to help realise a potentially defendable total. The hostile, talented opening pair of Jack Flavell and Len Coldwell made life difficult for the early Warwickshire batsmen but Barber (66) and Amiss (44) weathered the storm to take Warwickshire to relative safety. When the score stood at 138/5, there were seven overs left and

17 runs required, and Warwickshire's wicketkeeper and future captain, Alan Smith, calmly steered Warwickshire home in the 57th over. Bob Barber was nominated man of the match by Peter May, but there were some like Don Kenyon who thought it should have gone to Cartwright.

This earned Warwickshire, as Gillette Cup winners, one more match to round off their season, a 50-over game against the West Indian touring team at Edgbaston. West Indies, batting first, made 257, Joey Carew making 78 and Seymour Nurse completing a century in the last over. Warwickshire put up a good fight to make 238, Barber scoring 63 quick runs and Amiss making 78. Rudi Webster was expensive in his final match for Warwickshire, going for 61 from ten overs before departing for a medical post in New Zealand. Mike had problems again with Lance Gibbs, being stumped off him for 4.

One of the major problems that Warwickshire had been facing for some years was the decline in attendances, which had dropped in the last 20 years from two and a quarter million to just over half a million. The solution was crystal clear as far as their prescient secretary Leslie Duckworth was concerned. 'We must face the fact', he said in a blunt address to the Forty Club before the start of the 1967 season, 'that we are providing a spectacle the public does not want. At the same time we must acknowledge that we know what the public does want – they have told us so through the medium of the Gillette Cup games – and if we want to survive and preserve the happiest of games, we should play it the way it was intended to be played and the way the public understand and love it.'[156]

At the beginning of 1967 MCC sent a team of young cricketers to Pakistan and Dennis Amiss, David Brown and Neil Abberley

156 *The Story of Warwickshire Cricket,* Leslie Duckworth.

were included in their number. Seven matches were played, of which four were won and the remainder drawn. All three Warwickshire players acquitted themselves well, Amiss coming second in the batting averages to Mike Brearley, the captain, and Brown picking up 18 wickets at 22.50. Abberley, unfortunately, had to return home after suffering a cracked finger from a beamer in the second match after he had scored 92 in the first innings.

CHAPTER 21

Swansong as Warwickshire Captain

THE 1967 season was to be Mike's last as captain of Warwickshire and the results obtained were rather disappointing. The team finished tenth in the County Championship with five victories, four defeats and 17 drawn games. Championship cricket was played at Edgbaston on a Sunday for the first time. Warwickshire were, however, particularly unlucky with the weather, having four of their first seven matches abandoned in one of the wettest Mays on record. Dennis Amiss topped the Warwickshire batting averages with 1,260 runs at 54.78 and was second in the national averages to Ken Barrington. He played in two Tests against the Indian tourists and one against Pakistan, and toured Pakistan in the winter with the MCC Under-25 team. Mike was the only other player to make over 1,000 runs (1,360 at a lower than usual 34.87) and, in spite of scoring 173 not out against the Pakistani tourists, was not selected for any of the Test matches.

He did, however, play in and captain a couple of representative matches, one for an England XI against a Rest of the World XI and another for an England XI against Pakistan. Jim Stewart missed a large part of the season through illness, including his own benefit match, but performed well enough in the games he played in. Bryan Richardson, the younger brother of Peter and Dick, who had been with Warwickshire since 1963, showed some improvement and made a century in each innings against Cambridge University. Bob Barber's appearances were infrequent but he was always a valuable addition to the side with his all-round batting, bowling and fielding ability. John Jameson's and Neil Abberley's performances fell off slightly and both failed to make 1,000 runs in Championship matches.

The brunt of the bowling was again borne by Tom Cartwright, Jack Bannister and David Brown, Cartwright taking 132 wickets at 15.84 and finishing fourth in the national averages as the leading wicket-taker in the country. In one match at Swansea in August against Glamorgan he was practically unplayable and had match figures of 15-89, his best ever performance. According to his team-mate Jack Bannister, some fine batsmen like Garry Sobers wouldn't take him on, especially in limited-overs cricket, and would wait for his spell to end before going on the attack. That wasn't so easy in the longer form of the game, as he was seemingly indefatigable. Bannister took 72 scalps at 20.87 and Brown 62 at 22.46. Brown also toured Pakistan with the MCC Under-25 team. Barber was the county's best spin option with 19 wickets at 25.52 and Jimmy Allan also bowled but was expensive.

Yorkshire eventually won the County Championship, but their win was tainted by some deplorable gamesmanship in the match against Warwickshire towards the end of the season in which they employed time-wasting tactics to deny Warwickshire a win. Fred Trueman bowled three no-balls in his final over, probably to prevent a further over from being bowled, and was reportedly upset because one of them was not called. The match ended as a draw, with Warwickshire needing a further nine runs for victory, which another over may have made possible, as John Jameson had just hit Tony Nicholson for a magnificent straight six in his 36 not out. As a result of these unsporting tactics, Yorkshire salvaged two points from the game, which ironically were not needed in the end as they finished ten points ahead of Kent. Even the respected cricket correspondent of the *Yorkshire Post*, Jim Kilburn, despite his deep love of Yorkshire cricket, was highly critical of the Yorkshire players, writing, 'They made no effort to hide their delaying tactics. They walked slowly to bowling marks, to positions in the field and between overs. They were provocatively tardy in retrieving the ball from the boundary and returning it to play. Spectators grew increasingly discontented and abusive and the whole atmosphere of the game degenerated to disillusion with the basic principles of sport.' Warwickshire made no official complaint, but MCC ordered an inquiry, to which Cyril Goodway, chairman of the Warwickshire ground sub-committee, who had watched the last day's play, was invited to attend for his opinion. This ultimately led to Brian Close losing the England captaincy for his stubborn unwillingness to accept that he had done anything wrong and also for his ugly confrontation with a Warwickshire spectator as he was leaving the field. It was a great pity, as tactically Close was a brilliant captain. The captaincy then passed back to Colin Cowdrey for the tour of the West Indies, Mike having made it clear that he was definitely not going back on his intention to retire. His son Neil had been born in July and the prospect of winters away from his family now had little appeal.

Warwickshire did not even have the consolation of a good run in the Gillette Cup, getting beaten by Somerset by 24 runs in their first match.

There was another double tour in the summer of 1967, India coming first for three Tests followed by Pakistan, also for three. England won all three Tests against India, Amiss and Brown playing in the last two. Pakistan lost two and drew one, Amiss playing in the final one and his Warwickshire team-mate Ibadulla playing in the first two for Pakistan as an opener.

CHAPTER 22

A New Career

AND SO at the end of the 1967 season Mike left the club he had graced with his presence for the last 11 years, having unselfishly declined the offer of a benefit or testimonial, partly because Tom Cartwright was having his benefit in 1968. He then spent the next two years working for Derrick Robins, a sports promoter and self-made entrepreneur who had a loose connection with Warwickshire, having played a couple of games for them in 1947. Robins was also chairman of Coventry City Football Club and ran his own cricket team, Derrick Robins XI, which played matches against visiting touring teams and undertook overseas tours to South Africa, New Zealand and Sri Lanka. He was interested in hiring Mike as a leading international sportsman to promote a new product line in his Banbury Buildings company, prefabricated squash courts, to cash in on the 1970s boom in that sport. According to Mike, the venture was not a great success as prefabricated courts with asbestos roofs did not create a warm enough playing environment in the winter and did not always fit in with architects' requirements. The concrete walls, however, were much more durable than their plaster predecessors and it was this concept that Mike was later able to utilise when he set up his own squash club in 1972.

Mike spent part of the summer of 1968 playing club cricket for Leamington and also played one match for Warwickshire in the Gillette Cup, making a duck in their semi-final win over Middlesex. Warwickshire, now under Alan Smith's captaincy and strengthened by the acquisition of West Indian Test players Rohan Kanhai and Lance Gibbs, went on to win the Gillette Cup Final against Sussex. Deprived of Tom Cartwright and Jack Bannister through injury for this match, Dennis Amiss was called upon to bowl 12 overs to fill the breach. Chasing 214, they slumped to 155 for the loss of six wickets before a partnership of 60 between Amiss and the captain saw them over the line. Despite this one success and the arrival of these two West Indian Test players, Warwickshire had a disappointing season, finishing 15th in the County Championship.

Kanhai and Gibbs were highly talented additions to Warwickshire's squad. They both hailed from Guyana, and were great characters but could be argumentative with one another. Dennis Amiss recalls them discussing vehemently almost any subject in the back of his car when returning from away matches. He says he often threatened to pull over and make them walk back to Birmingham if they didn't stop. They would halt temporarily then start up again five minutes later. Both were magnificent players though, and the club was lucky to have the services of these two world-class performers.

Dennis also remembers a lively discussion between Rohan Kanhai and Jack Bannister over whether Ted Dexter had scored over 4,000 Test runs in his career. Jack was sure he had and Rohan was adamant he hadn't and money was wagered on the outcome. To settle the matter, Jack had a *Wisden* brought from his car and when it transpired that Jack was right, Kanhai promptly scooped up all the money, put it behind the bar and laughingly ordered drinks all round.[157]

157 Conversation with Dennis Amiss.

Dennis Amiss was recalled to England's side for the first Test against Australia, but made a 'pair' and was dropped for the rest of the series. He had to wait three years for another chance.

An important development took place in 1967, the formation of the Cricketers' Association, a players' union founded by Somerset's Fred Rumsey. This was not initially welcomed by MCC, as they realised it would inevitably present a threat to their monopolistic control of the game, and a certain amount of pressure was put on Somerset to bring their employee to heel and to nip the idea in the bud. Fred recalls how he was invited to dinner by the chairman of Somerset at his club, expecting to be told in no uncertain terms to drop the issue. At dinner the chairman told Fred that he had had a call from MCC telling him to order Fred to desist in this activity. 'What did you say to them?' asked Fred, fully anticipating the chairman to take MCC's side. To Fred's pleasant surprise, however, the chairman replied, 'I told them to f... off."[158] The Cricketers' Association was to considerably improve the lot of the players, one of its first achievements being to establish the free movement of players between counties. Jack Bannister became the association's first honorary secretary and later its chairman.

Mike did not play in any Championship matches for Warwickshire in 1969 but turned out for them regularly on Sundays in the newly formed John Player League without making any significant scores apart from 43 not out in a win over Somerset. This new format had been introduced to meet an increasing demand for 'results cricket' and, like the Gillette Cup, was successful in helping to bring the crowds back. It was inevitably to have an adverse effect on attendances at Championship matches though, the number of which had been reduced to 24. Matches in the John Player League were of 40 overs per side with no bowler

158 As related by Fred Rumsey at a Dorset Cricket Society meeting.

allowed more than eight. Each county played all the others with four points for a win and one for no result. In its inaugural year Warwickshire finished in ninth position, having suffered by having four matches washed out. Mike also played in their only Gillette Cup match, scoring 36 in their defeat by Essex.

Warwickshire finished fourth in the County Championship, Glamorgan winning it for only the second time in their history. Kanhai and Amiss were the only two batsmen to pass 1,000 runs in the Championship and John Jameson made 1,000 in all matches. David Brown showed the most improvement, finishing third in the batting averages, but Bob Barber and Jim Stewart failed to achieve their former high standards with less frequent appearances. This would be the last season at Warwickshire for both of them, Barber having decided to develop a business career outside cricket and Stewart opting to change counties. 'Things did start to get a bit awkward towards the end when I decided to only play 30 days a season,' says Bob, 'as when I came in I was keeping regular players out.'[159]

Cartwright was, as usual, Warwickshire's most successful bowler with 95 Championship wickets at 16.07 and over 100 in all matches. Bill Blenkiron, who had joined Warwickshire in 1964, showed great improvement with 67 wickets at 22.94 and Norman McVicker, joining the county from Minor Counties side Lincolnshire, made an immediate impact with 64 wickets at 20.95. Brown took 41 wickets at 23.04, his availability limited by Test appearances. Once again, Warwickshire were deficient in the spin bowling department, Barber having lost some of his potency and Gibbs with only 18 wickets seldom being available because of his place in the West Indian side which toured England that summer.

159 Conversation with Bob Barber.

CHAPTER 23

1970 – Welcome Back!

MIKE WAS, however, clearly missing county cricket and in early 1970 he approached Alan Smith with the simple request, 'Would you mind if I came back?' Alan was only too happy to agree as several major players had left.[160] Their key wicket-taker Tom Cartwright had joined Somerset after the chairman of that county Colin Atkinson had offered Tom a coaching position at Millfield School where Colin was deputy headmaster. Warwickshire had also offered Tom a similar position, but he felt ready for a change of environment. With the support of Jack Bannister, in his role with the Professional Cricketers' Association, Tom was given exemption from the requirement of having to spend a year out of the game. Tom's departure was a serious blow to the county, as he had made over 10,000 runs and taken over 1,000 wickets since joining as a 16-year-old in 1952. Jim Stewart, who joined Warwickshire on the same day as Tom, had moved on to Northants and Jack Bannister, who also started on the same day, had retired to concentrate on his bookmaking business and to pursue a broadcasting career.

An agreement was reached with Derrick Robins that Warwickshire would pay Mike's salary during the summer months but Mike would work for him that autumn. The relationship

160 Conversation with Alan Smith.

between Mike and Derrick Robins eventually ended when Mike decided that his long-term future lay elsewhere. Like most self-made men (Robins had started his business with a cement mixer in a field), he was a demanding employer who liked to get his own way and this did not always fit in with Mike's plans. He had been keen for Mike to make himself a candidate for the captaincy of MCC's forthcoming tour to Australia and also for him to become a Test selector, which was being mooted at the time, as these prestigious roles would obviously benefit his company commercially. Mike had firmly decided against any further tours and felt that the role of selector would be too time-consuming. 'I'd never get home,' he said. He was, however, grateful for the knowledge he had gained working for Robins, which was to stand him in good stead when a few years later he went into business on his own.

Mike thus returned to Warwickshire on a full-time basis at the beginning of 1970, resuming his previous number four position in the batting order and pushing Dennis Amiss down to number five. Both had good seasons, Dennis finishing above Mike in the Warwickshire averages with 1,351 runs at 42.41 compared with Mike's 1,479 runs at 36.97. Kanhai again headed the list with 1,500 runs at 68.18 and six centuries. John Jameson had an excellent season with 1,821 runs in all matches and Neil Abberley also passed 1,000 runs. Lance Gibbs' season was rather disappointing and he took only 48 wickets at 31.89. David Brown and Bill Blenkiron were the most successful bowlers with 66 and 68 wickets respectively. Warwickshire dropped four places to eighth in the Championship table and came fifth in the John Player League. In spite of a half-century by Mike, they were knocked out of the Gillette Cup in the first round by Nottinghamshire, thanks to 70 not out from Sobers.

South Africa had been scheduled to tour England in 1970 but, because of threats to disrupt the tour on account of the country's apartheid policy, it was always uncertain whether it would go ahead.

After much debate and the prohibitive costs involved in providing security and protecting grounds, even including the use of barbed wire, it was finally cancelled by the Cricket Council under strong pressure from the government. Edgbaston had not been immune from protests and in January 1970 it was revealed that weed killer had been mischievously put on the wicket. Despite attempts to repair the damage, it took five of the season's 12 pitches out of commission. Warwickshire's president Sir Oliver Leese described it as 'a monstrous impertinence' and the unanimous feeling among the counties and MCC, blind to the bigger picture, was that politics had no place in sport and the tour should proceed.[161] In February a decision was taken for security reasons to reduce the number of South Africa's fixtures from 28 to 12, with Warwickshire, in addition to hosting a Test match, one of only three counties to retain a fixture, the others being Lancashire and Surrey. The Warwickshire committee's view was that, although no one was in favour of apartheid, it was much more likely to combat this policy by inviting South Africa's cricketers here into a multi-racial society than by ostracising them. It was, however, decided that the club's overseas players, Ibadulla, Kanhai and Gibbs, would not take part in any matches against the tourists. This, ironically sparked off a complaint to the Race Relations Board about reverse discrimination. Eventually, however, in the face of mounting controversy, the tour was cancelled. The Stop the 70 Tour organisation led by Peter Hain had triumphed with its threats to disrupt matches and South Africa were condemned to the cricketing wilderness for the next two decades. Colin Schindler's book *Barbed Wire*

161 *The Story of Warwickshire Cricket*, Leslie Duckworth.

and Cucumber Sandwiches gives an excellent account of the whole episode.[162]

Instead a series of five matches was arranged between England and a Rest of the World XI, which included five of the best South African players. The strong Rest of the World team won four of the matches, England one, but in spite of the cricket being of a high standard, this proved to be an anodyne solution and, in the absence of any national rivalry, attendances were poor. David Brown played in the second and third of these matches and Dennis Amiss in the final one.

162 *Barbed Wire and Cucumber Sandwiches,* Colin Schindler.

CHAPTER 24

Championship Runners-up Again

WARWICKSHIRE ENJOYED an excellent season in 1971, finishing on equal points with Surrey, but had to settle for second place because Surrey had won more matches. With hindsight, had Warwickshire not declared against Surrey earlier in the season at the Oval, setting them a target which they achieved in the last over, they may have won the Championship, but they had no regrets, as they believed this was the right way to play the game. Mike had a splendid summer, scoring almost 2,000 runs in all matches with six centuries, including one against the Pakistani touring team. He finished fourth in the national averages and topped the Warwickshire batting averages with 1,689 runs at 49.67 ahead of Rohan Kanhai who scored 1,452 runs at 48.40. John Jameson also had another good season with over 1,000 runs as did a new star on the horizon, John Whitehouse, in his first season. Jameson was selected for two Test matches against India, after having earlier made a double century against them for Warwickshire, but had the dubious distinction of being run out in three of his four innings, once unluckily at the non-striker's end when the bowler's fingertips deflected the ball on to the wicket.[163]

---

163 Conversation with John Jameson

Dennis Amiss also missed several games on account of Test calls against the Pakistani and Indian tourists and failed to make his 1,000 for Warwickshire. In the bowling department Lance Gibbs was an outstanding success with 123 wickets at 18.84. He was voted Cricketers' Cricketer for 1971 and also featured as one of *Wisden*'s five Cricketers of the Year. At last Warwickshire had solved their problem of finding a decent spin bowler but ironically only Norman McVicker of the pace bowlers performed well with 71 wickets at 26.38. David Brown was injured for a large part of the season and Bill Blenkiron unaccountably lost form. The team was again ably captained by Alan Smith, who combined his job with his duties as an England selector. In the limited-overs competitions Warwickshire finished bottom of the John Player League and lost to Kent in the semi-final of the Gillette Cup in a rain-affected game. In the second round they had come up against Lincolnshire who had Sonny Ramadhin playing for them, but he was given rough treatment by his former team-mate Kanhai (126) and Mike (88 not out). They put on 157 for the third wicket and Ramadhin finished with figures of 0-68 from his 12 overs. McVicker was principally responsible for bowling out Lincolnshire, his former county, with 5-26.

CHAPTER 25

Champions at Last

THE SEASON of 1972 was a great one for Warwickshire as they won the County Championship for the first time since 1951 and only the third time in their history. They were unbeaten and won nine of their Championship matches in spite of winning the toss on only four occasions. The number of Championship matches had been reduced from 24 to 20 to accommodate the growing popularity of limited-overs cricket, which many counties now saw as the financial saviour of the game. The addition of two more West Indians to the Warwickshire squad, left-handed batsman Alvin Kallicharran and wicketkeeper Deryck Murray, who had been put in contact with the club via fellow West Indian Rudi Webster, undoubtedly strengthened the batting. Kanhai had an excellent season, scoring five centuries and finishing second in the national averages.

At the beginning of the season, Dennis Amiss, who had not been able to command a regular first-team place, asked Alan Smith if he could open the innings. Alan agreed and Dennis scored a century in his first outing in this position against Middlesex. This was to give his career a new lease of life and he went on to score six centuries, top the Warwickshire batting averages and make the opening spot his own. He was also named as Man of the Series in the first one-day international matches with Australia, although in spite of his outstanding form, he was not selected for any of the Tests. Kallicharran and Mike both scored over 1,000 runs in all matches, but John Jameson and John Whitehouse underperformed relative to the previous year.

With the arrival of a new wicketkeeper, captain Alan Smith was able to indulge in his preference for his own medium-pace seam bowling and, with his ungainly run-up and windmill action, topped the Warwickshire bowling averages with 20 wickets at 22.45. 'When Deryck Murray joined the club', says Alan Smith, 'the chairman said to me, "That should suit you," as he knew I liked bowling.' Norman McVicker was the most successful pace-bowler with 63 wickets at 23.74. David Brown was again hampered by injury and took 34 wickets at 26.52. Bob Willis, who had joined the county from Surrey, but was not allowed to play until the beginning of July, performed moderately with 25 wickets at 29.28 but finished the season spectacularly with 8-44 against Derbyshire, including a hat-trick. Lance Gibbs had a relatively disappointing season by his standards with 50 wickets at 26.48, but was the county's most successful spin bowler. At the end of the season, the county bade farewell to 'Billy' Ibadulla. He had joined Warwickshire in 1954 where he was a permanent member of the side in all 19 seasons as a more than useful all-rounder and an outstanding close catcher. On retirement he took over from the former Surrey player Laurie Fishlock as coach of St Dunstan's College in East London. He later emigrated to Otago, New Zealand, where he coached several of their future Test players and still lives.

A new one-day 55-overs competition was launched in 1972, the Benson and Hedges Cup. It was organised on a regional basis with five teams in four groups who would play each other on a league basis, with the top two in each group going into a knockout competition. To make the number of teams up to 20, Minor Counties North and South teams and Cambridge

University were included. After coming second in their regional group, Warwickshire defeated Glamorgan in the quarter-final, but were well beaten by Leicestershire, the eventual winners, in the semi-final.

They got their revenge over Leicestershire in the second round of the Gillette Cup, beating them by three runs in a match in which Mike made 66 not out. Kallicharran saw them through the third round against Glamorgan with a fine 88 and they beat Worcestershire by eight wickets in the semi-final thanks to 67 from Amiss and 85 not out from Kanhai. Despite good innings from Whitehouse (68), Kallicharran (54) and Mike (48) in the final, a memorable innings of 126 by Clive Lloyd saw Lancashire worthy winners. This was the match in which John Arlott memorably described one of Lloyd's drives as 'the stroke of a man out on a Sunday morning stroll knocking the head off a thistle top with a walking stick'. Warwickshire enjoyed little success in the John Player League, finishing in 12th position.

Following a couple of early season centuries and scores of 40 and 78 not out for Warwickshire against the Australian tourists, Mike got a surprise recall to the England side at the age of 38 after a gap of six years and he played in the first three Tests. In the first, which England won, he made scores of 10 and 34, falling on both occasions to Dennis Lillee. He also took a difficult catch high above his head on the long leg boundary to dismiss Ian Chappell for a duck in Australia's first innings. In the second at Lord's, which England lost, he was dismissed twice for 34 and 30 by Bob Massie, who returned figures of 8-84 and 8-53 on his Test match debut. In England's second innings Mike, with his sound defensive technique, was the only one to offer any resolute resistance as, according to Mike, Massie swung the ball both ways in humid conditions and it was a job merely to survive. The third Test, which was drawn, was Mike's last for England. He scored

17 and 15, being dismissed both times by Lillee. For the first time in his life he had contemplated switching to contact lenses, but had deferred the decision after having been selected for England.

The year 1972 was also an important one for Mike off the cricket field, as he embarked on a brand new business venture, the purchase of Wootton Court in Leek Wootton, near Kenilworth, with the intention of converting this former spacious mansion on a five-acre site into a hotel and squash club. He had initially planned to go into this venture with Jack Bannister as a sleeping partner and they had originally been pursuing a property in the Wolverhampton area, which fell through after they were 'gazumped'. Wootton Court was brought to their attention and it turned out to be a much better bet. Mike decided to go it alone after mutually agreeing with Jack that a one-sided partnership would be unlikely to work. Mike felt he had learned enough about squash court construction to create such a business, although he and his wife Diana had to learn the hospitality side of it on the job, not without the occasional mishap. Coinciding with a tremendous interest in the growth of squash, the club was soon highly successful and was the 'in-place' to be in the 1970s for the 'youth and beauty' of the towns of Warwick, Leamington, Kenilworth, Coventry and the surrounding villages. Within a few years there were ten squash courts, four grass tennis courts, a snooker room and even a cricket net where Mike's son Neil was able to learn the basics of the game. From time to time various cricketing associates of Mike's lodged there, including Rohan Kanhai for one summer. It was also a perfect venue for wedding receptions and private parties, and a lively atmosphere was provided by weekly discos, these having replaced the string trio Mike had originally engaged. Mike maintains he had no idea what a 'disco' was when the word was first mentioned to him, but it rapidly took off under the supervision of a talented local DJ. As a natural ball player, Mike quickly picked up the game of squash himself and was soon a prominent member of the Wootton Court five-man first team. Few permanent staff were employed and most of the catering and bar work was done by Mike and Diana themselves, plus some casual labour in return for free accommodation. Mike says it was very hard work but rewarding, especially in the early days when Mike was still playing cricket full-time. It was also a nice environment for their young family to grow up in. Mike and Diana ran Wootton Court for 14 years before selling to another hotelier.

CHAPTER 26

The Final Three Seasons

WARWICKSHIRE WERE unsuccessful in retaining the Championship title in 1973, finishing seventh in the table, largely because their four West Indian players were all on Test match duty in England in addition to which Dennis Amiss played in all six Tests, three against New Zealand and three against West Indies. Bob Willis also played in the final Test and the captain Alan Smith missed several matches as an England selector. For many games this left John Jameson, John Whitehouse and Mike to bear the brunt of the batting. Jameson, with a wholehearted commitment to attacking play, had one of his best seasons ever, scoring 1,948 runs at 48.70 in all matches (only Worcestershire's Glenn Turner scored more) and over 1,500 of them for Warwickshire in the Championship. Mike was the only other player to score over 1,000 for the county. Whitehouse had another rather disappointing season, as did Neil Abberley.

The fast-bowling attack was spearheaded by Willis, Norman McVicker and David Brown. These three were the principal wicket-takers, Willis with 43 at 18.95, McVicker with 45 at 23.53 and Brown, bowling off a shorter run, 57 at 26.52. Alan Smith, having relinquished his wicketkeeping duties, took 23 at 28.82. With Lance Gibbs injured at the start of his last season for Warwickshire and playing for the West Indies for the greater part of the remainder, two young off-spinners, Peter Lewington and Eddie Hemmings, represented the spin bowling department with moderate success.

Neither did Warwickshire distinguish themselves in the three limited-overs competitions, failing to reach the knockout stage of the Benson and Hedges Cup, losing to Worcestershire in the second round of the Gillette Cup and coming next to bottom in the John Player League.

Warwickshire started 1974 with much the same squad as the previous year with the exception of Lance Gibbs, who had retired from county cricket, and McVicker, who had been released. The breach opened by Gibbs' departure was filled amply by off-spinner Hemmings, who took 82 Championship wickets at 20.84. Brown put in his habitual share of hard graft to take 44 at 23.52 and Willis the same number at 21.56, although injuries and Test calls restricted his appearances. Left-arm medium-pacer Steve Rouse, later to become Warwickshire's groundsman at Edgbaston, topped the bowling averages with 27 wickets at 18.11.

Amiss headed Warwickshire's batting averages with 620 runs at 47.69 with Kanhai close behind with 757 runs at 44.52. Amiss, who played in all six Test matches against the Indian and Pakistani tourists, made 1,510 runs in total at an average of 53.92. Jameson, who had toured the West Indies with England during the winter, playing in two Tests, was the most prolific run-scorer with 1,420 Championship runs at 41.76 and 1,932 at 48.30 in all matches. The highlight of his season was an unbroken second-wicket partnership of 465 between Jameson and Kanhai against Gloucestershire, which could have been even greater but for the newly introduced 100 overs first-innings restriction. Jameson scored 240 not out and Kanhai 213 not out. This followed on the heels of a partnership of 231 by the same pair in the previous match against Lancashire. Mike and Alvin Kallicharran also made

1,000 runs, but Kallicharran's batting was below par for most of the season. Mike had started the season well with a century against Glamorgan and 98 against Northamptonshire in May but suffered a run of mediocre scores thereafter. It was becoming clear now that, although still a good player, he was no longer quite the dominant force he had once been. This was to prove his penultimate season. He was now 41 and retirement again beckoned – this time for good.

Warwickshire finished a disappointing ninth in the Championship and did poorly in all three limited-overs competitions. They fell at the first fence in the Gillette Cup, losing to Nottinghamshire by four wickets and came 11th in the John Player League. They finished third in their group in the Benson and Hedges Cup, thus failing to qualify for the quarter-finals. Apart from having reached four Gillette Cup finals in the past and winning two of them, their failure to excel consistently in limited-overs cricket, particularly the John Player League, is difficult to understand, as they possessed a decent bowling attack and some of the fastest-scoring batsmen in the country with players such as Bob Barber, Jim Stewart, Jameson, Kanhai, Kallicharran and Mike.

In 1975 David Brown took over the Warwickshire captaincy from Alan Smith, who gave up playing to pursue a career in cricket administration. He was already an England selector and became secretary of Warwickshire in 1976 and ten years later chief executive of the Test and County Cricket Board until his retirement in 1996. The county had a miserable year, slipping to 14th in the Championship table and underperforming in the limited-over, competitions.

In the Championship, after an innings defeat by Lancashire in the opening match, they won four of their next seven matches but finished the season with a run of defeats and draws. Kanhai, although appearing less frequently, topped the batting averages with 1,053 runs at an average of 87.75. Amiss with 1,422 at 47.40 and Kallicharran with 1,247 at 38.96 were the only other two to pass 1,000 runs. Whitehouse had a good season with 846 runs at 32.03, but Jameson a poor one and Abberley completely lost form and was rarely selected. Mike, in his last season, played on fewer occasions and failed to make a century for the first time since joining the club. One of Warwickshire's main problems was their failure to dismiss sides twice. They were handicapped by the absence of Willis for most of the season through injury and he only took 13 wickets. Once again, Brown shouldered the burden of the bowling with 72 wickets at 26.79, although Hemmings bowled a lot more overs for his 58 wickets. The other off-spinner Peter Lewington, who returned after a season's absence, took 56 wickets and the newcomer Steve Perryman, a right-arm medium-pacer, 45.

In the Benson and Hedges Cup they reached the semi-final after winning all their group matches and easily beating Essex in the quarter-final, only to lose to Middlesex by three runs after needing six off the final over with three wickets standing. Rouse was run out off the first ball, Hemmings failed to score off the next three and was bowled by John Price off the fifth and Perryman, who needed to hit a six off the last ball, could only get a two. Mike was absent for this match but played in all the other games. They also lost by over 100 runs to Middlesex in the second round of the Gillette Cup, Mike Brearley making 82, Graham Barlow 76 not out and Fred Titmus taking the wickets of Kallicharran and Kanhai in his 4-14 from 12 overs. Their best achievement in a poor season was to come sixth in the John Player League. In this competition Jameson scored centuries against Lancashire and Somerset and also equalled the record of 19 sixes in the tournament set by Brian Close the previous year.

CHAPTER 27

MJK – A Man for All Seasons

AND SO for Mike it was 'goodbye to all that' after over 20 seasons of first-class cricket. It had been a fantastic journey with more than its fair share of highs and lows. As long as he was available, his place in Warwickshire's county team was a certainty but he was never able to hold a permanent place in England's Test side. Mike had his moments at Test level, though. It is probably fair to conclude that he was an uncertain starter, especially against real pace, but once he got in, he was very difficult to dislodge and, in the right mood, he could take bowling attacks apart. Although Mike had all the shots, with the exception of the hook, his favouring of the leg side was his trademark. His rationale for this approach was based on the fact there are generally more gaps on the leg side to be exploited and, even if at times it looks inelegant, what matters is not 'how' but 'how many'.

'The 50s and 60s were terrific years for county and Test cricket and it was wonderful to be part of that era,' reflects Mike.

'There were a lot of great players and characters in the game. Although I thought Tyson the quickest, I would rate Fred Trueman and Brian Statham as the best English fast bowlers I faced, but there were a lot of other very good ones who couldn't get into the Test side because of these two. Jack Flavell, Len Coldwell and Les Jackson come to mind. Of the medium pacers,

Derek Shackleton, Ian Thomson and our own Tom Cartwright stand out.

'These three were nearly always in the top ten of the bowling averages at the end of the season. The best English leg-spinner early on in my career was Eric Hollies and I regret having him for only one season at Warwickshire. Tony Lock, Jim Laker and Fred Titmus were all fine bowlers, although Lock's action was always suspect until he was forced to modify it. On the world stage Wes Hall, Charlie Griffith and Peter Pollock were probably the most hostile of the fast bowlers. Richie Benaud was undisputedly the best leg-spinner and Lance Gibbs the best off-spinner. As far as batsmen were concerned, I would rate Colin Cowdrey, Tom Graveney and Ted Dexter as the best for England. Internationally, Bobby Simpson and Graeme Pollock were outstanding but the very best, in my and probably everybody else's opinion, was Garry Sobers, although later Rohan Kanhai ran him close. Of the fielders, there was no one to compare with Colin Bland, who was also no mean batsman.' When asked who the best captains were Mike played against, he answers laconically, 'The ones with the best teams!'

Leslie Duckworth in *The Story of Warwickshire Cricket*, published in 1974, well before Dennis Amiss had overtaken Mike's aggregate and shortly before Mike had retired, wrote:

> 'Warwickshire has never had a batsman – and it is doubtful if any county has either – who has scored runs so prolifically as MJK Smith. In his first sixteen seasons he exceeded the aggregate of every previous Warwickshire batsman except Quaife, taking his total to 24,562, compared with Quaife's 33,872, which took him more than twice as many seasons – thirty-five. Dollery in sixteen seasons made 23,457 and the only other batsman to have topped 20,000 runs is Wyatt

> – 21,597 in seventeen seasons. People have often marvelled that a player wearing spectacles could have performed such scoring feats as have marked Smith's career. He first had them when he was seventeen and expressed a quiet but firm conviction that they had never been a disadvantage to him. He admitted his weakness against fast bowling, especially at the start of an innings, but contended that it never had anything to do with eyesight.'[164]

One area in which Mike has been considered suspect was his running between the wickets. He was run out 26 times in his career and according to Ray Hitchcock, the last survivor of the 1951 Championship-winning side, 'Mike wasn't the best chappie to run with. He used the term "Go" and 22 yards away, you'd think, 'Did he say, "Go" or "No".' He also used to beckon you with his hand without saying anything which, according to John Jameson, could be a bit confusing.[165]

As a fielder, Mike was a natural athlete and good in any position, but as a close catcher at forward short leg he was truly exceptional. 'He took some amazing catches,' says former team-mate David Brown. 'He was absolutely fearless. He stood so close without any protection.'[166] 'It's a dangerous position,' says Mike, 'and not everybody wants to field there. There's no point putting someone there who doesn't fancy it. He'll never catch anything. Kenny Barrington was a brave batsman who took a lot of knocks but I knew he was reluctant to field at forward short leg so I never asked him to go there, and without naming names, there were one or two in the Warwickshire team who I wouldn't ask to field there. It's very much a specialist position and some

164 *The Story of Warwickshire Cricket Club*, Leslie Duckworth.

165 Conversation with John Jameson.

166 Conversation with David Brown.

players don't have the right physique or appetite for it.' Mike only got really hurt once in that position when a pull by one of the Yorkshire batsmen fractured his wrist as he protected his head in self-defence. It put him out of the game for a few weeks but it didn't put him off, although he admits that towards the end of his career he was starting to question the wisdom of fielding in that position. Regarding his technique, Mike maintains he never stood too close but, when fielding to a spin bowler, he would move in a yard at the last moment if he saw the ball was pitched up. 'The danger ball', says Mike, 'is the leg-stump half-volley. The batsman can pick this up and hit it with real power, giving the fielder no time to react. If the batsman goes to hook or sweep, the fielder has a fraction of a second longer to take evasive action.'

But Mike's greatest attribute was as a captain. Ian Wooldridge once wrote of him: 'He has a quite exceptional gift for welding prima donnas, nerve cases and barrack room pros into a Test team that will follow him to the end of the earth.'

Many of his contemporaries have sung his praises. Colin Cowdrey considered him one of the best captains he ever played under. Geoff Boycott, not one given to excessive eulogy, says this about him, 'Mike is a fantastic person and brilliant man-manager. He is a man of the people. You'd never know he'd been to public school. He wasn't a bit posh. People wanted to play for him.' Boycott has never forgotten receiving a letter from Mike as a schoolboy after having sought his advice about batting in glasses. He recalls:

> 'When I was about 16, I realised my eyesight was getting worse because I couldn't properly see what the teacher was writing on the blackboard. I was worried it might finish off my ambition to become a professional cricketer; so, at

> the suggestion of my Uncle Algy, who had always taken a keen interest in my cricketing development, I wrote to Mike Smith, asking him about playing in glasses. I got a nice letter back from Mike a few days later, saying batting in glasses was fine but I needed to get ones with shatterproof lenses. So I did this and wore glasses from then on up till about 1968 when I went over to contact lenses. They hadn't been available at the start of my career. I was also playing football and had already had some representative honours at junior level but I had to give that up because you can't play football in glasses. Anyway, the time when players were doing both was coming to an end and cricket was my priority. When I went to South Africa with the England team in 1964 under Mike's captaincy I was only just starting my Test career and I found it a bit difficult – the pitches were a lot faster than I'd been used to, so you didn't have as much time to play. I'd been raised on much slower wickets in England. Mike gave me a lot of encouragement. He was a very good captain, perhaps not quite as shrewd tactically as Brian Close, but a super bloke to play for.'[167]

Fred Titmus was full of praise for Mike and considered him a much better captain than Cowdrey or Dexter, especially when it came to field placing. 'He would have a chat with you and suggest things and you would come to a joint decision. Ted's idea of a joint decision was him telling you what to do and you doing it. Even Colin Cowdrey sometimes liked to direct you and be in charge. That always upsets a bowler. Mike accepted that if you were a Test bowler, you probably knew where you wanted your field setting and he would leave it to you. If you're playing for

167 Conversation with Sir Geoffrey Boycott.

England, you shouldn't need to be told how to bowl.'[168] When asked about this, Mike's terse reply was, 'You don't want your bowlers to be unhappy, do you?'

David Brown once said of him, 'Mike, for my money, is the best skipper I have ever played with. Without driving, he draws more reserves out of a player than any other captain I have known.'[169] He also maintained that a young cricketer could not find a better example on and off the field. In 1965 Mike had *Better Cricket for Boys* published, a book which gave guidance to young cricketers on all aspects of the game, in which, while appreciating the value of coaching, he stressed the importance of building on one's own natural ability. Around this time, as a role model, he was also involved in an anti-smoking campaign via a cartoon strip in which he advised youngsters that the best way to stop smoking was to never start. Mike himself has never smoked.

Mike possesses an extremely calm temperament and almost always kept his emotions under control. 'I saw Mike really angry only once,' says John Jameson. 'It was in a match against Hampshire which had petered out into a draw and Colin Ingleby-Mackenzie instructed "Butch" White to deliver a series of bouncers at Mike, presumably out of frustration. When the match ended, Mike really had a go at Colin.'[170]

Tom Cartwright, although younger than Mike, had already been with Warwickshire for five seasons before Mike arrived to take over the captaincy from Eric Hollies in 1957. 'He brought about a great improvement,' says Tom. 'Mike was a nice bloke to play for. He appreciated other people's abilities and he let them get on with it. His team was always happy. You could never fathom Mike. He is an enigma. He's never courted glamour. It's not his

---

168 *My Life in Cricket,* Fred Titmus.

169 *The Story of Warwickshire Cricket,* Leslie Duckworth.

170 Conversation with John Jameson.

style, and he's never had it. And therefore he's never had the recognition of how good a player he was. If somebody had said to me while I was playing, "You can pick any team to win the Championship next summer, out of all the county cricketers you've seen," he would be my first name down. Without any question. Nobody played like he did on bad pitches. When you meet him he's vague, and you think he's having an off day or putting it on. But when you saw him with a bat in his hand, he was electric.' On comparing Mike to Tom Dollery, Tom had this to say, 'He was a very intelligent cricketer, but I'm not sure he had the same ready wit as Tom Dollery had at making things happen on the field. Sometimes with Mike it drifted a bit.'[171]

Dennis Amiss, who played with Mike for many seasons, says in his autobiography, *In Search of Runs*: 'He looks aloof and it can take time to get to know him, but for years he dominated the conversation in our dressing room. Absent-minded, but a great player, especially of spin. He may go down in cricket history as the man who invented the 'lap' stroke from outside the off stump through midwicket or square leg. Indeed throughout his career he was a strong on-side player and to him the off side was known as "the cissy side".'[172] Mike could be rather vague about field placings, though, preferring to let fielders make up their own mind within certain parameters. Roy Virgin of Somerset, who only played once under Mike's captaincy for a combined XI, recalls asking Mike if he wanted him forward or backward of square-leg. 'Just float around somewhere,' was Mike's advice.

John Jameson laughingly recalls a match against Lancashire at Blackpool in 1973 when, in an innings of 161, Mike took left-arm spinner David Hughes apart with his famous 'lap' shot. In

171 *Tom Cartwright: The Flame Still Burns*, Stephen Chalke.

172 *In Search of Runs*, Dennis Amiss.

Mike leading a no-smoking campaign for boys.

Hughes's first over he hit the first five balls for four. Hughes had pitched successive deliveries increasingly wider of the off stump, but it made no difference. Mike simply dispatched them to varying parts of the on-side boundary depending on their width. An exasperated Hughes appealed to his captain, David Lloyd, with the words 'Where do I bowl at him?' He was advised to try a straight one. He did and Mike blocked it. John also recalls a match at Edgbaston against Yorkshire where Fred Trueman bounced Mike and he cut him for four. 'How do you bowl at him when he's in a mood like that?' said Fred ruefully.[173] When asked why he never tried to hook the ball, Mike replies, 'I never played the hook stroke. I would just duck. Nowadays, with helmets, I would play differently.'

Tom Cartwright remembers once teasing Mike about his favourite shot. A new stand at Edgbaston was being built called Extra Cover. The players were talking about it in the dressing room and Mike asked where it was. 'Extra cover,' said Tom, 'the part of the ground where you never hit the ball.'[174]

Opponents also held Mike in high esteem. This is what Doug Padgett, formerly of Yorkshire, says about him, as relayed to the author by his son Neil:

> 'What anyone thinks of Mike as a player must be irrefutable. He has written his record in the annals of cricketing history for both Warwickshire and England, a great batsman. We always knew whenever we played Warwicks that we must get MJK out cheaply if we were to win. Mike was always an easy-going man, a gentleman, good company, knowledgeable about the game with time for players and public alike. He was a player with a passion for the game who played hard but fair.'

Mike played 50 Tests for England, captaining in 25 of them. Of the 25, five were won, three lost and 17 drawn – not such a bad record

173 Conversation with John Jameson

174 *Tom Cartwright: The Flame Still Burns*, Stephen Chalke

with a series win in South Africa and a drawn series in Australia – often without some of England's best players. Whilst this may seem a high proportion of draws, it should be remembered that five of them were on lifeless wickets in India, four were on very good batting wickets in Australia and three were badly rain-affected four-day Tests in New Zealand. It is not unreasonable, however, to regard Mike as a fairly defensive captain who had a general preference for pace and seam bowling as opposed to spin. One criticism which has been levelled at him is that he did not make sufficient use of the leg spin of Barber and Barrington in Test matches, although he used them frequently with success in state and provincial matches.

While Mike always tried to win, he was prepared to close a game up at Test level if there was little chance of victory and his declarations were never very generous, especially if a series was at stake. Bob Barber's view is that Mike was probably a bit too defensive when England were fielding. However, in county cricket he was always looking to contrive a result with a sporting declaration, sometimes in spite of opposition from some of his bowlers, like Cartwright and Bannister. 'I remember a game against Hampshire', says Bob, 'when we were discussing the declaration and they said, "What if Roy Marshall smacks us all round the park and gets a century?" and Mike said, "What if he gets a duck?" In the event, Mike declared, Marshall got a century and Hampshire won. But Mike was always willing to make a game of it and get a result.'

David Brown confirms Mike's determination to try and produce a result. 'Mike was a superb captain but sometimes we bowlers didn't agree with his declarations – we thought them too generous.'[175] When asked if his approach to captaincy differed in Test cricket from county cricket, Mike said that in Test cricket it did depend to some extent on the state of the series. If you were

175 Conversation with David Brown.

one up you didn't want to lose that advantage. In county cricket, however, with a points-based system favouring victories, it was important to try for a win whenever possible.

After Mike's retirement, that exceptional writer John Woodcock, the Sage of Longparish, paid tribute to Mike in the 1976 edition of *Wisden*. Under 'MJK Smith Lays Down His Bat', he writes:

> 'On how many cricketers may it be said, at the end of a long and distinguished career, that he made no enemies? Precious few, is the answer to that – but Mike Smith is one of them. Between 1951, when he first appeared for Leicestershire, and 1975, when he played his last game for Warwickshire, he became one of the players' favourite players. It took some time to dawn that he was as good as he was, or such an excellent man. His appearance, I think, had something to do with this. To see him emerging from the pavilion in the Parks, as an outwardly gauche and gangling undergraduate, and to watch him taking guard, face screwed up behind those rimless spectacles, was not a convincing introduction. But he began very soon to be marked down as no ordinary batsman.'

He continues:

> 'We are embarked upon Smith's virtues again now, and there were plenty of them. If one above all others accounted for his popularity with his contemporaries, it was his consistency. No matter who he was with, or where it was, or when, he was always the same man – absolutely fair and as unselfish a captain as England ever had. His players knew exactly where they were with him, which meant every bit

> as much to them as their acceptance that he was a good enough cricketer to be in the side. Had he played as much for himself as the great majority of successful batsmen did he would have undoubtedly scored more runs than he did. It is more apparent now than it was at the time that the selectors got rid of him too soon, partly perhaps because he was too independent for their liking. He did things his own way, whatever the "establishment" may have thought of it, although as harmonious a partnership of captain and manager I have toured with was when Smith and David Clark were paired together in India in 1963/64.'[176]

No one is better qualified to judge him as a county captain than Warwickshire's secretary, Leslie Deakins. In 1967, on the occasion of Mike's first retirement, he wrote:

> 'He will not be readily replaced or easily forgotten and it is certain that the very happy, sometimes successful, sometimes disappointing, but never dull 11 years of his captaincy will long be remembered at Edgbaston.'

Let Alan Smith, who succeeded Mike as Warwickshire skipper, have the last word: 'Mike was not a demanding or strict captain. He was not ruthless but he liked winning. He is rarely ruffled, always cheerful, easy-going and loyal. He frequently gives the impression of being absent-minded and forgetful and this in itself is a major source of dressing-room laughter. I remember one occasion when we were sitting in a narrow box and Mike had a pen in his hand and was writing numbers in the margin. We all thought he was doing mathematical calculations to decide on the

---

176 *Wisden Cricketers' Almanack 1976:* 'MJK Smith Lays Down His Bat' *(extract),* John Woodcock.

best time for a declaration when suddenly he came out with, "It's cheaper to fly – the air fares between London and Glasgow are less than the train fare." Everybody liked playing for Mike. He was a very fine player – probably the best player of off-spin in the country. Don Shepherd said he was the hardest to bowl against, as Mike would chip it between fielders. He wasn't the easiest person to run with though. "No … Yes became Go … Guess,"' laughs Alan.[177] On his retirement Alan paid tribute to him as follows:

> 'Purely as a batsman and also as a close-to-the-wicket fielder, he has earned the respect, admiration and gratitude of spectators around the world. But, more importantly, wherever he has been, whomsoever he has met, he has instantly made friends. No player in the last 25 years has been more universally popular. Hard-bitten professionals have been prepared to walk over a cliff if he so decreed as captain.'[178]

---

177 Conversation with Alan Smith.

178 *The Story of Warwickshire Cricket*, Leslie Duckworth.

Bibliography

Amiss, Dennis with Carey, Michael, *In Search of Runs* (Readers Union, 1977)

Amiss, Dennis with Graham-Brown, James, *Not Out at Close of Play* (The History Press, 2021)

Arlott, John, *John Arlott's Cricket Journal* (Heinemann, 1958)

Arlott, John, *John Arlott's Cricket Journal 2* (Heinemann, 1959)

Arlott, John, *John Arlott's Cricket Journal 3: Cricket on Trial* (Heinemann, 1960)

Arlott, John, *The Ashes 1972* (Pelham Books, 1972)

Bannister, Jack, *The History of Warwickshire County Cricket Club* (Christopher Helm, 1990)

Baxter, Peter and Hayter, Peter, *England in the West Indies* (BBC Books, 1991)

Boycott, Geoffrey and Hotten, Jon, *Being Geoffrey Boycott* (Fairfield Books, 2022)

Chalke, Stephen, *Tom Cartwright: The Flame Still Burns* (Fairfield Books, 2007)

Chalke, Stephen, *Micky Stewart and the Changing Face of Cricket* (Fairfield Books, 2015)

Chalke, Stephen, *At the Heart of English Cricket* (Fairfield Books, 2001)

Chalke, Stephen, *The Way It Was: Glimpses of English Cricket's Past* (Fairfield Books, 2008)

Clarke, John, *With England in Australia: The MCC Tour of 1965/66* (Stanley Paul, 1966)

Duckworth, Leslie, *The Story of Warwickshire Cricket* (Stanley Paul, 1974)

Edrich, John, *Runs in the Family* (Stanley Paul, 1969)

Fortune, Charles, *Cricket Overthrown* (Bailey Brothers and Swinfen, 1960)
Fortune, Charles, *MCC In South Africa 1964–5* (Robert Hale, 1965)
Kelly, Rob, *Hobbsy: A Life In Cricket* (Von Krumm, 2018)
Hollies, Eric, *I'll Spin You A Tale* (Museum Press, 1955)
Jones, Tim, *Don Kenyon: His Own Man* (Amberley, 2015)
Knowles, Ray, *South Africa Versus England: A Test Cricket History* (New Holland, 1995)
McGilvray, Alan, *Backpage of Cricket with Norman Tasker* (Lester-Townsend, 1989)
Mackay, Ken, *Quest for the Ashes* (Pelham Books, 1966)
McGlew, Jackie, *Cricket Crisis* (Hodder and Stoughton, 1965)
Miller, Douglas, *No Ordinary Man* (ACS Publications, 2013)
Modi, Rusi, *Cricket Forever* (Rusi Modi, 1964)
Oborne, Peter, *Basil D'Oliveira* (Little Brown, 2004)
Parry, Richard and Odendaal, André, *Swallows and Hawke* (Pitch Publishing, 2022)
Ross, Alan, *Through the Caribbean* (The Pavilion Library, 1986)
Rumsey, Fred, *Sense of Humour, Sense of Justice* (Fairfield Books, 2019)
Schindler, Colin, *Bob Barber: The Professional Amateur* (Max Books, 2015)
Schindler, Colin, *Barbed Wire and Cucumber Sandwiches* (Pitch Publishing, 2020)
Short, Graham, *The Trevor Goddard Story* (Purfleet Productions, 1965)
Smith, EJ, *'Tiger' Smith of Warwickshire and England* (Readers Union, 1987)
Swanton, EW, *Last Over* (John Blake Publishing, 1996)
Swanton, EW, *Swanton in Australia With MCC 1946-1975* (Collins, 1975)
Swanton, EW, *West Indies Revisited* (Heinemann, 1960)
Titmus, Fred, *My Life in Cricket* (John Blake, 2005)
Waite, John, *Perchance to Bowl* (Nicholas Kaye, 1961)
Wadhwaney, KR, *Indian Cricket Controversies* (Diamond Pocket Books (P) Ltd., 2017)
Williams, Charles, *Gentlemen and Players* (Weidenfeld and Nicolson, 2012)
Wisden Cricketers' Almanack, 1955–76 editions

Appendix A

Match results during Mike Smith's career at Warwickshire

Captain	*Year*	*Championship*					*Gillette Cup*	*B & H*	*John Player*			
		Pos	*P*	*W*	*L*	*D*			*Pos*	*W*	*L*	*D*
MJK Smith	1957	11	28	9	7	12						
MJK Smith	1958	16	28	3	7	18						
MJK Smith	1959	4	28	13	10	5						
MJK Smith	1960	15	32	4	12	16						
MJK Smith	1961	12	32	9	10	13						
MJK Smith	1962	3	32	12	5	15						
MJK Smith	1963	5	28	10	3	15	KO 1st round					
MJK Smith	1964	2	28	14	5	9	Lost in final					
MJK Smith	1965	11	28	5	5	18	Lost in semi-final					
MJK Smith	1966	6	28	8	8	12	Won final					
MJK Smith	1967	10	28	5	4	17	KO 2nd round					
AC Smith	1968	11	28	7	8	16	Won final					
AC Smith	1969	4	24	7	3	14	KO 2nd round		9	6	6	4
AC Smith	1970	8	24	7	6	11	KO 1st round		5	8	6	2
AC Smith	1971	2	24	9	9	6	Lost in semi-final		17	5	11	0
AC Smith	1972	1	20	9	0	11	Lost in final	Lost in semi-final	12	7	8	1
AC Smith	1973	7	20	5	5	10	KO 2nd round	3rd in group	16	4	8	4
AC Smith	1974	15	20	5	5	10	KO 2nd round	3rd in group	11	7	8	1
D Brown	1975	14	20	4	10	6	KO 2nd round	Lost in semi-final	6	9	7	0

Appendix B

Warwickshire County Championship results against other counties during Mike's captaincy, 1957–67

	Played	*Won*	*Lost*	*Drawn/ abandoned*
Derbyshire	22	7	8	7
Essex	22	3	5	14
Glamorgan	18	7	2	9
Gloucestershire	22	10	3	9
Hampshire	18	4	6	8
Kent	17	4	6	7
Lancashire	21	4	8	9
Leicestershire	22	10	0	12
Middlesex	17	4	4	9
Northamptonshire	19	3	7	9
Nottinghamshire	22	8	3	11
Somerset	18	9	2	7
Surrey	18	4	5	9
Sussex	18	8	5	5
Worcestershire	22	3	9	10
Yorkshire	18	4	6	8
Total	**314**	**92**	**79**	**143**

Mike did not captain all these games, as he was sometimes away on Test duty or playing in other representative matches and very occasionally injured, but he did captain the vast majority. What is striking is the high number of drawn games. Three days was clearly not long enough for four innings even without interruptions for rain and bad light. Sides like Lancashire, Yorkshire and Surrey who had several Test players in their ranks were the most difficult opponents although they also had a poor record against Northamptonshire and Worcestershire.

Appendix C

Career record – MJK Smith

Batting

	M	*I*	*NO*	*R*	*HS*	*Av*	*100s*	*50s*
Test	50	78	6	2,278	121	31.63	3	11
First-class	637	1,091	139	39,832	204	41.84	69	241
Limited overs	140	130	17	3,106	97*	27.48	0	15

Bowling

	O	*M*	*R*	*W*	*Best*	*Av*
Test	35	4	128	1	1-10	128.00
First-class	80.1	14	305	5	1-0	61.00

Catches

Test	53	**First-class**	595	**Limited overs**	40

Index